THE COASTAL GARDEN

THE COASTAL GARDEN

DESIGN INSPIRATION FROM WILD NEW ZEALAND

ISOBEL GABITES

 potton & burton

First published in 2015 by Potton & Burton
98 Vickerman Street, PO Box 5128, Nelson, New Zealand
pottonandburton.co.nz

© Isobel Gabites

ISBN 978 1 927213 26 1

Editing and design concept: Jane Connor
Printed in China by Midas Printing International Ltd

Contents

Salt-scented

I've sailed around New Zealand's coasts and around the Pacific Islands—from Vanuatu in the west to Tahiti in the east—and to each stretch of coast my memory has assigned a scent. The smells of land, when you've been at sea for days or weeks, are instantly both astonishing (especially when you can smell a country coming before you can see it) and evocative. What is that smell? Smoke from houses or industry? Wet humus in forests? The earthiness of landslides? The sweet scent of burning coconut husks or the heady wafts of frangipani or tiare on the breeze? The mind captures the moment and it is with you for life, enriching the excitement of landfall.

What did New Zealand's explorers smell? We know that most European colonisers, relieved to at last make landfall, sailed into the smokiness of forest-clearance fires. Before those times it may have been wafts of guano or seal that tainted the air, and the heavy, dank, earthy forest scents. Nowadays, that might be the privilege of those approaching Fiordland, but the dry dust of sheep manure and the tang of resinous pine will be more pervasive along most of New Zealand's coastline.

Perversely, once ashore, with an onshore breeze to help, it is the sea we smell—salt, rotted seaweed, rich mudflats—and I'm convinced hot sand has its own smell! And what about the soundtrack? Screeching gulls, boat motors, shouts of children and the waves, which can be soporifically lapping their way up a soft slope of sand or roaring angrily with a rumbling intensity that can be heard kilometres inland.

This is the zone I'm interested in and whose inhabitants I'm writing for—the ones in the salt-scented zone.

The native way

Many gardens in New Zealand use native plants, but how would you define an exemplary native garden? To my mind there's no particular style. It isn't naturalistic necessarily, nor organised in a particular way, but it does reflect ideals and principles. It shows that the gardener respects the natural processes and patterns of the place. The garden is in tune with the materials, textures and traditions that make the place special. There is a unique connection with the natural world being made in a way that works 'here' but that may not work 'over there'.

Above all, garden is pure theatre. To enthral the audience it really must have a good story to tell, and if the characters telling the story fail to shine, the story falls flat. The actors vary from diva to chorus but they all have a part to play, and above all the entire garden should hang together in an integrated way so the audience understands there are sequences, plots, climaxes and areas of respite, but all within the over-arching gambit of a coastal environment.

All this is tempered by whether there is anything remotely resembling 'natural' New Zealand on the horizon to give the play a context. If the

The boulders set the scene and the cast is assembled, leaving just the sculptures to add their theatrical sparkle.

Getting the best out of a few well-chosen species is often the best approach in a small space. This means knowing what their needs are. These sun-demanding plants are clearly thriving in their sunny location.

garden is in an urban environment or a pastoral landscape, there are few straws of heritage or naturalness to clutch. However, if we can understand the physical and climatic circumstances of the place (its seasonality, soil fertility, extremes of climate, drainage, processes of dune formation and so forth), and match that to what we know about the tolerances of native species, we can still conjure up a garden that 'works'. The task I set myself in writing this book is to assist with that learning and matching-up process as best I can.

Not everyone is lucky enough to see the truly wild bits of coastline and be able to relate the plants growing there to the potted specimens in garden nurseries. So weird garden choices are sometimes made and disappointing results often dishearten even the best-intentioned. Thus, insight into natural coastal environments is foremost in this book. Knowing a bit about where the plants originate; knowing a bit about the coastal conditions of those places, even if you have never been there, and recognising whether plants have particular adaptations to those conditions; knowing what other plants would naturally grow alongside these ones—these all add up to making better-informed choices that result in a healthy garden.

The tending of gardens can involve artifice, but an amount of ingenuity can be applied to create a more subtle intervention. While one approach showcases human talents, the alternative showcases Mother Nature's talents.

Making coastal gardening even more challenging is the way 'developed' land forces us to start from scratch. Perhaps soft edges have become hard; perhaps consolidated fill has replaced mud or sand. We need to apply our knowledge of coastal plants in new ways and forge a new future. On the other hand, if we are restoring or rehabilitating a damaged and weedy natural environment, we could do with some knowledge of the past.

When the Department of Conservation was inaugurated in 1987, with great loss of expertise from the 'elders' of the Department of Lands and Survey, and the Forestry and Wildlife services, those who retained their jobs were sometimes bitter towards the new bloods like myself. I vividly recall meeting one such ex-Wildlife Service elder (it was my first month on the job), who, in front of as many staff as possible, put me to the test. 'So, what do you say are the three impediments to conservation in New Zealand?' Phew! Big question. 'Physical impacts, like fire, or exotic pests,' I said. Yes. He had to accept this. 'Greed,' was my next halting reply, hoping I was on the same wavelength as he was. Yup, he grunted. And the third? 'Well, ignorance, of course.' I passed the test. It was such a tense and important moment, as the young generation faced off with the old, that it has stayed ingrained in my memory.

Apart from making sure we always use water to put out a beach bonfire at the end of the day, there is little an individual can do about fire; authorities and recreational planners need to decide where people can and can't go in order to lower the risks. As for greed, well, that fuels the nation's economy and is an ongoing threat to our heritage that requires campaigns, government policy and strong leadership to overcome. Out of *my* league. But ignorance? Well, that's something we can tackle as individuals, sharing our knowledge to benefit the natural world.

As I age and find myself more frequently using phrases like 'I can remember when' or 'When I was young', I'm confronted with the terrible reality that most youngsters in New Zealand today will never experience beaches where birds are building nests in the sand or be able to go floundering in shallow coastal creeks, and even the traditional pastime of whitebaiting has been fishing itself out of existence. But then, our parents in their turn had already lost sight of the memory of coastal cliffs smothered in guano from nesting flocks of seabirds, or of the migrations of eels overland to the sea that could make entire paddocks writhe and quiver with flapping bodies. When you don't know what you're missing, you don't grieve for it. When you don't grieve for it, you've ceased to care. And that, whether we acknowledge it or not, is ignorance.

If, with books like this one, we can present gardeners with an inkling of the country as it was, interpret why it was like that, and add a bit of plant knowledge and an injection of imagination, we can not only create well-designed gardens, but we can also tap into what it means to be in New Zealand at the same time.

Native gardening isn't about replicating and perpetuating the wild environment, as in most cases the garden is small and in isolation, and is designed to suit a built environment. Over the years I've found that there are several motivations behind great native gardens of any scale, which at the end of the day are a reflection of the owners' or gardeners' passions. Those with a sense of grief over lost heritage are personally moved to give something back, or they live at a location so close to—or encompassing—a bit of wild New Zealand that they feel a responsibility to heal, nurture and enhance it. People who enjoy learning in a hands-on way get to understand the horticultural requirements of native plants by using them. There is botanical interest in each and every plant. Gardening

Domesticity of wild things takes practice and patience, but remember it is a relationship. Make the space to *enter* your garden so you can get to know each other better.

with native species, especially locally appropriate ones, is a statement about pride of place and pride in being uniquely Kiwi.

I often meet people who plant with native species because they 'don't need watering' or they 'look after themselves'—not a valid motivation. It is rare to meet a native plant that doesn't respond well to the same amount of nurturing and horticultural care that exotic plants receive when they are in a garden setting.

I've often been asked if I'm a 'purist' about native plants. I've never been very sure what is meant by that, but the last time someone asked me, they had just been proudly describing their duneland property. They had planted it in exotic trees that, after several decades, were finally doing quite well, especially the 35 phoenix palms—and, they quickly added, knowing my interests, so were the native nikau palms they'd planted in some hollows.

In my mind's eye, I saw instead the wild shrublands of pre-European times, shaped by salt-scorching and representative of the geologically young dunes, too young to have established native forest on them, in an area too dry and drought-prone to support the humidity-loving nikau palms. Yes, I thought, perhaps I am a 'purist', for I fail to understand the logic of struggling with foreign species in an extreme environment in a way that utterly ignores the history and physical conditions of the place, instead imposing a totally anthropocentric imprint of one individual's desires on a landscape. So there, it's out, my hand of cards exposed.

As a gardener, I have misgivings about the ride we are being taken on by commercial forces. A strong horticultural industry based on cultivars and hybrids of native species exists, producing ever-glossier, more colourful and startling variations on pure species. But this is an industry driven by economic imperatives, feeding gardens where colour and form dominate. There is more to gardening than this, and I really believe that until we fully explore the potential of the pure species and use them in ways that are alluring, connect us better with our landscape, and expose us to the entire spectrum of plant forms in nature, then we are in danger of being swamped by market forces in the sanctum of our own backyard.

Remember, many plants aren't economically viable to sell, simply because their propagation is difficult, their seeds are expensive to collect and their growth success is unpredictable. The ardent industry folk who do constantly explore new techniques and take risks to make a widening range of native plants available to us should be encouraged. The kindly folk who collect their own seed and share the results with friends and neighbours, however, will always be the mainstay of great gardens. And a great garden is one where plants thrive (not just survive), where wildlife is encouraged, and where the often disastrous interaction between nature and humans merges briefly into an intimate and constructive relationship in which both parties flourish.

One of the reasons I'm interested in gardening with native species is that in many parts of the country our gardens still have the potential to contribute to the welfare of our natural heritage. Native gardens near natural remnants and reserves form part of the habitat of birds that are transporting seeds back and forth. This is a great mechanism for introducing invasive weeds, too, so the fewer exotic species in the garden, the better. Those gardens in close proximity to natural areas may also be effectively expanding the habitat for native insects, which are often dependent upon a particular native species during some part of their life cycle.

For me, the exciting design challenge is how to re-evaluate the native plant associations that might occur naturally in a place and rework them so they are aesthetically pleasing and in scale with a suburban or rural–residential environment. In this way your garden is relating in a design sense—and an intellectual sense—to the physical landscape that underlies the human overlay, helping maintain the incredible diversity of the natural environment within this string of islands we inhabit.

I've explored these ideas in a previous book, *The Native Garden: Design themes from wild New Zealand*, and now I want to zoom into the zone that most of us live in—near the sea—and offer some background knowledge and some ecologically based ideas of how we can make great—not just great, but fantastic—gardens in such a challenging environment.

Perhaps this approach doesn't seem relevant in deep suburbia. Perhaps that is the domain of 'colour and form'. Plants still need to relate to their physical conditions, however, so think of your ambitions with native species as expanding your repertoire and of the ideas in this book as being fuel to the imagination.

Bon voyage

Bringing rare plants such as *Tecomanthe* into cultivation can create powerfully symbolic garden statements.
OPPOSITE The blueprint for this nikau garden is the carpet of seedlings that amass below nikau in the wild. Some of the best ideas are the least original!

PART ONE

Coastal location

CHAPTER 1

An approach to the coast

Much of the gardener's mind is exercised by plant knowledge—knowing what a species' needs are and adapting the garden conditions to suit it; investigating whether the new treasure needs added protection, improved soil perhaps, or whether it might require special pest-control measures. Another approach is to investigate the conditions of the garden, figure out what plants would naturally thrive in such a place and apply some creativity to making those plants attractive within a garden setting.

There are two key steps in this journey. The first is building up an understanding of the big picture of climate, soil and time—the features that, collaboratively, result in natural associations of plants sharing similar circumstances. There has to be something in this for gardeners. Surely we can find some place nearby where we can learn what Mother Nature might have done with *our* circumstances.

The second step is more challenging: recognising what changes to those 'natural circumstances' humans have wrought (soil loss, perhaps, or changed drainage, or recontouring the landforms) and how we should adjust our plant choices accordingly. Fortunately, more often than not, human-induced changes replicate some early stage in natural colonisation of 'new' ground, and we would do well to mimic what would happen naturally as plants first colonise this 'new' ground and slowly, over time, develop a complete vegetation cover.

I have seen many planting guides over the years that list the tolerances of native species (sun-demanding, shade-tolerant, frost-sensitive) but too often fail to deliver any insight into natural plant associations. They give no hint as to why some plants might be well suited to certain

Species have diversified over time to help overcome environmental challenges. For example, wharariki (mountain flax) is better adapted to rocky crevices than its swamp-bound cousin harakeke; kowhai has a prostrate form that survives salt-storm abrasion; rock-hugging small-leaved pohuehue is more resilient that its larger-leaved forest relative pohuehue.

'mega'-conditions. Will these plants do well on limestone or better on greywacke loess soils? Are these the best choice for my stiff, puggy clay soils or have they evolved for excellent drainage? The first part of this book endeavours to give the big picture—or at least a simplified version of it—and an insight into the processes of succession and time, which on the coast are a great guide and inspiration to the home gardener and the restoration movement alike. The information about individual species imparted along the journey is then of more relevance than your average nursery catalogue.

If you look at a relatively undisturbed area of native vegetation, you'll see that the species it contains have characteristics that make them suited to the physical and climatic conditions. Furthermore, the vegetation is being constantly tested. Frost, salt, infertility, drought—these are extremes that can restrict a plant community to just those species with adaptations to help them survive such stresses.

Let's call the locations dominated by one or more of these growth-limiting stresses 'zones'. It is quite easy to recognise coastal zones once you get your eye in, and knowing where you sit within the zones will go a long way to helping you select suitable plants and avoid expensive losses.

The easiest coastal zones to identify are those along the hard rocky shores of the west coast of New Zealand, because with hills intercepting the onshore prevailing winds, the actions of sea spray, salt-burn, sediment deposition and air movement off the hills create distinctive banding that can be recognised at a distance. The following few pages, therefore, look at this hard-coast scenario, comparing the western coastal processes with those of the eastern coast, and then understanding what zonation occurs along a sandy coastline.

Rocking in the wild west

Cook Strait and the west coasts of both islands are renowned for their relentless, prevailing, onshore, west-to-northwest winds. Often you can see the cloud of salty spray whipped up off the breaking surf and hazily hugging the coastal cliffs. It is wind that dries the ground and physically abuses plants, and salt that burns where it accumulates on foliage, damaging soft new buds. On the open west coast this 'coastal zone' generally extends about

1 km inland or 120–130 m up the coastal hillslopes, whichever is achieved first. (These distances increase in the most exposed wind funnels around the coast and obviously decrease in sheltered harbours.) Even in farmland, this zone can be identified by salt-burn and shaping of macrocarpa shelter belts. I use the term coastal here simply to recognise the role of salt in the mix, yet as we will explore in depth later, there are many other vegetation zones adjacent to the shore where, although they are close to sea water, salt simply doesn't direct the action.

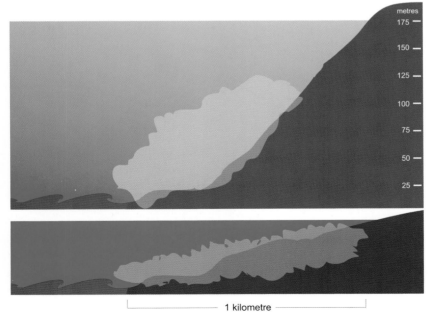

Onshore westerlies blowing in clouds of salt spray create a 'coastal zone' that extends far inland and up coastal mountains.

Within the coastal zone there is a 'severe salt edge' (A) adjacent to the shore, where plants need to be adapted to constant salt-burn and abrasion in order to succeed. Out of necessity, they are succulent (especially plants growing right in the splash zone of wind-driven waves), ground-hugging and springy or flexuous in form, and are likely to include a range of annual herbs that quickly race through their life cycle when conditions are tenable. This is a zone of tension: the constant humidity that plant growth requires is a salt solution that can cause damage as it dries and encrusts leaves and also, as a solution, sucks moisture out of plants by osmosis. Plants have to wear armour, use physiological cunning or simply hide to outwit salt.

Beyond the 'severe salt edge', you still experience the wind but without quite the same salt sting in its tail. In this 'close coastal zone' (B), plants may be subjected to occasional salty storms but damage is less often fatal. The single-tier shrubland or low-stature forest that survives here typically comprises round-crowned, multi-stemmed species. In New Zealand you won't find tall, straight trees, such as the Norfolk Island pine; rather we have squat resilient species crowded together to present a smooth canopy to the wind, with wrinkly or leathery foliage to minimise wind and sun damage. There is a noticeable preponderance of shrubs and trees with flowers at the terminal tips of branches (rather than flowering within the crown), as many species rely on the wind to disperse their seeds. It's a showy zone with many garden-friendly plants.

FAR LEFT To our great shame, New Zealand has few locations where we find a continuum of native vegetation between the shore and the hilltops. Paparoa National Park, near the north of the South Island, is one such location. Here, the zonation of west coast vegetation is clearly recognisable. LEFT A. 'Severe salt edge', B. 'Close coastal zone', C. 'Nikau belt', D. 'Hilly country'.

The colour palette of the close coastal zone on rocky shores is rather muted, apart from the flowering, with dull olives and browny greens reflecting the various wind-protection measures the plants have, such as oily or leathery leaves.

Inland of the close coastal zone is a far more benign area, which I call the 'nikau belt' (C). It exists because of its proximity to the coast but is not shaped by salt in the same way as the close coastal zone. This is where the onshore winds lose their energy, dropping their loads of dust and sand. In most hilly places this coincides with the area at the foot of the hills where nightly draining of cool air prevents frosts, moisture feeds the soils and the onshore winds, moisture-laden from their travel across the ocean, begin to rise and form rain clouds. It is the lack of that limiting factor of salt—combined with humidity and mild conditions— that makes the 'nikau belt' the most luxuriantly rich forest in the country.

The species that thrive here are fast-growing broadleaf species that produce much leaf litter, which breaks down rapidly into nutritious humus. Humans love this zone, too, which has resulted in the loss of most of its native forest cover, but the nikau palm, hard to kill, remains in the landscape as a ghost of those forests and an indicator of the climatic conditions. The palette of the native vegetation in the 'nikau belt' is fresh greens and yellow-greens—truly a delight.

Creating the backdrop to these areas that are influenced in some way by the coast is the 'hilly country' (D). Here, it is colder, cloudier and wetter, and growth seasons are getting shorter. You cannot really associate this zone with the coastal environment other than to acknowledge that the rain that falls on it has been generated while travelling across the ocean! Persistent rain leaches the soils of their nutrients and

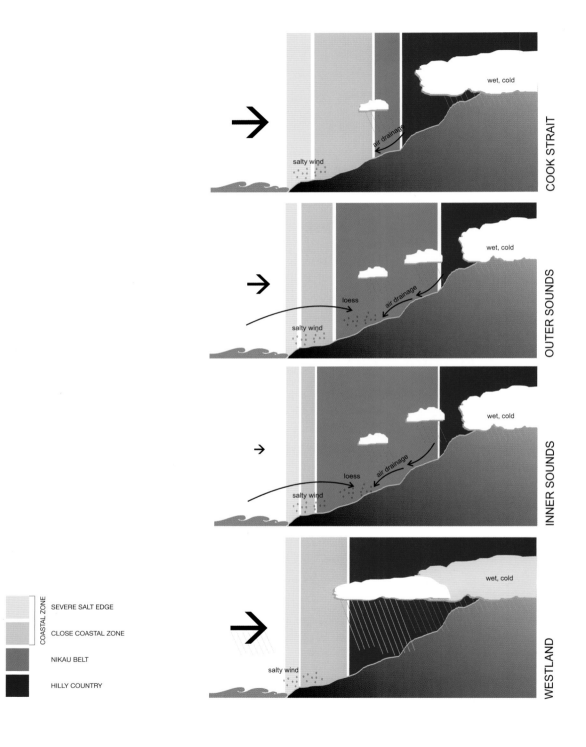

COOK STRAIT

wet, cold

air drainage

salty wind

OUTER SOUNDS

wet, cold

loess

air drainage

salty wind

INNER SOUNDS

wet, cold

loess

air drainage

salty wind

WESTLAND

wet, cold

salty wind

COASTAL ZONE

SEVERE SALT EDGE

CLOSE COASTAL ZONE

NIKAU BELT

HILLY COUNTRY

While the diagrams opposite are based on a simplified 'open coast', the widths of the zones described do vary greatly around the country. For example:

Out in the wind funnel of Cook Strait, the headlands rise steeply out of the sea, meaning that the 'severe salt edge' is quite narrow, but the 'close coastal zone' overall is broad in these harsh conditions as salt winds are driven hard up the slopes. The windshorn bush of the coastal zone is a tough blend of *Olearia* and *Pittosporum* species.

Inside the Marlborough Sounds there is still the odd gust screaming out of the valleys, picking up williwaws of salty water that lash the shore during gales, but generally conditions are much calmer. Here the 'severe salt edge' is even narrower and the 'close coastal zone' of wrinkly-leaved trees and shrubs is also narrower than on exposed coastlines. The so-called 'nikau belt' is far more dominant, especially in the bays, and noticeable because the dominant tree in this zone in modern times is the conspicuously bright, fresh-green kohekohe.

And here, right in the depths of the deep sounds of Marlborough, so calm and serene is the ocean that we find hill forest growing to the water's edge. In addition, the hills are bigger, attracting much more rain than falls in the outer sounds, and salt is generally washed off well before it causes damage.

Down the South Island's west coast at Haast, the coast is pounded by ferocious onshore winds. Not surprisingly, there is a tightly woven canopy of resilient coastal shrubs—mostly colourful stunted trees with waxy or oily leaves, such as horopito, kamahi and five finger, bearing the brunt of the salt spray. It is noticeable that the rimu forest of the hill country marches to within metres of the beach. How can a temperate rainforest association cope with being so close to the sea? It can because Haast receives 4.5 m of rain per year and the salt just washes off. It is too cold for a nikau belt down here, so there is an abrupt jump from coastal scrub directly into tall conifer forest.

a whole new set of growing conditions prevail. If the hillslope soils are extremely thin, only beech trees or kamahi thrive; otherwise there will be conifer–broadleaf forest with its attendant vines, ferns, tree ferns and epiphytes. Even from a distance the zone is distinguishable from the areas closer to the coast by its raggedy treeline and the colour palette: the greens here are dark and black but not without flowering highlights such as the summer-red glow of kamahi and rata, or the springtime splashy white garlands of clematis and winter fiery-orange climbing rata.

Eastern hard rock

The eastern hard-rock coasts north of East Cape pretty much share this zonation. Further south, however—almost from Gisborne through to Dunedin (except for a moist stretch near Kaikoura)—the physical factors that constrain plant growth include some new

additions: drought and frost. For vast stretches of the Wairarapa and Canterbury coasts, the mountains are at such a distance that the drainage of air at night does not affect the coast, and night skies are often clear in the rain shadow of distant mountains, so frosts are frequent. The prevailing winds are relatively dry (having travelled across more land than sea) and are oriented along the coastline. Dry, warm winds, rolling across the Canterbury Plains especially, can be game-changers for sprouting vegetation during the spring growing months. Except for the occasional really sheltered pocket, or where mountains are close to the coast, drought and frost eliminate the possibility of having a 'nikau belt'.

Not only is zonation here reduced to 'severe salt' and 'close coastal'—grading inland into either cold-tolerant hill-country bush, kowhai forest on the limestone hills or drought-tolerant alluvial-plain vegetation with no 'nikau belt' in between—but the composition of the

EAST COASTS

wet, cold

dry winds, frosty

salty wind in storms

COASTAL ZONE

SEVERE SALT EDGE

CLOSE COASTAL ZONE

DRY INLAND

HILLY COUNTRY

vegetation is also subtly different from the west coast. Gone (or reduced) are the frost-sensitive species of the west, such as whau, kohekohe, nikau (unless tucked into gullies), rengarenga and milk tree. Increased are the species that cope well with drought—small-leaved, wiry shrubs such as matagouri, shrubby tororaro, tauhinu, *Pomaderris*, *Carmichaelia*, leafless vines and kowhai species—although in all honesty there is so little natural vegetation left on the east coast it is difficult to describe what it may once have been like. Uplift of the Wairarapa coast has provided farming-friendly terraces, and the Hawke's Bay–Poverty Bay coastline is so dry that, once cleared, it is extremely difficult to develop woody vegetation cover over it again.

The sandy zones

So far this chapter has been explaining the hard coastlines of the country, but two very long extents of sandy coast on the west coast of the North Island (in Northland and south of Wanganui) need their own explanation.

Dunelands accumulate where the prevailing winds blow onshore and where the land, both onshore and offshore, has a gentle gradient, allowing unhindered sea currents, wave action and air flow. You need these things to draw sand up the beach, then unobstructed wind will drive the dunes inland.

The Paekakariki–Wanganui stretch of duneland extends much further inland than the salt-influenced coastal zone described previously. The land is low-lying so it receives less rainfall than 'hilly country'. With low rainfall and a greater distance covered by the nightly air drainage down off the hills, drought and frost become really important growth-limiting

factors. The 'severe salt edge' and the broader 'close coastal zone' certainly exist, extending as far as 1 km from the coast, but the naturally occurring plant mix generally excludes frost-sensitive species such as taupata, akeake, ngaio or pohutukawa.

Legend:

COASTAL ZONE
- SEVERE SALT EDGE
- CLOSE COASTAL ZONE
- DRY INLAND
- HILLY COUNTRY

salty wind

droughty, frosty

wet, cold

The broad gap between the coastal zone and the 'nikau belt' is tucked in at the foot of the 'hilly country' or occurs where river catchments allow cold air to drain away from the hills. It is filled with a drought-tolerant, wind-resistant vegetation that is dominated by small-leaved, hardy species such as kanuka, mapau, totara and kowhai where the gap is exposed to the wind, but with pockets of broader-leaved species such as drought-resistant titoki, five finger or kaikomako in the lee of the dunes. The understorey plants are small-leaved, such as small-leaved coprosmas, mingimingi and weeping matipo, to name a few.

In contrast to the Kapiti–Horowhenua dunelands, the Northland dunelands rarely experience hard frosts, so you'll find the shrubland there merging into a coastal forest that *can* contain taupata, ngaio and akeake in abundance.

As we will see, there is more to coastal vegetation and coastal gardening than just dealing with salt. The processes of dunelands and sandy bays, rocky shores and headlands, sheltered harbours and sluggish estuaries, and tidal creeks, and the transition to the vegetation just beyond the salt-influenced zone, all contribute to the coastal character and a coastal 'sense of place'.

The sections that follow cast a more focused spotlight on these different coastal environments. But keep the big picture of 'zones' fresh in your mind as an overlay, like the cast net of the fisherman in which a startling diversity of fish may be flapping.

CHAPTER 2
Lifescapes

Northern Australia has its softly whispering coastal forests of casuarina trees that create music from the relentless trade winds fingering the needle-fine leaves. Tropical islands are fringed by coconut palms, well designed to shed the torrential tepid downpours they rely upon for survival, and their fruit are perfectly seasoned sailors, able to migrate to new palm-friendly beaches. The tightly enmeshed dwarf canopy of woody shrubs and mega-herbs of the southern ocean islands create both springboard and storm-proof caves for seabirds. In the subtropical paradise of the Kermadec Islands, broken branches resprout with a vigour rarely seen in temperate climates.

Each coast has its own communities (sporting roots, legs and wings), drawn together in response to unique circumstances, sometimes grim, sometimes benign. Inevitably, the 'character' of a place is a portrayal of lives and losses, and geological legacies of erosion and creation, which we recognise as 'landscapes' but could more accurately be called 'lifescapes'.

The previous chapter has introduced the broad concept of zones that are determined by particular forces in nature that curtail growth (perhaps salty wind, salty groundwater or hard frosts) or allow survival of plants that have certain adaptations. We

can take a few steps even further back and view the bigger landscapes that frame these zones—indeed, that are *defined* by these zones. In the same way that readers can analyse a good novel, assessing the merits of its plot and the themes and inter-relationships that make the story stick, so can we analyse the interplay that makes a particular coastal landscape the way it is. Nevertheless, the ultimate test of a good book is whether it was a good read. The ultimate test of a landscape is whether its natural character resonates with us, no matter how complex its history. When

people talk about celebrating a 'sense of place', this is often what they are meaning—the expression of all those serendipitous events through time, climate changes and evolution that have culminated in a unique 'personality' of a stretch of coast.

Of course, what we see these days is greatly influenced by the activities of mankind over hundreds of years, but in New Zealand, so recently colonised by *Homo sapiens*, we are fairly good at interpreting which alterations in coastal patterns are due to our influence (or that of our tag-along animals), allowing us to be judgemental over our landscapes. Are they 'wild'? Are they 'modified'? And if modified, can they still be 'wild' if they regenerated with a full seed source available to them? Are they diminished by replacement of native species with exotics? What are we losing that our grandchildren will not even know has been lost? These are engrossing questions for even humble gardeners to wrestle with if they so desire.

A recent trend in urban landscape design has been to peel back the layers of modification to rediscover what natural patterns there once were. It may reveal a stream that has been culverted for decades and that it can be planted with swathes of restiads and rushes. Or perhaps it is the recognition that ponds are a process, not just a reflection of the sky, and can be allowed to mature into raupo swamps or flaxlands. This is not restoration in the conservation sense, where entire habitats and communities are restored to ecological viability, but it is a sign of respect of lost histories. Again and again, the garden designer finds that understanding the past enriches the present.

The following pages dip into the diversity of coastal regions, listing plants that, in conjunction with landform and climate, impart the character that makes each region such a different experience.

Northland–Coromandel

Diverse, picturesque, weathered: these are just some of the hallmarks of the indented Northland coastline, which also includes coastal forest almost to the water's edge. Petticoat frills of Pacific oysters, colourful volcanic hillside clays, and an abundance of foodstuffs for birds of the bush and sea are all characteristic. Sandy bays have raised beach benches where shells decorate the necklace-like strand lines. Buffalo grass and kikuyu have choked growth on so many coastal hillsides that the natural vegetation is to be treasured.

Trees and shrubs

Akepiro, *Olearia furfuracea*

Broadleaf, kapuka, *Griselinia littoralis*

Carmichaelia australis

Coastal maire, *Nestegis apetela*

Coprosma macrocarpa

Elingamita johnsonii

Golden tainui, *Pomaderris kumeraho*

Hebe diosmifolia (endemic to Northland)

Houpara, *Pseudopanax lessonii*

Kanuka, *Kunzea robusta*

Karaka, *Corynocarpus laevigatus*

Karo, *Pittosporum crassifolium*

Kohekohe, *Dysoxylum spectabile*

Kowhai, *Sophora microphylla, S. fulvida*

Manuka, *Leptospermum scoparium*

Nikau, *Rhopalostylis sapida*

Olearia albida

Pale-flowered kumarahou, *Pomaderris hamiltonii*

Parapara, *Pisonia brunoniana*

Pohutukawa, *Metrosideros excelsa*

Prickly mingimingi, *Leptecophylla juniperina*

Pukanui, *Meryta sinclairii*

Puriri, *Vitex lucens*

Tall mingimingi, *Leucopogon fasciculatus*

Tauhinu, *Pomaderris amoena, P. phylicifolia*

Taupata, *Coprosma repens*

Taurepo, *Rhabdothamnus solandri*

Tawapou, *Planchonella costata*

Wharangi, *Melicope ternata*

White maire, *Nestegis lanceolata*

Ground plants and climbers

Buggar grass, *Austrostipa stipoides*

Celmisia major var. *major*

Coastal tussock, *Chionochloa bromoides*

Fuchsia procumbens

Gahnia lacera

Kaiwharawhara, perching lily, *Astelia solandri*

Kauri grass, *Astelia trinervia*

Mercury bay weed, *Dichondra repens*

New Zealand linen, *Linum monogynum*

Peperomia, *Peperomia urvilleana*

Poor Knights lily, *Xeronema callistemon*

Rasp fern, *Blechnum* (=*Doodia*) spp.

Rengarenga, *Arthropodium cirratum*

Shore bindweed, *Calystegia soldanella*

Shore kowharawhara, *Astelia banksii*

Small-leaved pohuehue, *Muehlenbeckia complexa*

Tecomanthe speciosa

Turutu, *Dianella nigra*

Northern estuaries

Here, Old Man Time has accumulated his sediments, slowed the flow of rivers, and determined that we live by the ebb and flow of soupy water. These gentle places require commensurate sensitivity for their survival. They are usually encircled by clay hillsides that are parched in summer, and slippery and sticky in winter. A palette of olive-greys and browns, running through from totara forest to mangroves and rushland fringing the water, would be rather sombre if not for a seasonal spangling with yellow blossoms or fruits, and the rainbow-plumaged kingfishers darting about. Mangroves have always been a feature in northern estuaries but have increased their distribution dramatically through the interplay of increased nutrient-laden sediment from land runoff and the arrival of semi-aquatic exotic grasses that can capture the mangrove seeds and provide perfect nursery conditions.

Trees and shrubs

Cabbage tree, *Cordyline australis*

Golden tainui, *Pomaderris kumeraho*

Kowhai, *Sophora chathamica*

Mangeao, *Litsea calicaris*

Mangrove, *Avicennia marina* subsp. *australasica*

Manuka, *Leptospermum scoparium*

Mapau, *Myrsine australis*

Pale-flowered kumarahou, *Pomaderris hamiltonii*

Saltmarsh ribbonwood, *Plagianthus divaricatus*

Tall mingimingi, *Leucopogon fasciculatus*

Tauhinu, *Pomaderris amoena*, *P. phylicifolia*

Totara, *Podocarpus totara*

Ground plants

Glasswort, *Sarcocornia quinqueflora*

New Zealand iris, *Libertia ixioides*

Oioi, jointed wire rush, *Apodasmia similis*

Sea rush, wiwi *Juncus kraussii* var. *australiensis*

Shore primrose, *Samolus repens*

East Cape–Poverty Bay

With the abrupt emergence of high hills from the sea, there is only a narrow strip of lowland coastal habitat available around this coastline, and this has been shared for a long time now with humans. Little natural vegetation remains, although many unused areas are reverting to manuka scrub and pohutukawa still cling to the land's edge. The virgin vegetation would not have been too dissimilar to that of Northland and Coromandel, but the East Cape is drier and generally more exposed to wind so there is a higher proportion of drought-tolerant species evident. The subtropical species have dropped out.

Trees and shrubs
Carmichaelia williamsii

Kaikomako, *Pennantia corymbosa*

Kamahi, *Weinmannia racemosa*

Karaka, *Corynocarpus laevigatus*

Kohekohe, *Dysoxylum spectabile*

Koromiko, *Hebe stricta*

Kowhai, *Sophora tetraptera*

Manuka, *Leptospermum scoparium*

Mapau, *Myrsine australis*

Pohutukawa, *Metrosideros excelsa*

Raukumara, *Brachyglottis perdicioides*

Titoki, *Alectryon excelsus* subsp. *excelsus*

Wharangi, *Melicope ternata*

Ground plants
Chionochloa flavicans

Microsorum scandens

New Zealand iris, *Libertia ixioides*

Oplismenus hirtellus

Toetoe, *Austroderia* (=*Cortaderia*) *fulvida*

Turutu, *Dianella nigra*

Hawke's Bay–Wairarapa

This is a harsh environment for vegetation—long, hot, drought-prone summers with dry winds coursing across mostly pastoral coastal environments, or frostily bitter winters with driving southerly storms. Coastal forest, where it survives, crouches low and fits snugly over the hillslopes. Only when the forest is removed do we become aware of an infinite number of seepages and springs issuing from the sedimentary layering of this eastern seaboard that provide sustenance for cabbage trees. Peppering the coastal hillsides, it is often cabbage trees that create the landscape memories, while on the coastal terraces and deeply incised gullies, it is groves of Maori karaka orchards that are a legacy of the human landscape. This is a part of New Zealand where the tightening squeeze between eroding shorelines and pastoral land is most noticeable and the fringe of natural coastal vegetation the most vulnerable. Grasses and sturdy, wind-resistant shrubs impart much of the character of this narrow zone.

Trees, shrubs and climbers

Akiraho, *Olearia paniculata*

Brachyglottis greyi

Castlepoint daisy, *Brachyglottis compacta*

Chionochloa beddiei

Clematis forsteri

Gaultheria antipoda

Karaka, *Corynocarpus laevigatus*

Kohuhu, *Pittosporum tenuifolium*

Kowhai, *Sophora tetraptera*

Mapau, *Myrsine australis*

Muehlenbeckia complexa

New Zealand jasmine, *Parsonsia capsularis*

Ngaio, *Myoporum laetum*

Olearia solandri

Pimelea villosa, P. prostrata

Pittosporum ralphii

Puka, *Griselinia lucida*

Tall mingimingi, *Leucopogon fasciculatus*

Tauhinu, *Ozothamnus leptophyllus*

Taupata, *Coprosma repens*

Titoki, *Alectryon excelsus*

Ground plants

Carex flagillifera

Craspedia viscosa

Gossamer grass, *Anemanthele lessoniana*

Pingao, *Ficinia spiralis*

Sand wind grass, *Lachnagrostis billardierei*

Spinifex, *Spinifex sericeus*

Toetoe, *Austroderia (=Cortaderia) toetoe*

Wahlenbergia ramosa

Palliser–Wellington

The crumple zone between two different tectonic motions gives Wellington its buckling and jagged landscape but also its raised-terrace beach platform gifted by the massive earthquakes of the nineteenth century. The wind funnel of Cook Strait insists that vegetation must be firmly tethered or wedged into rock crevices and clay cliffs, but the hard-rock shoreline, shingle beaches, loess-coated hillsides and greywacke headlands also ensure that there is great diversity in microenvironments. The variety of plants may not be great after 160 years of intensive settlement, but the variety of niches for plants provides the gardener with lots of inspiration.

Trees, shrubs and climbers

Akiraho, *Olearia paniculata*

Clematis afoliata, C. forsteri

Cook Strait kowhai, *Sophora molloyi*
(cultivated form is known as
'Dragon's Gold')

Coprosma propinqua

Kaikomako, *Pennantia corymbosa*

Mahoe, *Melicytus ramiflorus*

Ngaio, *Myoporum laetum*

Pohuehue, *Muehlenbeckia complexa*

Silver tussock, *Poa cita*

Tauhinu, *Ozothamnus leptophyllus*

Taupata, *Coprosma repens*

Ground plants

Craspedia minor (white flowers),
C. *uniflora* var. *maritima* (yellow
flowers)

Golden spaniard, *Aciphylla aurea*

Haloragis erecta

New Zealand linen, *Linum
monogynum*

New Zealand iris, *Libertia edgariae*

Sea holly, *Eryngium vesiculosum*

Wharariki, *Phormium cookianum*

Western dunelands

From Farewell Spit to the Kapiti–Horowhenua coast, Kaipara's Poutu Peninsula or Ninety Mile Beach, sand is piling up against New Zealand, fed from an ample supply from eroding mountain ranges and volcanoes. This is, predominantly, a very large expanse of silica, as the heavier, darker minerals have either been left behind in the rivers of the Tararua Range or have spewed out from the Waikato River but failed to travel much further around the coast, unlike the lighter-weight silica grains. Tell-tale accumulations of pumice from the Taupo eruption of AD 180 peppering the western beaches are clues to the origins of much of the sand, but there are old offshore volcanoes that also contribute. The dynamic landscape formed from prevailing winds toying with this huge amount of sand is fundamentally unsuitable for human settlement, but that hasn't stopped us—only historic tsunamis have had the power to overcome the magnetic attraction extensive stretches of sand have for humans. It is a dimpled patchwork quilt of wet and dry, hill and swale. Although the dry dune forest was most likely burned and altered well before European settlement, associations that are unique to dry dunes can be found in most of the old bush remnants today, namely korokio, akeake, narrow-leaved maire, *Coprosma crassifolia*, totara, kanuka and titoki.

Trees and shrubs

Akeake, *Dodonaea viscosa*

Akiraho, *Olearia paniculata*

Bracken, *Pteridium esculentum*

Broom, *Carmichaelia australis*

Coprosma areolata

Coprosma crassifolia

Kanuka, *Kunzea robusta*

Kohuhu, *Pittosporum tenuifolium*

Korokio, *Corokia cotoneaster*

Kowhai, *Sophora microphylla*

Mapau, *Myrsine australis*

Matagouri, *Discaria toumatou*

Narrow-leaved maire, *Nestegis montana*

Prickly mingimingi, *Leptecophylla (=Cyathodes) juniperina*

Rohutu, *Lophomyrtus obcordata*

Sand coprosma, *Coprosma acerosa*

Sand daphne, *Pimelea villosa*

Tauhinu, *Ozothamnus leptophyllus*

Titoki, *Alectryon excelsus*

Totara, *Podocarpus totara*

Ground plants

Asplenium polyodon

Microsorum scandens

Pingao, *Ficinia spiralis*

Sand wind grass, *Lachnagrostis billardierei*

Selliera rotundifolia

Spinifex, *Spinifex sericeus*

Trip-me-up, *Carex testacea*

West Taranaki–King Country

Black sands and cannonball boulders are the only remnants of rhyolitic volcanoes eroded by rivers and flushed out to the coast, where the pounding west coast surf rearranges them into beguiling patterns and textures. There is, nevertheless, a strongly felt sense of resilience along this coastline. It seems ironic that erosive forces leave us with powerful landscapes of buttresses and big boulders. The vegetation, too, is bold and resilient at first glance, but with so much surf spray in the air year-round, there is an opportunity for lots of 'softer' plants—ground ferns, nikau palms, whau and giant herbs. There is a lushness to the vegetation that weds perfectly with the muscular landscape.

Trees and shrubs

Kawakawa, *Piper (=Macropiper) excelsum*

Kiekie, *Freycinetia banksii*

Kohekohe, *Dysoxylum spectabile*

Napuka, *Veronica (=Hebe) speciosa*

Nikau, *Rhopalostylis sapida*

Rangiora, *Brachyglottis repanda*

Taurepo, *Rhabdothamnus solandri*

Toropapa, *Alseuosmia macrophylla*

Totorowhiti, *Dracophyllum strictum*

Whau, *Entelea arborescens*

Ground plants

Common maidenhair fern, *Adiantum cunninghamii*

King fern, *Psitana (=Marratia) salicina*

New Zealand jasmine, *Parsonsia heterophylla*

Parataniwha, *Elatostema rugosum*

Shore hard fern, *Blechnum blechnoides*

Marlborough Sounds

The outer sounds have been likened to the bleached hills of the Mediterranean, the inner sanctum of the sounds like a journey into primeval Aotearoa. For all its ruggedness, this coastal landscape is hugely changed—felled, forested, grazed, burnt for generation after generation. Thankfully, small pockets of history remain—the bay that James Cook visited repeatedly for restocking and repairing his ships still has the same tall trees he admired, even if jetties, monuments and tourism paraphernalia now litter his pristine shoreline. And 'pockets' is a useful word to describe the natural vegetation character, which varies so markedly from that on exposed, wind-whipped headlands to that within sheltered, warm bays. There is a constant sense of reversion from farmland to bush throughout the sounds (although much of the scrubland comprises invasive exotic shrubs), and this somewhat scruffy and lackadaisical look is part of the nature of the place.

Trees and shrubs

Akeake, *Dodonaea viscosa*

Akiraho, *Olearia paniculata*

Dracophyllum urvilleanum

Inaka, *Dracophyllum longifolium*

Kanuka, *Kunzea ericoides*

Kohekohe, *Dysoxylum spectabile*

Kohuhu, *Pittosporum tenuifolium*

Ngaio, *Myoporum laetum*

Tawhirikaro, *Pittosporum cornifolium*

Broadleaf, *Griselinia littoralis*

Tauhinu, *Ozothamnus leptophyllus*

White maire, *Nestegis lanceolata*

Ground plants

Cook's scurvy grass, *Lepidium oleraceum*

Gossamer grass, *Anemanthele lessoniana*

New Zealand linen, *Linum monogynum*

Shore spurge, *Euphorbia glauca*

Turutu, *Dianella nigra*

Wharariki, *Phormium cookianum*

White climbing rata, *Metrosideros perforata*

Eastern Marlborough–Kaikoura

Along the east coast of New Zealand there are large areas where limestone has formed from the sediments and bio-matter that were gently laid down in deep basins off the shores of Gondwana. Over time, these beds have been uplifted to give us an exquisite landscape of fossiliferous and chalky reefs and cliffs. Rivers flowing from limestone valleys turn the sea milky. The sky somehow always seems paler and milkier too. Bleached whale bones once littered settlement beaches, but these days encrusted paua shells and sun-withered ringlets of kelp are the storm-tide flotsam. It is a landscape of curiosities, and the vegetation also has its intriguing characters.

Trees and shrubs

Akiraho, *Olearia paniculata*

Coprosma grandifolia, C. lucida

Mapau, *Myrsine australis*

Ngaio, *Myoporum laetum*

Broadleaf, *Griselinia littoralis*

Titoki, *Alectryon excelsus*

Tree fuchsia, *Fuchsia excorticata*

Veronica traversii

Ground plants

Lobelia (=Pratia) angulata

Long-hair plume grass, *Dichelachne crinita*

Marlborough rock daisy, *Pachystegia minor*

New Zealand lilac, *Veronica (=Heliohebe) hulkeana*

Tasman Bay–Golden Bay

Huge tides and beds of coarse golden sand provide so many sparkling, textured, memorable beachscapes through the tidal flux of the day that this is one of the most scenic parts of New Zealand. Clear blue skies are a feature here, and although the winters are extremely cold, it is rare for frosts to bother the coastal vegetation. Frost may lie on the sand, but often there will be enough of a hillside behind for air to drain down and protect the land itself. It is patterns that dominate the coastal character here—patterns of draining sandflats imprinted with sand ripples; tapestries of black mussel spat across golden rocks; tufts of tussock peppering estuary mudflats; skeins of seabirds.

Trees and shrubs

Akeake, *Dodonaea viscosa*

Akiraho, *Olearia paniculata*

Black beech, *Fuscospora solandri*

Hard beech, *Fuscospora truncata*

Kanuka, *Kunzea ericoides*

Makaka, *Carmichaelia australis*

Matai, *Prumnopitys taxifolia*

Prickle heath, *Leucopogon fraseri*

Prickly mingmingi, *Leptecophylla (=Cyathodes) juniperina*

Saltmarsh ribbonwood, *Plagianthus divaricatus*

Sand daphne, *Pimelea villosa*

Tall mingimingi, *Leucopogon fasciculatus*

Ground plants

Buggar grass, *Austrostipa stipoides*

Grey saltbush, *Atriplex cinerea*

Helichrysum lanceolatum

Libertia ixioides, L. mooreae

New Zealand linen, *Linum monogynum*

Shore lobelia, *Lobelia anceps*

Shore primrose, *Samolus repens*

Shore spurge, *Euphorbia glauca*

West Coast

The elements of the hard rocky shore of the South Island's west coast are similar to those of the North Island except the landscape is bigger, the mountains more immediate and higher. Here, the spray hugs coastal cliffs almost permanently, and the wet coastal vegetation responds in kind with a beautiful richness in ferns and (in the northern, warmer portions of the coast) nikau. With so much wetness, however, the soils are very leached, and trees tolerant of low fertility, such as kamahi, hutu and horopito, are very much favoured. Harakeke (swamp flax) is probably more common than wharariki (mountain flax). Salt-resistance is essential nevertheless, so the waxy-leaved trees and shrubs also dominate the mix: broadleaf in particular thrives here. Ground-creeping mat herbs and creeping ferns pour like fluid through cracks and basins in the severe salt edge. There is a wonderful diversity of flowering shrubs, daisies, ground ferns and tree ferns, climbing rata, and small trees with dramatic flowering, such as olearias and kamahi. It is a boldly showy environment in so many ways—certainly not a place for fainted-hearted gardening!

Trees and shrubs

Brachyglottis rotundifolia var. *ambigua*

Broadleaf, *Griselinia littoralis*

Climbing rata, *Metrosideros fulgens*

Horopito, *Pseudowintera colorata*

Hutu, *Ascarina lucida*

Kamahi, *Weinmannia racemosa*

Kawakawa, *Piper (=Macropiper) excelsum*

Nikau, *Rhopalostylis sapida*

Pigeonwood, *Hedycarya arborea*

Southern rata, *Metrosideros umbellata*

Tree fuchsia, *Fuchsia excorticata*

Ground plants

Gunnera monoica

Harakeke, *Phormium tenax*

Wharariki, *Phormium cookianum*

Deep South

Cold, yes. Windy, yes. Snowclad? Sometimes. When you get rain accompanying onshore winds, as you usually do down south (all year round), conditions are ideal for tree growth, and this area is renowned for its lush forest undergrowth of tree ferns and shrubs. Yet trees so close to shore are inevitably bent and misshapen into crouching, wind-resistant caricatures of trees. Manuka, totara, olearia, horopito—it seems the only criterion for which a species forms coastal forest is that it must be able to be contoured and shorn by the wind. Shrubland maintains the aerodynamically smooth canopy required for survival, and ground-hugging shrubs such as *Celmisia rigida* or Lindsay's daisy survive the best. With so many storms crashing through, it is little surprise that there are sandy beaches at the base of cliffs where erosion material accumulates even without large rivers supplying the raw materials. Here, pingao grows more luxuriantly than in any other part of the country. So this is a landscape of tortured vegetation, of strange ironies of beach and hard rock, of fringing, swirling skirts of giant kelp and of a richness of wildlife inhabiting the edges where nutritious cold currents collide with the land.

Trees and shrubs

Broom, *Carmichaelia petriei*

Horopito, *Pseudowintera colorata*

Kamahi, *Weinmannia racemosa*

Kanuka, *Kunzea robusta*

Kowhai, *Sophora microphylla*

Mahoe, *Melicytus ramiflorus*

Mountain akeake, *Olearia avicenniifolia*

Mutton-bird scrub, *Brachyglottis rotundifolia*

Ngaio, *Myoporum laetum* (as far south as Dunedin)

Pigeonwood, *Hedycarya arborea*

Prickly mingimingi, *Leptecophylla (=Cyathodes) juniperina*

Raukaua simplex

Stinkwood, *Coprosma foetidissima*

Shore hebe, *Veronica elliptica*

Teteaweka, *Olearia oporina*

Tree fuchsia, *Fucshia excorticata*

Ground plants

Bindweed, *Calystegia tuguriorum*

Celmisia rigida

Geranium sessiliflorum var. *arenarium*

Harakeke, *Phormium tenax*

Kiwakiwa, *Blechnum fluviatile*

Libertia peregrinans

Lindsay's daisy, *Celmisia lindsayi*

New Zealand iceplant, *Disphyma australe*

Pingao, *Ficinia (=Desmoschoenus) spiralis*

Poa maniototo

Remuremu, *Selliera radicans*

Sand tussock, *Poa billardierei*

Shield fern, *Polystichum neozelandicum*

Shore lobelia, *Lobelia anceps*

Shore primrose, *Samolus repens*

Shore spleenwort, *Asplenium obtusatum*

Shore spurge, *Euphorbia glauca*

Sickle spleenwort, *Asplenium polyodon*

Silver tussock, *Poa cita*

Toetoe, *Austroderia (=Cortaderia) richardii*

Canterbury–Banks Peninsula

The challenging contrasts of dry nor'westers and stormy sou'easters on arid substrates are manifest in grey shrubland that merges inland into woodland across the broad sweeps of Canterbury's shingle coastline, resilient pingao on dunes, and oily or leathery-leaved trees on steep banks. But tough conditions produce extreme speciation—that, and the isolationist history of Banks Peninsula as an island, has resulted in some special treats for Cantabrians. Flattened, leafless prostrate broom and leafless pohuehue, mat coprosma or *Convulvulus waitaha* are examples. The raised shingle beaches in some ways sport the most interesting native vegetation: an entanglement of 'grey' shrubs such as *Coprosma dumosa*, *C. crassifolia* and matagouri, shrubby tororaro choked with clematis, native jasmine, pohuehue, *Convulvulus waitaha* and that old battler leafless bush lawyer. The volcanic clay cliffs of Banks Peninsula are more orthodox, dominated by akeake, ngaio, kowhai, kanuka and hebe.

Trees and shrubs

Akeake, *Dodonaea viscosa*

Coprosma crassifolia, C. dumosa, C. propinqua

Helichrysum lanceolatum

Kowhai, *Sophora microphylla*

Makaka, *Carmichaelia australis*

Mat coprosma, *Coprosma petriei*

Narrow-leaved lacebark, *Hoheria angustifolia*

Ngaio, *Myoporum laetum*

Olearia avicenniifolia, O. paniculata, O. fragmentissima, O. fimbriata

Shrubby tororaro, *Muehlenbeckia astonii*

Veronica salicifolia, V. strictissma

Ground plants and climbers

Bush lawyer, *Rubus cissoides*

Clematis afoliata, C. marata

Convolvulus waitaha

Leafless bush lawyer, *Rubus squarrosus*

Leafless pohuehue, *Muehlenbeckia ephedroides*

New Zealand jasmine, *Parsonsia capsularis*

Pohuehue, *Muehlenbeckia australis*

Prostrate broom, *Carmichaelia appressa*

Sand tussock, *Poa billardierei*

Shore spurge, *Euphorbia glauca*

Silver tussock, *Poa cita*

PART TWO

Wild lessons

CHAPTER 3
Sand country

Sand is being manufactured from rock around our country all the time and fed down rivers or stockpiled at the foot of cliffs, and it is being recycled from vast offshore deposits from previous ice ages. So with such proliferation of the stuff, why aren't all our beaches sandy? Think of all those rocky coastlines through the Marlborough Sounds, and yet there are very few sandy beaches to be found. In contrast, other stretches of New Zealand are comprised entirely of sand, with the nearest rocky outcrop miles away. And having got sand onshore, how do we learn to live with it? Gardening on a material that is the ultimate end product of the physical destruction of useful minerals—and which moves around a lot—does not bode well for soil-loving gardeners.

Each type of sandy deposit, whether it is a beach in a cove or a dune on an exposed shore, has been formed by processes that influence what vegetation it can support and therefore what gardening potential it has. Because the approaches are so different, I have divided sand country into three parts: the dry duneland, the truly wet areas and the sandy bays. What the different vegetation types associated with wet and dry sand environments do have in common,

however, is an incredible successional drive to change and mature into something different. The more we understand this, the happier we will be to embrace change within our own properties.

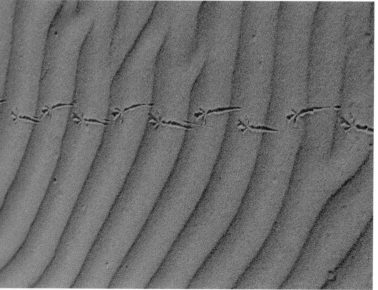

Dry duneland

Scorched feet as you dash between cool grass to soothing sea water; gritty sandwiches; gritty floorboards; sagging guttering; glinting crystals and crumbling sand castles, scarves that flutter from the top of sand hills; and beach umbrellas threatening to roll along the shore like giant tumbleweeds. Further inland, and it's drifts of sand against the curb; small blowouts where cattle have nestled for shelter; old garage doors, paint peeling and abraded; drained flat paddocks bristling with rushes.

Of the 17,000 km or so of coastline in New Zealand, only 1100 km is duneland, which can extend many kilometres inland. It is that 1100 km that most people dream of over summer and that we love to live close to, even if it does mean sand through every nook and cranny. Duneland is quite a special coastal landscape with a great variety of features that the modern property owner needs to understand to get the best out of it. So let's look at the story of duneland in New Zealand in order to help us garden in this most difficult of gardening environments.

Dune creation

To get sand piling up along a shore at all, you need a combination of high wave energy (where waves are parallel to the shore and will accumulate sand at the beach rather than sweep it further along the coast), strong onshore winds (to move sand up the beach) and, of course, a supply of sand to begin with. Sand is the product of erosion of rock, so where there are rivers feeding material into the sea or where cliffs are being eroded, sand is being produced, either directly or by the grinding up of rocks into smaller grains by wave action.

Where there is a gentle sea-bed gradient off the coast, sand can move easily with the long-shore currents and will accumulate in shallow waters. Although it is the sea that transports sand along the coast or to a particular beach, it is the wind that forces it up the beach and piles it into dunes. Wind and dunes go hand in hand.

The North Island dunelands stretching along the Manawatu, Horowhenua and Kapiti coastline illustrate this wonderfully. These are our most extensive dunelands, continuous for 200 km from Paekakariki to Patea. Now, go back in time to the most recent glacial period, which lasted from around 18,000 to around 9000 years ago. At its peak, the shoreline was 120 m further out from the current coast, the climate was generally 5°C cooler, and all that extra land was relatively sparsely vegetated. Much of it was built up from greywacke gravels cascading out of snow-clad mountain ranges. As the climate warmed, and sea-level rose, that land became seabed, which provided a huge source of sand. Eventually, the sea-level rose to several metres higher than it is today, and by 6000 years ago, dunes were forming along the coast.

When dunes form, as long as there is an ongoing source of sand available, they extend the shoreline out towards the sea, building row after row of foredunes as the sand-binding plants do their job. For thousands of years this process continued, and there was either so much sand or so much wind (we can't be sure which) that these dunes became unstable and started heading inland. They shuffled inland, pushed by the wind, as much as 14 km* in northern parts of the region or up against the old sea cliffs towards the southern end of the region.

*This was happening when the coastline was 4 km inland from today's position, so these innermost dunes are now around 18 km from the sea.

TOP Dune stabilisation begins with sand-binders pingao, spinifex and sand sedge.
BOTTOM On exposed dunelands it takes a very long time for stabilising shrubs to coallesce into continuous ground-cover.

59

Dunes that move en masse across flat land are usually parabolic dunes—so called because a mobile dune crest forms, trailing arms behind it, making a crescent-like shape when viewed from the air. The sand erodes from between the trailing arms, creating sand flats that often scour down to the water table. Thus we end up with a landscape today of very steep-sided dunes, often aligned at right angles rather than parallel to the coast, interspersed with swamps, lakes and sand flats. These earliest post-ice-age dunes are generally the biggest and steepest, even today.

Over time there have been long episodes of these destabilised dune movements separated by long periods of stability, during which time scrubland could slowly evolve into forest over quite reasonably developed sandy soils.

In places, subsequent dune migrations have overlain the older dunes, but mostly the coastline has progressively moved seawards. Each new sequence of dune-building, destabilisation, migration and then restabilisation by vegetation has created its own landscape. We can see the results still, although we can't be sure of the reason for these periods of instability.

From the 1870s, when it became clear that west coast dunes in the Horowhenua–Kapiti region were on the move, a massive effort went into stabilisation using introduced plants. First marram grass, lupin and pines, and later coastal wattle (*Acacia sophorae*) and Sydney golden wattle (*A. longifolia*), were introduced explicitly for dune stabilisation, which has largely been successful, although at a cost to natural coastal character. They have, indeed, been too successful, as marram, lupin and acacia have continued to spread in an uncontrolled way along all our sandy coasts, suppressing native species and changing the forms of our dunes.

With less erosion occurring inland now, compared with the 1800s, there is less sand being supplied down rivers, so dune-building is slowing down. Ironically, this is also resulting in the permanent retreat of

On Chatham Island, previous cycles of dune-building and stabilisation are being overrun by the latest activity, triggered by grazing damage.

foredunes during storm events as there are no new sand sources to replenish the sand lost. To stave off erosion and optimise the chances of rebuilding stable dunes, a new phase of planting using native plants rather than exotics is underway throughout New Zealand. It began as something of a pipe dream, but as we refine the methodology and overcome technical issues of bulk-planting programmes on raw dunes, we are beginning to see real successes.

Nevertheless, we should never be complacent about the foredunes. The erosional effect of a rise in sea-level when there isn't a new source of sand available isn't a happy prospect. Perhaps a large earthquake could trigger an influx of sand? Let's hope it isn't accompanied by a tsunami, which would destabilise large extents of duneland. In the early 1980s, an El Niño climate event caused dune blowouts and erosion along the west coast of the North Island, reminding us that there is little we can do to stabilise dunes completely when there are at least three major natural factors involved in their creation—ocean currents and waves, wind *and* sand supply.

Less organised than the parabolic dunes that form when prevailing winds cause blowouts are transgressive dunelands—the mobile dunes and sand drifts that can form when erosion is at its peak and sand is blowing in all directions. They are most common along the Wanganui coastline, on west coast beaches in Northland and on Stewart Island/Rakiura—areas where wind strengths are constantly high. It's extraordinary seeing cliff-top dunefields, but these are common sights in parts of Taranaki. Along stretches of the Wairarapa coast there are dunelands confused by two strong wind directions: the fearsome southerlies that blow sand ashore and also a predominant offshore wind that refuses to cooperate with orthodox dune-building processes.

It is easy to understand why revegetation of fields of mobile sand is more problematic than in the more regular landforms of foredunes, rear dunes and parabolic dunes, where there are relatively large areas of sheltered habitat available. Instead, vegetation in trangressive dunelands extends from small scattered pockets and it is not until the pockets coalesce that the entire field is stabilised.

Tombolos are dune linkages between the mainland and islands, or between two islands. We can see some classic ones in Wellington (Lyall Bay area), Mahia (between Mahia Peninsula and the mainland) and in Northland (Aupouri Peninsula, Karikari Peninsula). In such places the shallow water between the mainland and the island had been collecting and trapping sand as it moved along the coast to the point that the accumulated sands rose above water

'Charles Slight leased the Paekakariki Hotel from Mrs Tilley. Under a clause in the lease he was to receive approximately 200 pounds if he could find some means of holding the drift sand then encroaching the sand-dunes. He later went off for a brief period to South Africa and the Boer War. While he was there he gathered lupin seed which he brought back with him and planted on Paekakariki Beach. The seed germinated and flourished. We used to collect the resulting seed pods and spread them over dunes near the creek south of Paekakariki. This was the beginning of sand holding in New Zealand. Seed was later sent from Paekakariki to New Brighton, Canterbury, and has now spread through the country.'

Robert Kent, 1885–1910, in *The Celebration History of the Kapiti District,* by Olive Baldwin

TOP TO BOTTOM Pingao, spinifex and sand sedge.

level. (In the Wellington example, a massive earthquake also uplifted the area, hastening the process.) Once the sand is above sea-level, it is up to the prevailing winds to determine the form the land link will take. The examples given have all been subject to recent (early European) destabilisation, forcing new dunes over the top of older ones, but most have subsequently restabilised.

Dune mobility has created a patterned landscape that, while comprising many specialist habitats for plants, was full of interconnections, so plant populations were rarely isolated. Overlaying such specialisation was the natural succession that occurs with time as vegetation cover matured, soils formed and swamps slowly infilled. Always, the limiting growth factors were related to proximity to the beach.

A landscape of four dimensions

Duneland, then, is a process of dunes both migrating inland from the coast and building out seawards at the same time. The legacy of all this activity is a diverse landscape. You could call it a four-dimensional landscape. Distance from the onshore, salt-laden winds and those piles of infertile sand determines what vegetation is possible. The increasing distance inland corresponds also to an increase in time, with its subsequent maturity of vegetation cover. And every duneland feature, whether it is dry dune, swamp hollow or sand flat, is going through its own successional changes as time passes. Confusing? Yes, but a botany student's dream, as succession is spread across the countryside like pages in a textbook laid across the ground.

The diagram opposite illustrates in simple terms the relationship between time and distance from the shore as dunes stabilise and vegetation matures. Although it reveals the sequence along the Kapiti coast, the successional process will not vary much for other large west coast dunefields in New Zealand.

The youngest dunes are colonised by the sand-binding pingao (*Ficinia spiralis*), spinifex (*Spinifex sericeus*) and sand sedge (*Carex pumila*), which can cope with salt- and sand-laden winds and low fertility. Indeed, often it is simply the presence of spinifex snaring the drifting sand that creates dunes in the first place. Although there is little seaweed on sandy coasts, these beachfront plants do gain some nutrient from rotting driftwood

62

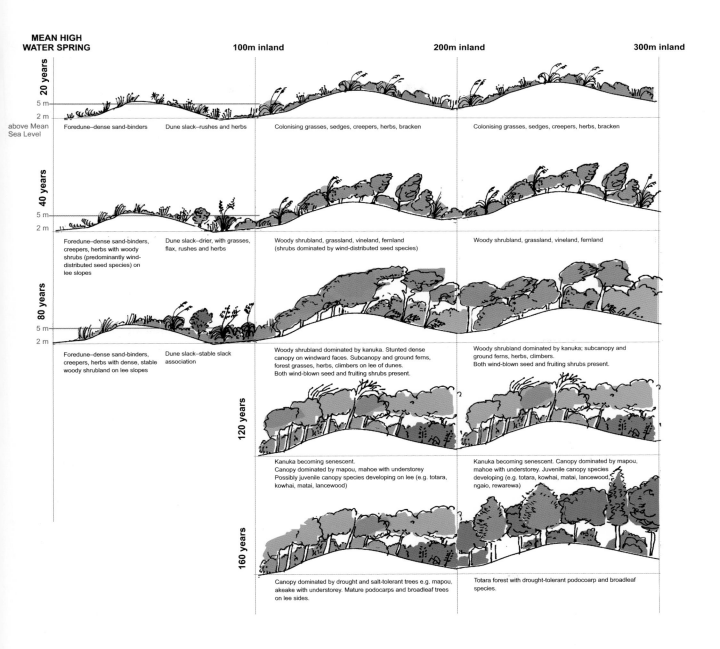

MEAN HIGH WATER SPRING

100m inland   200m inland   300m inland

20 years

5 m
2 m
above Mean Sea Level

Foredune–dense sand-binders   Dune slack–rushes and herbs   Colonising grasses, sedges, creepers, herbs, bracken   Colonising grasses, sedges, creepers, herbs, bracken

40 years

5 m
2 m

Foredune–dense sand-binders, creepers, herbs with woody shrubs (predominantly wind-distributed seed species) on lee slopes

Dune slack–drier, with grasses, flax, rushes and herbs

Woody shrubland, grassland, vineland, fernland (shrubs dominated by wind-distributed seed species)

Woody shrubland, grassland, vineland, fernland

80 years

5 m
2 m

Foredune–dense sand-binders, creepers, herbs with dense, stable woody shrubland on lee slopes

Dune slack–stable slack association

Woody shrubland dominated by kanuka. Stunted dense canopy on windward faces. Subcanopy and ground ferns, forest grasses, herbs, climbers on lee of dunes. Both wind-blown seed and fruiting shrubs present.

Woody shrubland dominated by kanuka; subcanopy and ground ferns, herbs, climbers. Both wind-blown seed and fruiting shrubs present.

120 years

Kanuka becoming senescent. Canopy dominated by mapou, mahoe with understorey Possibly juvenile canopy species developing on lee (e.g. totara, kowhai, matai, lancewood)

Kanuka becoming senescent. Canopy dominated by mapou, mahoe with understorey. Juvenile canopy species developing (e.g. totara, kowhai, matai, lancewood, ngaio, rewarewa)

160 years

Canopy dominated by drought and salt-tolerant trees e.g. mapou, akeake with understorey. Mature podocarps and broadleaf trees on lee sides.

Totara forest with drought-tolerant podocoarp and broadleaf species.

63

and plankton foam blown inland—just enough to help them overcome nitrogen deficiencies.

Also blowing along the beach might be seeds of herbs and creeping ground-covers such as shore bindweed (*Calystegia soldanella*), sand piripiri (*Acaena pallida*), shore groundsel (*Senecio lautus*) and geranium (*Geranium sessiliflorum* in the South Island or *G. traversii* on Chatham Island)—all able to deal with the dry, infertile, drifting sands. Sedges and grasses soon take root, too, especially knobby clubrush or wiri (*Ficinia nodosa*), sand tussock (*Austrofestuca littoralis*), and perhaps sand wind grass (*Lachnagrostis billardierei*) or, through the North Island, the relatively drought-tolerant small toetoe *Austroderia* (=*Cortaderia*) *fulvida*. They can all deal with extremes, especially when they are tucked in among other plants. Knobby clubrush, spinifex and pingao are also extremely tolerant of frosty beaches.

Such growth begins to collect leaf litter as well as sand and perhaps creates odd pockets of shade. Thus begins the formation of a simple organic soil that can support larger woody shrubs. This is most likely to happen in the lee of steep foredunes. The first shrubby colonisers are most likely to be those with wind-blown seeds: sand daphne (*Pimelea villosa*), tauhinu (*Ozothamnus leptophyllus*), coastal shrub daisy (*Olearia solandri*) and bracken (*Pteridium esculentum*). As soon as these start to attract birds and provide adequate shelter for fruit-eating

TOP Knobby clubrush thrives on stabilised dunes. It doesn't spread as aggressively as spinifex, but nevertheless acts as a sand-binder, with its rhizomes expanding the clumps as sand builds up.
CENTRE Few people realise that the natural habitat of the common garden plant trip-me-up includes coastal dunes.
BOTTOM Sand coprosma helps stabilise the drift of dry, wind-blown sand, constantly growing taller to keep pace with sand accumulation.

geckos, we also start to see fruit-bearing species appear—only ones that are highly specialised for these conditions, such as sand coprosma (*Coprosma acerosa*) and small-leaved pohuehue (*Muehlenbeckia complexa*).

In time, the rear dunes may provide enough shelter for these plants to be joined by other woody shrubs: *Coprosma propinqua*, *C. crassifolia*, korokio (*Corokia cotoneaster*) and matagouri (*Discaria toumatou*), our only spiny native plant, once far more common in dry coastal settings than it is today and, usefully for this environment, a nitrogen-fixer.

The rear dunes at Farewell Spit are a close-knit mosaic of dry and wet habitats. However, you can see how the dry dunes are becoming clad in small-leaved (drought-resistant) woody shrubs such as *Coprosma crassifolia*, *C. propinqua*, korokio and kanuka.

Coastal shrubland will become dominated by small-leaved, drought-resistant divaricating shrubs such as korokio. Kanuka (most likely *Kunzea amathicola*, or *K. toelkenii* in the Bay of Plenty) will be in the mix and will eventually overtop these shrubs, changing for ever the vegetation from shrubland to treeland.

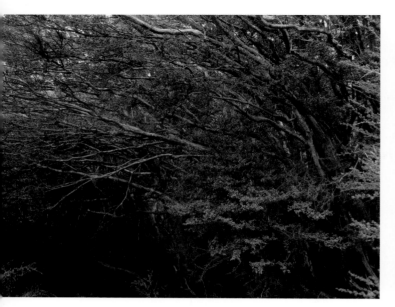

It provides the shade, shelter and, most importantly, the soil development suitable for another wave of dune dwellers—mapau (*Myrsine australis*), kowhai (*Sophora microphylla*), taupata (*Coprosma repens*), kohuhu (*Pittosporum tenuifolium*), akeake (*Dodonaea viscosa*) and akiraho (*Olearia paniculata*)—although they cannot develop to their full potential unless they are several hundred metres away from the shoreline and their roots are well above the salty groundwater. These are plants suited to aridity, low fertility and salt wind (having small, tough leaves, or leaves with waxy coatings or that are rich in oil glands). Akiraho, in particular, can live to a ripe old age, the trunks becoming more weathered and textured with maturity.

There may also be the beautiful rohutu (*Lophomyrtus obcordata*) in this maturing coastal forest—with its tiny leaves (suiting it perfectly to dune conditions) and dainty white flowers it is reminiscent

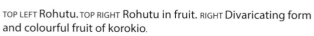

TOP LEFT Rohutu. TOP RIGHT Rohutu in fruit. RIGHT Divaricating form and colourful fruit of korokio.

of rata. Its stand-out feature, however, is its trunk. Like akeake, it grows with a spreading crown and horizontal branches, but the flaky-barked trunk, unlike the ruddy-coloured akeake, is white and, if you hold it, always seems strangely cold to the touch.

Curiously, there are usually moist conditions underfoot, probably due to the characteristic of sand that means it holds water at the surface. As a result, you'll find some of the hardy ferns here—*Asplenium oblongifolium* and *A. polyodon* are common, along with the leathery *Pellaea rotundifolia* and *Polystichum richardii* (one of the hard shield ferns). A surprisingly dainty resident here might also be the minuscule *Asplenium flabellifolium*, whose wee fan-like pinnae creep across the mosses and leaf litter in the dampest of dune hollows. Hound's-tongue (*Microsorum pustulatum*) is a stalwart, coping with both shade and more direct sunlight. In very dry areas it is likely to be hound's-tongue's cousin the narrow-fronded fragrant fern (*Microsorum scandens*), rather than the broader-fronded *M. pustulatum*, that clambers over the ground and up tree trunks.

Needing a cool root-run but also seeking the light is the New Zealand jasmine (*Parsonsia capsularis*). Some of the smaller duneland shrubs can carry an immense burden of jasmine, which gaily releases its feathery seeds into the fresh sea breezes. The small-leaved canopy lets in lots of light, so you'll find quite a few climbers enjoying this habitat, including pohuehue (*Muehlenbeckia australis*), the large-leaved and higher-climbing cousin of small-leaved pohuehue out on the foredunes, New Zealand passionvine (*Passiflora tetrandra*) and *Clematis forsteri*; *C. cunninghamii* may be present but is often overlooked for lack of the showy flowers of other clematis.

Some of the small-leaved shrubs that were precursors to the forest can persist in the now-shadier conditions, especially korokio and the small-leaved coprosmas (other than sand coprosma, which is sun-demanding). They create the hazy, dainty understorey so typical of drought-stressed forests. More small-leaved shrubs can join them, including tall mingimingi (*Leucopogon fasciculatus*) and poataniwha (*Melicope simplex*).

There is an exception to this 'natural' progression, and that is where mahoe (*Melicytus ramiflorus*) becomes the dominant canopy species early on. This seems to happen most commonly when bracken has been dominant in the previous vegetation phase. Bracken's deep fibrous root

TOP Fragrant fern. ABOVE New Zealand passionvine has the showiest foliage of any of our climbers.

Old poataniwha, gnarled by time, perched above a dune lake.

Eventually, though, as the dune forest ages and the underlying sands increase in fertility, there is a greater chance for the bigger canopy species to become established, for example, totara (*Podocarpus totara*), ngaio (*Myoporum laetum*), titoki (*Alectryon excelsus*), the fine-leaved white maire (*Nestegis lanceolata*) and, perhaps in frost-free northern dunelands, pohutukawa (*Metrosideros excelsa*). There is also scope by now for the broadleaf understorey species (but still those displaying salt-resistence) such as kawakawa (*Piper (=Macropiper) excelsum*) and five finger (*Pseudopanax arboreus*).

The overwhelming character of these wonderful coastal forests, all too rare now, is the lacy canopy dancing with light, created by myriad tiny or wrinkly leaves, and the spectacular textures of the bark of so many of the trees here.

Survival tactics create the duneland character

Rhizomatous or tap-rooting creeping growth, tiny or skinny leaves, low nutrient demands and slow growth are the duneland plants' secrets to a long life. The way most sand-binding plants grow is by pushing underground stems and roots out horizontally, then pinning them down with long taproots that seek out groundwater as far from the evaporative hot sand surface as possible. The effect that we see on the surface is drifts of plants; they may even be drifts created by a single plant that is spreading widely. There is relatively little diversity in the foredunes—more a patchy spread of this species or that species. And it is patchy—often a loose array of spinifex or pingao sprinkled across a sandy landscape, with the odd mass of sand coprosma appearing that might represent decades of growth, sand cover and re-emergence.

mats probably help trap enough moisture and provide adequate fertility for this broadleaf species to survive better than might be expected. However, mahoe is a tree with a very high turnover of leaf litter, which in rainforests breaks down readily for recycling into the soil. Not so in the dry dunes. Litter builds up, creating an impenetrable layer that makes it almost impossible for other seeds to germinate and push through. In the long run, the mahoe coastal stands are slow to progress and tend to be less diverse coastal communities.

LEFT Pingao (in the foreground) concentrates its creeping rhizome growth just under the surface, in contrast to spinifex (behind), which trails long stems for metres across the surface (although they often become submerged by drifting sand).

BELOW Behind the spinifex, introduced marram grass grows much like pingao. The bushy tussocks that form above ground level, however, are far more vulnerable to salt damage and blowouts than our sturdy native creeping sand-binders.

Soils from sand

When dunes remain stabilised for long enough, the sand itself becomes more stable through the chemical weathering of the sand grains. With the sorting of sand that goes on out at sea, you get more silica coming ashore than the other, heavier minerals, but any feldspars that are in the mix in the onshore dunes will break down with time into clay, and this clay acts to 'cement' the steep dunes in shape. Vegetation contributes to the chemical weathering process. The clay assists with holding organic material in the topsoil for the plants. It is a mutually satisfactory arrangement.

Diversity really only starts to occur away from the foredunes where enough shelter allows for shrub and herb growth amidst the taller sedges and grasses, but this diversity is overwhelmed by the sense of a close-knit tapestry of similarity as plants of similar growth forms and size compete for what little nutrition and moisture are available. Ironically, it is often elbow-to-elbow competition that allows their survival, as a close-knit ground-cover will survive the desiccating salt winds far better than individual plants will. The overwhelming need for plants to have small leaves results in a distinctive fuzz across the inland dunes. There is no place here for big, soft, floppy leaves.

Plants use the same suite of leaf adaptations in dunelands as they do anywhere to prevent stress: they minimise water loss from their leaves (curled, ribbed or hairy leaves to protect stomata); they economise on photosynthesis demands (small leaves); protect themselves from salt-burn (waxy coatings; gooey leaf buds); and they store water (succulence) and avoid losing it through osmosis (salt-, sugar- and oil-rich sap).

Out in the dunes, with so little respite from the sun, you will see more of the silvery hues that reflect the heat. You'll also find striking orange, russet and golden colours, indicating foliage full of stored oils. Green, of course, represents chlorophyll, the key to photosynthesis. It is thought that leaves containing less chlorophyll might reduce heat stress by minimising the risk of overexciting the photosynthesis reactors, which would demand more water.

TOP Spinifex. RIGHT New Zealand iceplant. OPPOSITE TOP LEFT Sand iris. OPPOSITE TOP RIGHT Knobby clubrush and *Leucopogon fraseri*. OPPOSITE BOTTOM LEFT *Selliera rotundifolia*. OPPOSITE BOTTOM RIGHT Shore bindweed.

Large duneland gardens

Nowhere does pest management, nutrient knowledge, strategic planning for shelter, planting and clever water use become more integrated than in dune gardens. Gardening here is rewarded by long-term vision and oodles of perseverence—combined with a love of sunshine and sea breezes.

Protecting the front line

Although very few of us live within the foredunes, their stabilisation is a community-wide concern, and a growing number of communities are pitching in with local authorities and industry to find feasible ways to prevent blowouts. The benefits of foredune reconstruction and protection are evident at some high-profile locations, a spectacular example being the foreshore at Mt Maunganui near Tauranga. Not only did the foredune plantings remain unscathed during ferocious storms in the 1990s, but they captured blowing sand to the degree that the road behind stayed clear—unlike the road a few hundred metres away.

Keeping people off developing foredune vegetation is a good idea, and zigzag paths will be less prone to blowouts and scouring than ones that take a more direct route.

It is likely that the shallow-gradient dunes under spinifex (far left) will be more resilient to the next storm surge than the over-steepened dunes under introduced iceplant (right).

Stabilising dunes is rather like the corporate team-building exercise to see how many items can be made out of a single paper clip in ten minutes. At face value, with only a few resilient plants to work with, options seem limited, and as a result engineered 'solutions' have often prevailed where property is at risk from dune erosion. The 'soft' options of using plants alone has worked with marram grass and lupin to a degree, and recent horticultural knowledge is allowing native species to gain ascendancy in erosion prevention. The paper clip exercise is stretching our ingenuity.

Marram grass clearly survives well throughout the country but it did not prove to be the ultimate solution for stabilising foredunes. The root system of the North Atlantic Ocean species of marram that we have here is a fibrous network that travels deep and wide in search of moisture. When growth tips of the underground rhizomes are covered with sand, this stimulates new rooting as well as new leaf growth, and thus the plant spreads and spreads, stabilising sand and arresting dune movement. The tall tussocks of marram, especially where they have naturalised rather than been planted, trap sand well, but then they also cause wind to eddy, leading to erosion. It is when marram dunes are eroded that the plant's downside becomes evident. The mat of roots that has stabilised the dune is now a liability, preventing the plants from readily regenerating. With roots exposed, the plant soon dies. Dunes then become scoured and steepened and thus likely to incur more blowouts.

Managing a blowout

Faced with a sudden blowout requiring urgent attention, what is the best course of action?
• Rabbit-proof the blowout.
• Erect some wind resistance, either by piling up manuka or cut lupin branches at the windward end, or with a windbreak fence.
• Plant a mixture of spinifex and sand tussock.
• Don't plant lupin (especially if it isn't in the area already).
• In the following autumn plant a mix of small-leaved pohuehue, sand daphne, sand bindweed and sand coprosma (keep up the rabbit eradication as these pests love coprosma).
• In our quest to stop blowouts, marram is still considered to be the most effective sand-binding plant in areas behind the foredune, with fewer disadvantages than some of the other introduced dune species.

73

Similarly, South African iceplant (*Carpobrotus edulis*) seems to provide great protection in stable conditions but, when storms erode and collapse mats of iceplant, redistribution and replenishment of sand cannot occur. Native spinifex and pingao, on the other hand, are better suited to quickly revegetating blowouts and trapping sand with their long surface runners. Over time, even though they are more sparsely vegetated, the dunes formed are smoother, create less wind turbulence and are less susceptible to blowouts. These sand-binders may not grow as densely as marram, but they punch above their weight in terms of results.

Other sand sedges and grasses once more abundant on the foredunes (in pre-rabbit days) include sand tussock (*Poa billardierei*), sand wind grass (*Lachnagrostis billardierei*), trip-me-up (*Carex testacea*) and sand sedge (*C. pumila*) (which likes the damp sand near the high-tide mark). The soft-leaved

shrubby herb *Euphorbia glauca* is also often described as a sand-country plant but tends to prefer the more sheltered and more fertile sandy beaches of sheltered bays.

Knobby clubrush should not be underestimated as a sand-binder, especially given its tolerance of both wet and dry conditions, but it is better suited to stable dunes where blowouts are unlikely.

A surprisingly tough customer, which also endears itself to gardeners, is sand piripiri, the native bidibid that is adapted to life by the shore. It has thicker leaves than its inland cousins and is well suited to wending its way through the taller sedges, building up into great mounds in places. The colour shifts through the seasons of its flowerheads (white) as they turn to seedheads (tawny brown), opening up some attractive colour-matching possibilities in small garden areas.

One of the reasons for the blind belief that introduced species were going to be better at their task than native ones is that we had also introduced animals and insects that grazed so heavily on our unprepared native species that entire populations failed. Rabbits demolished spinifex, pingao and sand coprosma. Stock chewed herbs and grasses. Certainly, some of the introduced plants continue to experience their own problems, such as the fungal blight that periodically knocks back lupin, but this is minor in comparison to the wholesale losses of native dune species. The upshot is that any native planting, be it gardening or restoration, needs to be accompanied by animal control (see page 212).

OPPOSITE TOP Sand wind grass. OPPOSITE BOTTOM LEFT Sand piripiri teamed up in a garden with trip-me-up and, OPPOSITE BOTTOM RIGHT, growing naturally with knobby clubrush.

Starting from scratch in the rear dunes

As anyone who has cut down trees on dunes can attest, once you remove mature vegetation, organic matter in the soil very quickly leaches away. With the clearance of the old coastal forests, the successional process has to begin all over again, especially on the younger dunes.

On the big old 4000–6000-year-old dunes you do sometimes find the old forest soils lingering on, providing a head start for new plantings. You can find 200–300 mm of dark organic topsoil and a slightly coloured subsoil even under pastoral grassland—a relic of a previous forest cover. Over thousands of years, minerals in the sand have weathered into clays, and this has helped soil development and also probably helped these older dunes retain their shape. Clays and organic matter in the sand increase water retention, so a wider variety of plants can be sustained by these older sandy soils.

On younger dunes the process of ageing can be fast-tracked, in a gardening sense, by improving water retention of the sand and providing shelter from salt winds. However, you still need to be mindful of your distance from the sea, and not expect to shift the successional matrix (page 63) closer to the salt zone than it would naturally be. There is little point in adding fertiliser since colonising dune species—as we will see shortly—are plants adapted to low fertility, and incautious addition of nutrients may be counter-productive.

And yet it does seem to be human nature to want to fast-track natural processes. Why we can't be satisfied to live amidst dune grasslands and shrublands is a mystery to me, as I look despairingly at the rows of Norfolk pines, Australian acacias, South African banksias and battered European macrocarpa hedges that disfigure perfectly adequate foredune landscapes. If we needed shelter that badly, why did we choose to live in the dunes? Worse, these tall trees can increase frost pockets, giving gardeners even more to fret about. However, a dense vegetation cover is more desirable than a sparse one that would be vulnerable to blowouts, so if we shift the emphasis from fast-tracking forest development to enhancing conditions for woody shrubland growth, then our aims are both ecologically realistic and culturally practical.

Dense planting of shrubs that will grow to be a similar height—such as manuka (*Leptospermum scoparium*), korokio, tauhinu, coastal shrub daisy or the taller kanuka, akeake, akiraho and mapau—is key, so that the sooner the crowns coalesce, the better (they can be thinned out later). Do read the pages at the end of the sand section (pages 85–98) that explain some of the nutritional eccentricities of dune plants, as finding the balance between fertilising for quick growth and producing hardy plants, and determining a sensible watering strategy, can spell the difference between success and failure.

The inland sandy forest garden

Even with so much emphasis on conserving water, we should never reach the stage where people avoid planting trees. Trees are the greatest investment in the future we have. They are assets to nurture. Why? Because 30–40 percent of rainfall is held temporarily in tree foliage. By slowing rain's passage into the soil, we slow stormwater surges, attenuate flooding and optimise the water uptake by roots of other plants. We are told to expect more and bigger storm events in the future, and the sums have been done—it is cheaper to plant more trees than it is to retrofit stormwater systems to increase their capacity. Plus, the tree is absorbing carbon dioxide, which has to be good.

What should we expect a forest on young dunes to comprise? Sadly, there is next to nothing left to learn from. Of 21,000 hectares of duneland in New Zealand, only 11 percent is still found in anything resembling a natural state. What we do know is that this forest was dominated by small-leaved and wrinkly-leaved trees (hardy in droughts), both in the canopy and the understorey. This was an open, feathery forest of dappled light and subtlety.

As already discussed in the section A landscape of four dimensions on page 62, the tallest trees in the mature coastal forest would have been totara, perhaps a few matai (*Prumnopitys taxifolia*), with kowhai, kanuka, kohuhu, narrow-leaved maire (*Nestegis montana*) and mapau sharing a lower canopy. Masses of fine-leaved New Zealand jasmine

Low-level planting has more drama when individual species are clumped together. It may not look 'natural', but for a large garden it can cut down the workload considerably. Just remember to avoid straight lines—maintain the sinuous forms of the dunes however you can and allow some sloppy growth that looks relaxed.

and passionvine cascading into the understorey of tall mingimingi, korokio and small-leaved coprosmas (such as *Coprosma crassifolia*, *C. areolata* and *C. propinqua*) provide the magical curtains of light, but there are also sturdier understorey species, including kawakawa and five finger. The fringes of the forest would have benefited the tough small tree daisies—akiraho in particular—with akeake and taupata taking the brunt of the salt wind.

On dunes thousands of years old, where the sand has become shallow and loamy, and can hold moisture and benefit from a nutrient cycle, more broadleaved canopy species can be supported. Thus, in frost-free areas in the northern districts, ngaio, karo (*Pittosporum crassifolium*), karaka (*Corynocarpus laevigatus*) and kohekohe (*Dysoxylum spectabile*) could enter the woodland garden, and possibly some tall spires of rewarewa (*Knightia excelsa*), which tend to herald the maturing of broadleaf forest into a podocarp forest. Through most of the Horowhenua dunelands it would have been too frosty for these species to become dominant, but towards the southern end of the Kapiti Coast dunelands, where air drains off nearby hills, frost diminishes and consequently there are more kohekohe and ngaio.

ABOVE *Coprosma crassifolia* imparts a subtlety and softness yet with an intimate, wiry structure that is quite captivating. It could be in danger of being overlooked in a garden, so would benefit from careful placement under taller trees or the shelter of buildings, where it is either silhouetted against dark shadow or its branchlets are back-lit. In the wild, it is not confined to sandy soils, but, along with korokio, is a dominant component of dune shrubland, later becoming an understorey shrub in the developing forest. LEFT Thin-leaved coprosma.

OPPOSITE TOP Hound's-tongue fern can create a dense carpet in both shaded and semi-shaded sites.
OPPOSITE CENTRE Asplenium ferns such as shining spleenwort thrive on dune forest soils with fresh humus. They are splendid candidates for bush edges as they do not mind partial sunlight.
OPPOSITE BOTTOM *Carex dissita* underlies kanuka, but it may just as easily be *C. comans* or *C. testacea*. FAR RIGHT Given some soil fertility and shelter, *Parsonsia heterophylla* will be preferred over *P. capsularis*.
BELOW LEFT A young totara canopy filters the light. Tall mingimingi and five finger share the understorey. BELOW RIGHT: Totara is our most drought-tolerant conifer and is usually dominant in the old dune forests.

In the wild, dune forests are often quite sparse, and grasses and ground ferns take precedence. These woodland glades seem like gardens in their own right. The ferns hound's-tongue, *Asplenium* species and *Blechnum filiforme* (which, like hound's-tongue, will scramble up tree trunks) will be common and adapt readily to garden environments.

The 'grasses' are likely to be a mixture of true grasses, such as meadow rice grass (*Microlaena stipoides*), and sedges, such as *Carex* species (*Carex testacea, C. dissita, C. dipsacea, C. flagellifera, C. comans*) or hook grass species (*Uncinia* spp.). Collectively, they can form a forest meadow where overhead dappled light can penetrate. Since coastal forest is generally a simple two-tier affair—just canopy and shrubby undergrowth—there is often more light here than in other forest types, so these 'meadows' are quite typical.

Small trees in gardens provide protection from prevailing winds and also shade and shelter on hot days. Tree height and flexibility of growth are the criteria for the former; the aim is to create an aerodynamically

smooth cross section that will raise the wind up and over your house with the least disturbance (and preferably without requiring constant pruning to get that balance right). Kanuka, akeake and taupata are very well suited to this role—if they grow too high, they self-regulate their growth, and if there is room, they will spread their branches to suit the wind strength and direction.

To create shelter for humans rather than buildings, you should plant trees on the lee side of a house rather than the windward side. It makes sense to plant a cluster, creating a canopy as the trees mature to shade and cool the ground below. This offers the opportunity for an underlay of vines like New Zealand jasmine, grasses, sedges and ferns for variety. Having a low-growing ground-cover that can cope with the intrusion of deckchairs and barbecues as required suits the beach lifestyle.

Vines come into their own in a coastal forest garden, especially New Zealand jasmine and passionvine. There are several jasmine species; the fine-leaved *Parsonsia capsularis* var. *capsularis* is the most common in drought-prone situations. In the wild it will just as readily be found climbing as forming large mounds. The scent of its flowers is divine, and then they are followed up by long, wispy seed capsules that are decorative in their own right.

Trees will need to be planted no less than 3 m apart, but because we are fast-tracking the natural succession through shrubland to trees, we need to provide the shelter the young trees would otherwise have received. If you can bear the sight of tree protection for the first few years, it will be worth it. Do not use plastic as it will heat up too much inside the growing space; fine netting is ideal. Growth is usually surprising in the lee of a house, and with added bonuses such as taps and water-storage tanks in close proximity, a woodland garden will soon take off.

If it is simply a hedge that is required, it is best not to use tree species. They'll demand a lot of water for large root systems, need constant pruning and, as they mature, the trunks lengthen and the hedge becomes 'gappy' at the base. Use shrubs such as korokio, coastal shrub daisy or *Coprosma crassifolia*. Even better, use small-leaved pohuehue to wend its way through the shrubs for a complete windbreak.

TOP Mature kanuka creating a delightful glade.
LEFT Even on its way to maturity, kanuka provides a splendid garden sight. If you can restrain yourself from pruning, the branches will be free to create their characteristic spreading form.

Preventing weedscapes

Along most of our developed coastal duneland, the vegetation is no longer native; introduced plants that serve the same role in succession have replaced our own. Marram grass is now the dominant sand- binder. Lupin, boxthorn (*Lycium ferocissimum*), South African iceplant and acacia species oust the native shrubs; South American pampas (*Cortaderia jubata and C. selloana*) overtakes the slower-growing native toetoe (*Austroderia* spp.). To turn the tide back towards the plants that originally inhabited our duneland, a lot can be gained from understanding what the features are that allow native species to survive or, even better, to thrive in the dunes.

It is important to replace all of these invasive weeds if possible or they will continue their spread far and wide. Your greatest ally is going to be the spray gun, because ideally you will target specific weeds and keep dead and dying plants *in situ* so their skeletons are providing shade and shelter for new young plants, as well as minimising the germination of their own dropped seed.

A managed 'roll back' from the windward edge will also minimise the reinfestation of your site. A plant like iceplant will soon shrink and wither when dead, so you must be prepared to move swiftly to plant new ground-cover. Start with the plants that will spread, and come back in a year or two to plant the woody shrubs or tussocks that will benefit from that ground-cover.

Plant densely and plant in winter, as water is the primary consideration for new dune growth. While sometimes useful on steep slopes where a shrubland or flaxland is being planted, coir matting will impede the establishment of spreading species that are so necessary on dunes closest to the shore.

TOP The downside of coir matting is that it prevents naturally sprawling plants from sprawling.
ABOVE *Carex testacea* is well established in this garden, but to avoid weeding headaches, now is the time to interplant with sprawling species such as sand piripiri or sand coprosma.

Small gardens in the dunelands

The main distinction made here between large duneland gardens and small ones is that the latter are more likely to be dominated by housing, carports, driveways and neighbours, and while still close to the beach and that permanent sense of playtime that accompanies sand, they are less likely to be as naturalistic as a duneland garden on a large property. If you were to zero in on the essence of dunes and pick out a few key ingredients that located your garden explicitly within duneland, there would probably be a sense of sandy texture, of dune forms, of lackadaisical sedges and tussocks, of sparse ground-hugging prostrate herbs, and certainly of exposure and harsh sunlight.

The marriage between gritty textures of hard landscaping, pottery or paths and tiny-leaved plants (left) speaks of sandiness even where sand itself is not present. The starkness of distant dunes, Sahara-like, with their clarity of form, can be evoked through relationships between simple architectural form and 'silhouette' planting, where the shadow of a plant cast in stark relief against a wall is almost as important as the plant itself. Not everyone finds this harshness relaxing, but the play of sharp-edged shadow and strong plant forms such as pingao is evocative of this face of duneland.

A more relaxing approach, perhaps, is where sprawling, crawling plants are permitted access to our formal spaces. The juxtaposition of wilful sand plants and built structures is both contradictory and slightly manic by nature, so why not play with this idea and exaggerate the consequences of this clash of wills?

As always in a small space, it is the combinations of plants—often very simple indeed, with perhaps only two or three intermingled species—that create the texture, colours and patterns that spell out the desired storyline.

Sand coprosma and sand daphne share the same wild environs but do not always elbow for room as intensely as in garden settings. In a practical sense you couldn't get better weed matting than this partnership.

Although pingao is most often found in a solo role in the foredunes, its growth in a garden setting could be bolstered by feeding it seaweed-enriched fertiliser or its spindliness compensated for by teaming it up

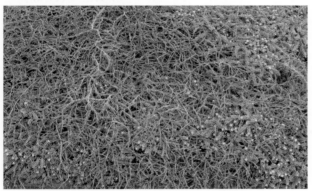

TOP New Zealand iceplant and pingao are encouraged to sprawl across the main entrance pathway, inviting visitors to navigate their way through a microcosm of beach to reach the front door.

ABOVE LEFT Sand coprosma and sand daphne.

ABOVE Sand piripiri and pingao.

LEFT Sand piripiri and sand daphne.

OPPOSITE TOP AND BOTTOM Small-leaved pohuehue.

with duneland ground-covers such as sand piripiri. The seedheads of piripiri share the golden glow of the pingao foliage while the piripiri foliage provides the more traditional 'garden greening'.

At a different time of year it is the white pompom flowerheads of sand piripiri that help it team up with other white-flowering ground-covers, such as sand daphne. It really is a 'plant for all seasons'; you simply choose which colour combination draws out the best partnership for your place.

Shore bindweed needs loose sand to creep through and rarely grows densely enough to suit a garden situation, but it can be blended with other ground-covers such as pohuehue, New Zealand iceplant or New Zealand spinach (*Tetragonia tetragonoides*)—plants with a flush of green to their foliage to great effect.

TOP *Geranium traversii* (left), from Chatham Island dunes, with *G. sessiliflorum* var. *arenarium* (right), which hails from Southland sandy coasts. These will have been selected for their purple coloration; foliage colours vary more in the wild. The sandy coast is one part of the New Zealand landscape where pink does occur naturally, so by all means celebrate this! CENTRE Shore bindweed. BOTTOM LEFT *Selliera rotundifolia*. BOTTOM RIGHT Sand iris can be used in bulk for a strong statement, but avoid the risk of going overboard.

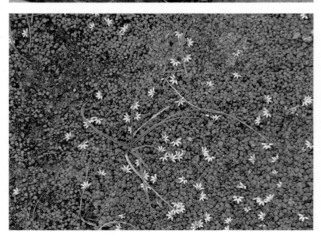

A special little plant that grows in the sand flats of North Island dunelands lends itself to intimate nurturing. *Selliera rotundifolia* is a delight—in miniature. Given a flat, damp site in full sun (perhaps a corner of the garden that is slower to drain after rain, or a large pot and saucer), this ground-cover, which is getting scarcer in the wild as it is outcompeted by exotic weeds, is a novel talking point.

Far more widespread and better known in New Zealand gardens is another sand-flat inhabitant, sand iris (*Libertia peregrinans*). Its shallow-rooting but spreading habit works well in the hard sand pans, but like most lilies, it will store enough moisture to get it through the scorching-hot, dry days as well as those days when the hard pans are slow to drain. This versatility means it will cope in most sunny garden situations and it needs no fertiliser whatsoever. The vivid intensity of sand iris does dictate its use to a large degree. So does its invasive lifestyle, especially in fertile soils. Some of the popular commercial cultivars excel in both regards.

The small sand garden does not need to be at ground level, and certainly the contrast between building and ground-level garden is so great that raising beds does help to inject a sense of scale that we are more accustomed to.

Nutrition, water and keeping it all together

Remember, sand is rock that has been broken down physically into its component minerals, which have then been sorted out at sea and the lightest ones brought ashore and blown up the beach. By the time dunes are formed, sorting of the sand has resulted in its being dominated by quartz grains. Depending on the rock source, there may be other minor minerals too: 'light' grains of feldspar, hypersthene and hornblende from greywacke rock; or 'heavy' minerals from volcanic rocks, which create black sand.

There could also be a fair amount of ground-up shell, boosting calcium levels. But there is very little organic matter. Not much seaweed grows offshore on sandy coastlines, and what plankton washes up the beach as foam would be rapidly leached out of the sand. Nitrogen and phosphorus are required for plant growth, but these are precisely the nutrients that are in short supply.

So where do foredune plants find their nutrition? This is the big contrast between rocky-shore life and sandy-shore life. You'll get to see that sandy-shore plants are often found on rocky shores as well, but many rocky-shore plants won't be found on sandy shores. Since the main difference lies in fertility, there must be some clever adaptation going on for specialised dune plants to grow on the scantiest of diets.

Phosphorus

Phosphorus is all-important to the plant world. Plankton 'foam' and rotting driftwood may supply a modicum of phosphorus along the beachfront but there usually isn't very much in a form that is available to plant roots.

Throughout the world there are plants living in very infertile soils that have developed a high sensitivity to phosphorus. They are especially efficient at extracting phosphorus from soils, although this efficiency means that too much phosphorus is toxic to them. Some foreign genera that display this ability include *Protea*, *Leucodendron*, *Banksia*, *Grevillea*, *Boronia* and *Acacia*. To date, known New Zealand examples are manuka, akeake and *Atriplex* spp., but there will be others not yet recognised. It is very important not to overfertilise

Birds and foam—the two greatest ready sources of phosphates on a sandy coast.

absorb; some grasses, coprosmas and totara rely on this and don't need root hairs). Species relying on mycorrhizal fungal associations for nutritional assistance in poor soils have fungal hyphae extending out into the soil, where they absorb nutrients that the roots themselves cannot access. Until these fungal associations develop, the young plant will noticeably respond to the application of phosphorus, unlike phosphorus-sensitive plants, which will already be optimising what they have. That's why, if coprosmas are already well established in the sandy soil, let them be—there is no point adding fertiliser as they probably have already developed the means to work with what they've got. But if you are planting out young nursery-raised plants, then scattering a very low dose of Magamp granules at the bottom of the hole may be a good idea. Not all nurseries add mycorrhizals to their potting mix, so the extra phosphorus may get the babies through a barren period—just not too much or the plants may not develop the desired long-term relationship with the fungi.

It is important to consider what plants to use if you are releasing greywater into a dune garden, as this inevitably contains high phosphorus levels. If you live on the property, that portion of the garden should not include phosphorus-sensitive plants. If you are merely an intermittent holiday-maker, it may not be a problem.

Another aspect of plant choice to consider in dry-dune gardens is the relationship between fertiliser and drought-tolerance. If you add fertiliser to a plant that is adapted for arid conditions and the plant puts on a spurt of foliage growth, it will increase the roots' demands for water and could overstress the plant. The perfect situation for arid dune plants is to allow them to become slightly water-stressed and not to

such species in case the phosphorus levels become toxic. Even adding a 'normal' slow-release fertiliser pellet to the planting hole of a very small phosphorus-sensitive species could kill it.

There are also plants that do their best to increase their uptake of phosphorus—either with abundant growth of fine root hairs (rushes and sedges use this technique) or by increasing the mycorrhizal fungi associated with their roots (the fungi break down mineral phosphates into something the plant can fertilise them. This will increase their ability to respond to the climate in the ways they have evolved to do so. This is a classic example of the benefits of learning what species grow 'naturally' in your environment, and knowing that they truly are best suited to cope. It is the first step towards a sustainable garden that isn't relying on human input to keep it alive.

Nitrogen

Legumes are plants with nodes on their roots containing bacteria that can extract atmospheric nitrogen from the soil, allowing these plants to make good growth in nitrogen-depleted soils. Other plants gain their nitrogen less directly from the activity of soil bacteria and algae. It may take a while before sand is stable enough and contains enough organic matter to support much micro-organism activity, so if you see lush growth on the foredunes, it is likely there are free-living nitrogen-fixing bacteria at work. Some dune plants also have the ability to store nitrates in their tissues in times of water stress, then feed on these when conditions improve.

Only low-nutrient-demanding species (including species with special abilities to extract food from minimal resources) will grow on the dunes until the soils are better developed. Unfortunately, our native duneland, grassland and shrubland flora do not have any nitrogen-fixing legumes, although the more mature coastal forest further from the severe salt edge does support a couple: kowhai and native broom (*Carmichaelia* spp.).

The yellow tree lupin (*Lupinus arboreus*), a legume introduced for sand-stabilisation purposes, is particularly successful on fresh dunes because of this nitrogen-fixing ability. Does it benefit our nutrient-poor coastal environment? Not in the foredunes, where it grows so densely that it excludes native shrubland species, so is only benefiting itself and decreasing our options for diversity. It certainly stabilises dunes, but at what cost?

Where it persists in the foredunes, lupin eventually enriches the sand with nitrogen, and both here and overseas, this tends to encourage invasion by non-native weedy species. Lupin is more useful inland, where it can become a nitrogen-enriching 'nursery-crop' for trees that can grow up through it and overshadow it. It is recommended for growing between rows of olives in sandy soil, for example, to be regularly harvested and

This blowout reveals two distinctly different rooting strategies: knobby clubrush has rhizomes with prolific wiry root hairs, creating a stable mat but one that is vulnerable when a sand blowout occurs; sand coprosma has strong, deep roots that anchor the plant—plus the spreading prostrate stems provide stability and bind moving sand. Both styles of root may reflect strategies to increase uptake of phosphorus.

TOP Pingao seems to respond well to a modicum of fertiliser but too much makes the plants look unnaturally lush and green—perhaps more suited to a garden setting than dune-restoration sites.

ABOVE The only fertiliser this planted area has received was a slow-release Magamp pellet in each plant hole—just enough to boost initial growth, and now nature does the rest.

mulched to increase soil fertility for the trees.

Low-nutrient-demanding species do respond well to sparingly low levels of nitrogen fertiliser. Pingao and spinifex will grow strongly in sand if urea fertiliser is applied. (Urea is a nitrogen-release fertiliser made commercially from ammonia and carbon dioxide, formed into pellets that break down in rain to ammonia and carbon dioxide again.) It is quite possible that in the past, flocks of shorebirds excreted enough natural urea to boost growth of the sand-binders living closest to the shoreline, but without birds around in the same numbers, a little bit of human assistance doesn't go amiss. Note that although additional nitrogen increases the volume of foliage of spinifex and pingao, it does not mean they will survive better; indeed, if you are planting out seed-raised juveniles, the best survival rates in the first few years will be displayed by the unfertilised plants. So, what is the intention? Fast-tracking dune stabilisation (in which case a bit of fertiliser may help)? Or re-creating a naturalistic duneland vegetation (in which case let nature do the gardening for you)?

Salt

Obviously a lot of salt is being blown inland, but the inability of pure sand to retain ions means the sodium and chloride of salt are quickly leached away. It is fortunate that salt doesn't reach toxic levels in the soils, as it does in salt marshes, since it means plants do not need to be specialised halophytes (salt-tolerant species) to live in the dunes. However, plants that can take up salts *are* better able to withstand dry conditions; when a plant can store salts, this enriched sap can prevent the loss of water from the plant due to osmosis—useful not only in saline soils but also in arid soils. Some of the coastal plants known to be good at extracting and storing salts include New Zealand spinach, *Atriplex* spp. and glasswort (*Sarcocornia quinqueflora*).

Organic matter

Certainly, one thing you do notice about plant-survival techniques in dunes is that the successful woody shrubs and large herbs are ones whose prostrate creeping forms allow their own leaf litter (and any other organic matter blowing around) to be trapped within the plant, thus providing their roots with organic matter. Sand coprosma, *Cyathodes parviflora*, sand daphne, *Pimelea prostrata*, coastal shrub daisy, small-leaved pohuehue and leafless pohuehue (*Muehlenbeckia ephedroides*), kanuka and manuka are all well suited to this function.

It is a sadly rare but heartening sight to see dunes where these plants form dense mats that stabilise sand hills and drench the landscape in their particular ruddy and orangey hues. Sunset on such beaches is a delight, as these shrubs glow with increased intensity in the low evening light. Gardeners are wise to follow their lead and plant very densely with ground-hugging, small-leaved woody shrubs to achieve the vital ingredients for life on dunes—cool root-runs, organic matter and self-sheltering, aerodynamic forms.

Half the plant matter created from photosynthesis during the life of a plant ends up in the soil, either as leaf litter, dead root fragments or root exudates. This is the material that soil microbes utilise, so it is the key to the soil life cycle. Although most dune species have tough, oil-rich leaves as part of their survival strategy and these leaves are slow to break down, contributing relatively little to soil nutrients when they do, the cumulative effect is large. Do not tidy up fallen leaf litter from a coastal garden—life depends upon it. We will look at the role of mulch once we have understood a bit better the role of water in the dunes.

In contrast to dry sand, wet peaty dune soils have a high organic content, being made up from poorly decomposed leaf matter, but this does not mean they are fertile. Their acidity and poor aeration lock up nutrients and they lack mineral nutrients anyway. Nitrogen is about the best they can offer.

Too much fertiliser in a zone where plants are generally adapted to low-nutrient, arid conditions can not only weaken the resilience or health of native species in the long term, but will also encourage invasion by exotic species (which have different tolerances to our natives), especially exotic annuals, which can seasonally swamp our mostly perennial, slower-growing coastal plants.

In sandy soils, top-dressing fertilisers leach through the sand quickly, so you would also be wasting money. If you feel the need to add fertiliser to foredune plants, use urea in preference to fertilisers with phosphorus content (such as poultry manure), or use slow-release pellets in holes dug for new plants.

The best form of soil enrichment is organic matter, which breaks down slowly and retains water. Gardening books will usually advise the addition of humus or compost to sandy soils for good plant growth, although admittedly they are talking to gardeners who want a diverse array of temperate plants suited to loamy soils. In well-aerated soils, microbial activity is greater and that compost disappears faster than in loams—you have to keep resupplying organic matter to maintain that lush vegetation. Unless you are growing a vegetable garden, why bother? If you grow the low-nutrient-demanding plants adapted to sandy soils, you may have less work to do in the garden!

TOP Germination of *Carex testacea* on an exposed beach is possible only in the lee of the parent plant, where seedlings are sheltered from both sun and wind. ABOVE *Selliera rotundifolia* with *Coprosma acerosa* 'Hawera' growing in a prostrate fashion (possibly because its root-run is restricted and shallow, but this helps make it an attractive ground-cover).

Water

The other essential ingredient often in short supply in the duneland is fresh water. Most of our biggest duneland areas are in dry parts of the country, but even in the wet south, dunelands maintain arid conditions for plant life. (This partially explains why duneland vegetation is so similar from one end of New Zealand to the other.)

What rain does fall won't be retained unless there is some organic material or clay in the sand. Sand grains allow water to drain through quickly, and little is retained as the soil pores are relatively large. In a clay loam, not only does water infiltrate more slowly, but more of it is retained within the tiny soil pores. Say 100 mm depth of water is sitting on top of both a sand and a clay loam. After several hours the water will have infiltrated to a depth of about 1.4 m in the sand. In the same time, water will have penetrated only about 700 mm into the clay loam, and it would take days for it to get as deep as it does in the sand.

All plants need water, especially while they are young and developing root systems. Drought-tolerant plants are simply species that have tricks to allow them to survive drought (such as dormancy or leaf-dropping)—they will consume as much water as other plants when it is to be had. As soils dry out again, plants find it harder and harder to extract water from the pores. Drought-sensitive plants will begin to wilt. Drought-tolerant plants, on the other hand, are ones that can extract a bit more water and utilise it more efficiently. Clearly there is a greater need to be growing drought-tolerant plants in sand than there is in clay loams.

Dune plants depend on being able to tap into a high water table. Tall plants (such as grasses and sedges) will tend to have deeper root systems, especially if they are sand-binders adapted for dry sand conditions. Pingao and spinifex have deeply penetrating taproots. Yes, the stems of spinifex creep horizontally for great distances through the mobile drifts of sand, but at intervals those stems send down extremely long taproots in search of water. (Such rooting systems are described as stoloniferous.) Their leaves are curled and, in the case of spinifex, hairy, to minimise water loss from the leaf surface. These plants don't provide much shade, allowing the sand surface to heat and dry out. Sun is a great enemy for dune plant life. Black sand heats up to higher temperatures than quartz-rich sand, reaching temperatures twice that of air temperature, even 70–80 mm below the surface.

Dogs know what to do—scratch away the uppermost layer of hot sand to find the cool sand below. Similarly, roots of dune species are rarely shallow but seek the cooler, deeper sand, and seeds germinate only where there are pockets of shelter and shadow that protect their vulnerable sprouts from being scorched. Only plants that creep across the ground, shading and cooling the sand with their own foliage, will reduce water loss from the sand and can afford to have shallower roots. Shallow-rooting sand plants are generally the ground-covers such as shore bindweed, small-leaved pohuehue, New Zealand spinach, New Zealand iceplant and sand daphne (and in shingles, the *Raoulia* and *Crassula* species). These differences in root systems are worth keeping in mind when you are planting shallow beds.

In-built strategies to combat drought

It's only recently that we've become aware that photosynthesis differs between species. As a rule, it occurs during daylight hours and requires open pores (stomata) to receive carbon dioxide; at the same time, the plant is also losing water vapour and oxygen through those pores. The wind and sun evaporate the water vapour faster, and this action drives a pump that draws water from the soil through the roots and up into the leaves. But, having to open pores on hot, windy days can readily result in water stress, when the demand for water cannot be met from what is probably already dry soil. As the water runs out and gets harder to remove from between sand particles, the plant wilts.

Drought-tolerant plants have several strategies to deal with this situation. One is to minimise evaporation to begin with by having hairy or curled leaves. Another strategy is to have a more efficient photosynthesis process that requires less water. This is the difference between C_3, C_4 and CAM (crassulacean acid metabolism) plants. There are three ways in which plants photosynthesise. C_3 carbon fixation is the 'normal' photosynthesis process but requires plants to grab as much carbon dioxide from the air as possible so they keep their stomata open all day, at the risk of evaporation of water; most temperate-climate plants are C_3 plants. In temperatures higher than 30°C, C_4 carbon-fixation plants come into their own. They are more efficient users of carbon dioxide, and use and lose less water, so are better able to cope with drought; C_4 plants include euphorbias, and *Chenopodium* (such as the the introduced coastal weed orache) and *Atriplex* species, along with kikuyu (*Pennisetum clandestinum*) and *Paspalum* grasses—exotic grasses that are already pervasive in the far north. Glasswort is another C_4 pathway plant.

CAM plants open their stomata only at night, not during the day, so water loss is minimised. Many succulents, cacti, epiphytes and aquatic plants do this. Yes, they still need sun for photosynthesis, but the carbon dioxide is stored in their cells as malate, waiting for the factory doors to open again in the morning. In New Zealand, plants known to use CAM pathways include akeake, aquatic plants in the genera *Isoetes* and *Lilaeopsis*, semi-aquatic *Scirpus* and *Eleocharis* species, *Microsorum* and *Pyrrosia* ferns, and probably also *Dendrobium* orchids, as their Australian cousins are CAM plants.

One strategy to outwit drought, as we've seen, is to ensure roots penetrate deeply into the damper sand or the water table. So is drought stress in the garden overcome simply by watering plants during the day?

Well, yes and no. Yes, if you can afford to waste so much water, but who can? Humans can no longer take water for granted in dry or seasonally dry climates. Bore water is no longer seen as a bottomless well to be tapped. If water is sprayed over plants on a hot day, you could immediately lose 10 percent through evaporation: most of it feeds the foliage and the rest slowly permeates back towards the water table—but possibly a different layer of artesian water than the one supplying the irrigation system. Certainly watering in the cool parts of the day will be a more *effective* use of water.

Even less wastage will occur if you trickle-feed to the soil rather than spray. But on pure sand, even that water is going to drain away in a very short time, and plants don't have time to utilise all they are given.

Surely the best approach is to reduce wastage by (1) growing drought-tolerant plants that can cope with little water; (2) minimising runoff and water repellency; (3) increasing the water-retention capability of the soil so less water is wasted; and (4) irrigating so that water gets where it is needed, slowly, and is used efficiently.

Water repellency
First, get water into the sand. This is frustratingly difficult, even though sand seems such a permeable substrate. Water runs off the surface as if off a duck's back, especially on older dunes. This simple fact is another argument not to level out dunes. Where there is a hollow for water to drain into (plus shelter from wind), there will be life and gardening will be fun! Where sand is flat, it remains challenging.

Terracing—lots of little level areas rather than few large ones—may overcome some of the runoff problems, although it is very difficult to make this look attractive in soft dune country and requires much gardening skill.

The cause of this water repellency seems to be the greasy build-up of soil micro-organisms (the very ones you want) across the surface. If you have added a large quantity of organic matter to the soil, you may get the same result as decomposing fungae build up.

In small urban gardens it is feasible to add a wetting agent (with water—so if you are in a sprinkler-ban zone, wait for rain) to break the surface tension and help water permeate the surface layer. Wetting agents are detergents, but not laundry detergents, which may be toxic to plants. They come as granular powders that biodegrade slowly, and after six months or so (or after a lot of heavy rain) you may need to re-treat the area. This isn't a very practical approach on large properties. Although I wouldn't recommend earthworks on dry-dune crests, it is sometimes feasible to mix clay into the top 200 mm of sand (use a rotary hoe).

Quite a number of large duneland subdivisions are combining peat from old swamps with the pure sand and redistributing this mix across the surface of new sections. This is of little real value unless water can actually be made to penetrate the surface, and in the meantime the organic matter, now able to decompose in its new aerobic state, makes that task more difficult.

Water retention in sandy soils
Having got water into the sand, now you want to keep it there—but not too much, as you have planted drought-tolerant species that would not appreciate being too wet. These need just enough water so that the stress period is shortened.

The rate at which water soaks into sand can be 100 mm depth per hour or more, but an optimal rate for plant uptake is around 10–25 mm/hour, so clearly we want the water to stay longer around plant roots. Surface attraction of water depends on particle size, so the more fine particles within the sand, the better—just not so much that they clog soil pores. Mixing in clay or organic fibres is the best approach.

There is a catch: introducing too much fine material to the top surface may act as a barrier to water infiltrating into the sand below (the capillary pressures holding the water within the fine loam are too great to overcome). Water may be held too long near the surface and not feed the deeper roots, which are the ones that get the plant through the hard drought times. Be sure to mix material deeply and thoroughly before a planting programme starts as you won't get another chance once plants have grown.

There is no doubt that increasing the organic content of the sand will enhance its water retention, but if we don't want to overfertilise the soil, how do we do this? Manure will work but may be too rich. A very good alternative is coco peat or coir fibre dust, which is a waste product from the process of separating coir fibre from coconut husks and is supplied to the garden industry as a mulch. Mixed into light sandy loams, it will increase the water-retention capacity and the amount of water available to plants. It decomposes slowly but will give young plants the time to become established. Adding 20 litres of coir dust to a square metre of sand will give the same level of water retention as mixing in a 100 mm layer of manure to the same area.

For small areas another option is to add water crystals to the top 200 mm. These must be pre-soaked before use. Maximum benefit is achieved when there are 100–300 g (dry) crystals per square metre, mixed into the top 200 mm of sand. This is an expensive approach, but a slurry of crystals added to planting holes can be a blessing, especially if you are not going to be around for the first few critical weeks of growth of the newly transplanted plant when it needs water the most. Layering the bottom of the planting hole with layers of newspaper to stop water draining deeper into the sand can also give plants a head start.

Irrigation

The principle of irrigation in sand gardens is to get water to where it is needed (the plant roots), to get it to them only when it is needed, and not to waste it. In many seaside towns there are sprinkler bans during the driest part of the year and that can include trickle-feed bans. Hand-held hoses may be allowed, but who has the patience to stand waiting for water to penetrate first any surface mulch and then into the root zone? Even the hardiest of drought-tolerant plants will want water if they start to wilt, and survival of new plantings may depend upon it. So there needs to be a solution to suit the circumstances of the owner as well as of the garden.

Irrigation specialists recommend a periodic soaking of the equivalent of 12 mm of 'rainfall' during dry months. Doing this by sprinkler irrigation during the day is wasteful as up to half may evaporate off the surface of plants and soil. If it goes on too quickly (draining away into the sand before plants can access it), as much as half will end up in the water table. Drip irrigation underneath mulch is ideal and should be timed for the coolest parts of the day (sunrise and sunset). You need more drippers per line in sand compared with other soil types, as you don't want the plant roots to be concentrated in spots—you want them well spread to support the plant in strong winds. Dripper lines are low-pressure systems, so you can have longer lines than you would if you were using a sprinkler system. One of the downsides of hidden irrigation is the ease with which you can overwater and waste your precious resource. Timers are a really good idea! So is using a soil-moisture sensor. These are ideal for the absentee owner as they will cancel a scheduled irrigation if it is raining or there is still adequate soil moisture since the last shower.

Assuming that you are planting the types of drought-tolerant species that would be growing naturally in dry sand, it should be feasible to give them a deep soaking once a month (rather than once a week). Some water stress will be fine—but when even these kinds of plants start to wilt, you know it's time for action.

If you are using, or considering using, greywater

The humpy scrumple of small-leaved pohuehue and shore bindweed makes a perfectly 'beachy' substitute for a lawn—and requires a lot less work.

for irrigation, remember there are potential problems with supplying it to drought-tolerant plants in sandy sites where the chemical makeup of the water is not controlled. If you can be sure you are not raising the phosphorus levels too high, then greywater is certainly an option. This works best where constant greywater supply is combined with plants that are not particularly drought-tolerant. However, they may be more susceptible to water stress when you go away on holiday during dry spells.

Irrigating holiday bach gardens

Here, I have to make the distinction between the holiday bach (small and informal, probably with small water tanks and the power turned off when the guests depart) and the 'second home' that happens to be near the beach (fully equipped, on mains water supply, with large rainwater tanks and the power often left on between visits). The latter can, in reality, be treated as if the residents were permanent and the same design and water-rationing considerations put into play.

But the small and humble dwelling is often a different kettle of fish, especially when the gardener visits only during dry summer months, when plant establishment is challenging. For starters, don't even bother with pot plants. I wouldn't condone having lawns either, except under already mature trees where there is shading through the heat of the day. Instead, concentrate on densely packed woody shrubs and sprawling ground-covers that have low water requirements, and put all the watering effort into a few specimen trees or shelter hedges.

Even there, don't rely on irrigation to get you through the lean times; use water crystals and mulch to retain and conserve what rain falls. If you use the roof rainwater for house supplies, leave a few buckets standing around outside to collect water for the garden while you're not there. Bach gardens are one location where using greywater for irrigation is a good option, assuming that the bach is being used only sporadically, but remember not to use washing and laundry chemicals containing phosphates.

Irrigation in urban gardens
Wherever possible, have an independent rainwater tank dedicated to garden water. It needs to be high enough above ground level to provide the required pressure to the irrigation system, so that may mean a row of small tanks on long legs rather than one large one. Alternatively, do what so many of our grandparents did—bury a large tank underground and pump water out.

The rain you are collecting off your roof won't be going to waste while it feeds your plants, but it won't be going back into the ground to replenish water tables either. You could bear in mind ways of letting as much water re-enter the ground as possible. Perhaps cobbles for paving and driveways rather than solid concrete with curb and channelling. Perhaps a dedicated rain-garden for any excess water from your tank overflow pipe (rather than putting it straight into the stormwater system).

In the smaller garden individual trees and shrubs can be singled out for special attention. Fill plastic dripper bottles (cut in half, with their spouts buried in the soil) for slow release at the base of a tree—if you can find an attractive way to do this!

Bore irrigation on lifestyle blocks
Have bore, will water. Some bores require a resource consent and policing of annual take, but many don't and it is tempting to use them every day or night to allow

While it is not always appropriate to grow trees in the foredunes, these gardeners have nevertheless approached the job sensibly: dedicated irrigation feeds each ngaio; mulch is concentrated around each tree; and their reward is eventual shade, allowing them to have a lawn in an arid environment, thus creating an attractive woodland garden. At this stage further irrigation should not be required.

any kind of growth to flourish. While groundwater circumstances vary enormously through duneland, and proximity to larger streams and rivers will have a bearing on replenishment of artesian water, in general terms, excessive bore use in arid climates is a dead-end path. To maintain both quantity and quality for future generations and unforeseen circumstances (perhaps more urgent a need than having a pretty garden), we need to be sophisticated in our bore useage.

We have already touched on the problems of getting water into a sandy soil. On large properties this issue is exacerbated and much irrigation water goes to waste. It is worth putting the effort into making little earth dams or wells around individual plants where water can collect.

The other common form of water wastage is continued watering long after the young plants are established, deep-rooted and quite able to fend for themselves for long periods of time. On large properties it makes sense to tackle planting programmes section by section. After irrigating a freshly planted area for several years, plant a new section and shift your irrigation system to that area, leaving the first section to grow without irrigation. Concentrate irrigation on the dry crests, not the damper hollows as these are less prone to drought anyway.

As plants grow they won't need water as frequently (assuming that you have, by clever irrigation management, encouraged their roots to grow deeply rather than remain at the surface), so you can reset the timers as the months pass, to deliver less and deliver it less frequently. As plants grow they'll start to shade

Bracken interspersed through knobby clubrush provides both seasonal interest and a nutritious stepping-stone for larger shrubs.

the ground surface anyway and reduce evaporation, so although they are bigger and still thirsty, their water-stress periods should be diminishing.

Large properties without irrigation
It's a common scenario: duneland farms become uneconomic and subdivision looms. Releasing the land from grazing sees a rapid growth of bracken, pohuehue, lupin or, worst of all, blackberry. How should the new property owner who wants to garden or plant shelter trees approach what they generally perceive to be a problem? Well, as long as you can keep the risk of fire away, lupin or bracken could be deemed to be assets.

Clearing bracken can be likened to a girl shaving her legs for the first time. She is committed, from that day forward, to shaving for the rest of her life. Better, perhaps, to have lived with a modicum of fine hair? Half the biomass of bracken is underground and the ferny fronds produced dry to a brittle rustle of stalks through winter. The intense autumnal coloration of bracken through this period is part of its attraction and certainly contributes to coastal character.

In the shrubland zone, bracken will mingle with knobby clubrush and pohuehue to create just the dense, resilient ground-cover needed to prevent sand blowouts. In the zone where you might expect trees to grow in due course, bracken can be interplanted with tree species and treated as a nursery-crop. In time, as trees overtop the bracken, it will either die out or become etiolated and easier to pull out. You may think this looks too scruffy—and it probably will for a few years—but it is also an effort-free nursery that has saved hours of work and watering and weeding around young trees.

Lupin can be approached in the same way—interplanted with taller-growing species—but it has the advantage over bracken of being more easily turned into a nutritious mulch and kept low for several seasons while young trees take hold.

Mulch

Dunelands are generally windier places than sandy bays, so let's look at the worst-case scenario of dunes with strong wind, dry sand, dry weather and no irrigation.

First, a reminder of what mulches are. They are not there to condition the soil or add organic matter to it; they are there to prevent evaporation of water from the surface, to cool the ground on sunny days (or to blanket it warmly on frosty nights) and to limit weed growth. They need to let rainwater in at the same time.

A thick layer of mulch (say more than 50 mm) is counterproductive, as rainwater, or irrigation spray, is held within the mulch and never penetrates the deep root zone. The finer the mulch, the more water it retains. And the finer the mulch, the more water it sucks out of the sandy soil below (by capillary action). Sometimes, fine mulches become quite water-repellent when their surface dries out, and rain can't penetrate at all! Particle sizes need to be larger than 5 mm for rain to be able to penetrate and to minimise loss of water once it's in the topsoil.

The ideal mulch in windy, sandy sites, then, is one that can be spread thinly (say around 30–40 mm deep) but that holds together and is heavy enough not to blow away. The mulch should offer mini-traps for rainwater so it doesn't just run away over the surface of water-repellent sand. And I would suggest that it should be a material in keeping with the dune environment—not stones.

Shredded bark and coarse wood fragments are a useful solution. The shredded bark holds together better

The fine detritus that accumulates around river mouths is a perfect mulching material.

97

than loose nuggets, and the coarse wood chips are heavier than the standard bark chips (and more interesting to look at). Mulched lupin can be useful for *in situ* surface protection in large-scale planting programmes, although it will need constant attention to prevent the next generation of lupin simply taking over. Don't move it to other sites if there are seeds on the plants.

In summary, on sand avoid the use of organic mulches that are fine and that break down quickly—too much biodegradable mulch overstimulates drought-tolerant plants and may undo the good work of planting them. Use coarse, heavy mulch and use it thinly, replenishing it regularly.

When you are planning a garden area in sand, always include ground-cover plants that will sprawl around and through the taller species. This is your best natural mulch. New Zealand spinach and piripiri are useful as they grow in shade as well as in full sun. *Muehlenbeckia axillaris* is less overwhelming than *M. complexa*, which will smother small plants and require more gardening attention.

Wet duneland

Dune swales

We've looked at dry dunes and the landscapes they create, but a large portion of duneland is actually quite wet. On a coastline where dunes are steadily building seawards, low depressions form behind the foredunes. These are called swales. What a lovely word swale is, looking and sounding like the gently rolling landform it describes. Swales aren't generally wet, but they don't dry out as quickly after rain as do the higher dunes, so they harbour a greater variety of plants. They are home to toetoe; there may be the odd clump of harakeke (*Phormium tenax*) if there is a seed source handy; and there'll certainly be rushes and sedges and scrambling vines.

This moist sand vegetation will also be found in bays where streams can become impeded by storm ridges of sand and debris. It is influenced primarily by fresh-water inputs rather than saline, but rooting is very close to a saline water table so the species are somewhat limited.

Cyperus rules! Giant umbrella sedge (*Cyperus ustulatus*) is totally at home in these conditions. There is probably no country in the world (outside the Arctic and Antarctic circles) that does not host *Cyperus* sedges. Giant umbrella sedge is found only in this country, however, and

Giant umbrella sedge is reasonably tolerant of a brackish water table and certainly lends an oriental flavour to pond and stream edges.

is always associated with water. We also have several introduced *Cyperus* species that have naturalised in the same habitats, but the key to recognising our native species is its dark nutty brown to black seedheads. It tends to like more water than your standard suburban garden can give it, but hollows or pond edges will bring out the best in it.

Sand flats

Where dunes aren't growing seawards but are instead being blown inland, each dune blowout and each migrating parabolic dune has the ability to create damp sand flats in their wake, where wind scours sand away down to the water table or to a hard pan. Water will pond on these flats in winter, or in some places more permanent shallow ponds may form. Close to the beach, sand flats are host to an extraordinary range of native plants—extraordinary because of their finely tuned habitat requirements, which revolve around the degree of dampness. Some herbs and orchids may require water for seed germination, some need year-round moisture for the adult plants, and others can tolerate only periodic wet feet. There seems to be a haven for every need. There isn't, however, much scope for woody shrubs in these hard-pan flats, which is why some of the smaller, less aggressively growing herbs have a sporting chance.

The loss of native landforms (ploughed, drained, bulldozed or smothered with exotic weeds) has compounded the loss of these coastal plants, already reduced through browsing. As you can imagine, the proximity of sand flats and wetlands to each other in the past allowed these plant species to shift about as conditions changed—and we certainly know they changed. Now both the duneland landscapes and the plant populations are so fragmented and dispersed

TOP The southern Taranaki coast has large sand flats that become lagoons at times. BOTTOM Sand flats on Farewell Spit.

that this ability to migrate to find the perfect habitat conditions has been lost. It has been estimated that more than 30 of our coastal herbs have been lost or have become endangered in this way, which is an appalling tally.

Managed landscapes, whether reserves or private gardens, are the last hope for a great many coastal species, yet they have to contend with the human

99

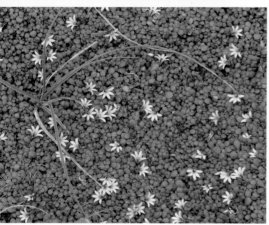

TOP Sand sedge leaves have a distinctively blue tinge. This is a surprisingly lush patch for this sedge, which is often more reminiscent of mange on a dog's back.
ABOVE *Selliera rotundifolia.*

displeasure with things ephemeral. How often do we see the rich diversity of tiny sedges, herbs and rushes that thrive along the fluctuating edges of a natural pond formed on consolidated sand (full when it rains, empty during the dry spells) forsaken for a bulldozed, deep and static waterbody? Ephemeral wetlands are something we could all benefit from learning about. Ironically, ephemeral ponds or shallow ponds with fluctuating water levels are themselves worth preserving because of their rarity, even though, as we will discover shortly, their prospects in the wild are often short-lived.

Some of their specialised plants resist human endeavours. The endemic sand spike sedge (*Eleocharis neozelandica*) will undermine the noblest attempts at artificial resuscitation as it is naturally short-lived and doesn't last long in garden situations. Its more widespread cousin, slender spike sedge (*E. gracilis*), is a better bet for damp parts of the garden. Another damp sand flat sedge is the odd-looking slender clubrush (*Isolepis cernua* var. *cernua*). The black seedheads at the tip of each stem have a slightly clownish look. In the wild these sedges would no doubt be joined by the shining star of the sand-binding community, sand sedge. No other plant binds sand so effectively, but because this diminutive sedge covers damp ground quite sparsely, it has never endeared itself to gardeners.

Oioi, or jointed wire rush (*Apodasmia* (=*Leptocarpus*) *similis*), is in its element on sand flats as it will grow wherever the water table is high (within 300 mm of the surface in summer) and can also tolerate being intermittently submerged. This water-table constraint is one that refers to the natural situation and is related to seed germination, but in cultivation oioi can tolerate a wider range of soil moisture content.

The pretty little sand buttercup (*Ranunculus acaulis*) is easy to propagate and makes a delightful pot plant as well as a plant for damp flats. Similarly, if you were moving through the Manawatu–Kapiti dunelands from sand flat to sand flat, the chances are you'd be walking across mats of *Selliera rotundifolia*, which looks very similar to the buttercup but is studded with lopsided, star-like white flowers in summer.

Dune swamps

Where there is permanent water appearing between the dunes, it may be difficult to determine whether we are looking at a sand flat scoured by the wind (with a hard pan impeding drainage) or a swampy area created when moving dunes blocked the path of a small stream. The end result is very similar, but like all duneland vegetation, think of it as a 'work in progress' because wet duneland is constantly going through its own successional development. This is a very important point to grasp. Gardeners often want static environments—reflecting ponds that are still reflecting in 20 years' time; rushlands that continue to grow bulrushes indefinitely; flax swamps that remain as pure flax without being invaded by bushes.

However, the natural world is a far from static place, and wet duneland the very least of all. By quickly looking at the general succession occurring in wetlands, we can learn what changes to anticipate— at the very least we can appreciate the likely age of a wetland or understand the growth factors such as drainage, seasonal water tables and likely wildlife that will call that stage of vegetation 'home'.

The process by which open water was created to begin with can make a difference to the course of change the vegetation will undergo. In some places perhaps, streams have been impeded by drifting dunes and swamps are formed. If water continues to flow through the swamp and can also drain into underlying substrates, it will be a more fertile, more oxygenated and less acidic environment than one where it is simply fed by the water table.

The 'flowing' swamp environment is conducive to growing harakeke along its edges. Thousands of hectares of harakeke once graced duneland hollows, enough for a booming rope-making industry right through to the 1920s, when competition from sisal and disease in the crop spelled its demise. Lost, along with its almost complete removal from the scene during the conversion of duneland to forestry and farmland,

TOP Tui enjoying the nectar of harakeke.

was the understanding of flax's role in erosion control and native ecosystems. Along streamsides, willow (*Salix* spp.) took its place. Sadly, willow contributed nothing to the food chain, and tui, bellbird and kaka no longer visited the duneland swamps.

The harakeke renaissance is coming! Clearly, strong-rooted plants that are flexible during floods (laying down over soil to protect it from erosion) are sought after. Small, new industries using both the fibre and gel of harakeke are slowly emerging and

101

need stock with which to expand. (And speaking of stock, apparently cows with access to flax foliage suffer less bloat!) Streamside planting of harakeke should be dense—perhaps 1.2 m spacing—to ensure the root systems form a protective mat. In swamp-edge or damp-soil situations, spacing can be greater, perhaps 1.8–2 m spacings.

When planting swamp edges or sand hollows, ensure you are not planting into permanently waterlogged soil. Although harakeke roots can penetrate the water table, they still need air and 200–300 mm of moist, rather than wet, soil should be available. If you have production in mind, choose the appropriate variants, as different flaxes are good for coarse- or fine-fibre uses. Eco-sourcing plants is wise where frosts are common as frost-tolerance of harakeke varies around the country.

The biggest challenge with a flax swamp is keeping the blackberry at bay, and even the native pohuehue can become a smothering pest. Flax is resistant to brushweed herbicides (the triclopyr range, such as Grazon, rather than the glyphosate types), so blackberry invasion can be controlled with spraying. In a large flax swamp, expect it to be years before you conquer blackberry, but do persevere as suppressed native species will respond well. Useful tips include cutting paths through the blackberry to give access for spraying, and spraying in spring once new leaf growth is established. If, however, the blackberry is close to bird-breeding or dragonfly-breeding areas, you can wait until February before spraying. The following year, respray any regrowth, and if pohuehue is proving a problem, dig up its roots, cut and paint

with herbicide. You will want to fill the gaps left as soon as possible. Purei (*Carex secta*) or *C. virgata* make good substitutes that are easy to move through if you need to return (and also resistant to the herbicides suggested), but the exotic grass known as Yorkshire fog (*Holcus lanatus*) can also be used. It will form a dense suppressing mat the first year, then you can expect ferns such as bracken to push through the following year and eventually overtake it.

In contrast to the 'flowing' swamp is the 'static' swamp, fed not by streams but by rainwater or the water table. If the wetland is effectively a perched pond over a hard pan, its depth will be dictated by rainfall, making it more vulnerable to dry spells. This limits the range of species that can thrive, and the pan will limit the introduction of shrubs and large plants, slowing down succession. It will be more acidic, and probably ideal for *Carex* species such as purei or, where the water-table fluctuation is greatest, *C. virgata*. Various rushes will join the sedges, and although harakeke may be scattered here and there, this is not its ideal habitat.

Looking superficially like an etiolated *Cyperus*, this is or marsh clubrush (*Bolboschoenus fluviatilis*), one of the few emergent rushes that tolerates salinity. It will also grow in damp soil.

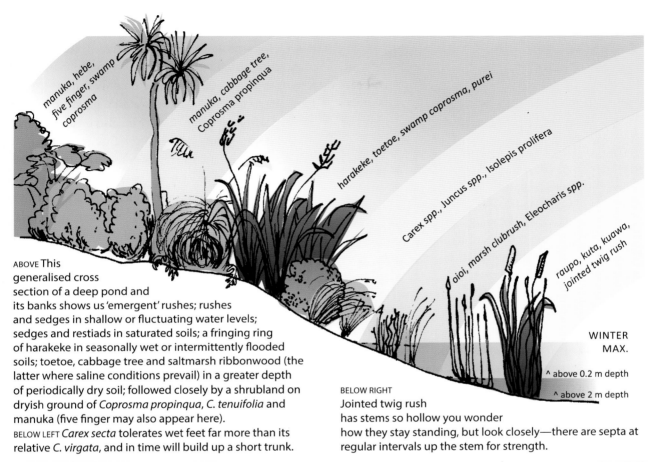

manuka, hebe, five finger, swamp coprosma

manuka, cabbage tree, Coprosma propinqua

harakeke, toetoe, swamp coprosma, purei

Carex spp., Juncus spp., Isolepis prolifera

oioi, marsh clubrush, Eleocharis spp.

raupo, kuta, kuawa, jointed twig rush

WINTER MAX.

^ above 0.2 m depth

^ above 2 m depth

ABOVE This generalised cross section of a deep pond and its banks shows us 'emergent' rushes; rushes and sedges in shallow or fluctuating water levels; sedges and restiads in saturated soils; a fringing ring of harakeke in seasonally wet or intermittently flooded soils; toetoe, cabbage tree and saltmarsh ribbonwood (the latter where saline conditions prevail) in a greater depth of periodically dry soil; followed closely by a shrubland on dryish ground of *Coprosma propinqua*, *C. tenuifolia* and manuka (five finger may also appear here).

BELOW LEFT *Carex secta* tolerates wet feet far more than its relative *C. virgata*, and in time will build up a short trunk.

BELOW RIGHT
Jointed twig rush has stems so hollow you wonder how they stay standing, but look closely—there are septa at regular intervals up the stem for strength.

Dune lakes and ponds

In the fullness of time, both sand-flat and dune-hollow swamps will develop into shrublands, but before we look at that, we'll take a look at the process deeper ponds go through to reach the same stage.

Ironically, water is the greatest limiter to growth we have (whether liquid or frozen). Many native plant guides offer cross sections showing relative depths different species can tolerate. Follow these guides closely (once you have become accustomed to the seasonal variation of the waterbody) to get the best results. Fewer losses will occur at planting time if the plants used are relatively mature, especially those species that will be inundated.

The few native rushes that can cope with water up to 1 m deep water include raupo (*Typha orientalis*), kuta (*Eleocharis sphacelata*) and jointed twig rush (*Machaerina (=Baumea) articulata*).

For any large trees to establish, one of two things needs to occur: the groundwater level needs to fall (giving the roots enough useable space to become established) or the ground itself needs to raise up. In a duneland pond or swamp, neither scenario is particularly unusual. Groundwater levels may fall if surrounding land uses remove vegetation cover, giving the wind more evaporative power; creation of artificial ponds nearby or digging of drainage ditches can also lower the water table over appreciable distances. But without human intervention, it is more likely that the ground level will rise, simply through the long-term accumulation of poorly decomposed fibrous foliage.

This build-up of material begins as soon as rushes colonise water. Look at raupo. Each year the entire plant dies off and collapses. In a pond with little flow and aeration, this material can break down only very slowly. The seasonal changes in a raupo swamp are one of its great visual attractions, but it surely represents a process of change. We know now that raupo grows more vigorously in enriched waters, so adjacent land use can also be playing its part in changing the pond environment.

The plants that will move in to colonise the slowly rising and drying edges, such as toetoe and purei, themselves become nurseries for further developments. Toetoe clumps expand outwards, creating a 'fairy ring' of young offshoots. You will often see young coprosmas or even five finger becoming established in the dense fibrous heart of an ageing clump of toetoe.

OPPOSITE **Typical succession from dune lake to swamp forest.**
1. To begin with, rushlands dominate the fringes of deep ponds.
2. Raupo quickly builds up a mass of dead leaf litter that infills the ponds, allowing harakeke growing around the edges of the pond to start colonising this 'new' ground. The vegetation that is going to take over this pond can be seen in the surroundings: a ring of cabbage trees denotes drier ground, and in the background a swamp forest dominated by kahikatea will provide the seed source for the forest that one day will fill the foreground.
3. Raupo is slowly replaced by harakeke and toetoe; shrubs begin to enter what is now a swamp rather than a pond.
4. On the seasonally saturated ground around the swamp edges, toetoe and manuka shrubland will dominate. Cabbage tree is their companion.
5. It takes little imagination to envisage the process this pond will take, surrounded as it is with a mature duneland swamp forest of swamp maire, kahikatea and pukatea.
6. The culmination of hundreds of years of duneland swamp succession: the large background trees are kahikatea (younger ones to the left, the round-topped blue- and bronze-coloured crowns of mature male and female, respectively, to the right); in front of them is a line of dark-green pukatea; in front of the pukatea is a mixture of bronze swamp maire, with pale olive-green tawa (*Beilschmiedia tawa*) and fresh-green kohekohe on drier ground.

TOP Swamp maire. TOP RIGHT Cabbage tree thrives in its preferred swamp- or pond-edge habitat. No matter where you are, plant cabbage trees only into hollows, not on dry elevated ground, to see them really perform. ABOVE Dried cabbage tree leaves made excellent kindling.

In the fullness of time, swamp forest establishes on what was once open water—perhaps taking only several hundred years if conditions are suitable and if the site is away from the worst of the salt winds.

There is only a handful of fresh-water swamp trees in New Zealand: kahikatea (*Dacrycarpus dacrydioides*), pukatea (*Laurelia novae-zelandiae*), swamp maire (*Syzygium maire*) and cabbage tree (*Cordyline australis*). None of these can endure scorching, dry salt winds, so dune ponds closer than around 500 m to the sea are unlikely to develop the whole way to forest unless the climate is a very wet one (with relatively few dry salty storms). Of these specialised trees, the most 'gardenesque' is swamp maire. What a perfect specimen tree: not too large, with a rounded, shapely crown and spreading branches, and gorgeous bright-red fruits that attract native birds. Needless to say, it must be kept damp year-round; it is also frost-sensitive.

The fringes of swamps and dune lakes are prime habitat for cabbage trees. With a steady supply of root moisture, their foliage can withstand wind and salt air without becoming scorched and tatty. Cabbage trees, or ti kouka, were integral to life for early Maori, so much so that they became imbued with deep symbolism and cultural gravitas. Pragmatically, they helped Maori keep warm and eat hot food, with dried ti kouka leaves providing a constant supply of excellent kindling. The dried flowerstalks of harakeke were used for stoking the fire; the dried stalks of kuta and raupo for thatching; and the seedheads of raupo to provide a flour-like food. Combined with the untold eel (tuna) and whitebait of the open waters, swamps were unquestionably beneficial to those whose lives depended on natural resources.

Translating the natural wetland into a garden setting, whether on a lifestyle-block scale or in a backyard rain-garden, is easy so long as you think of what is happening underground as much as above ground. Be prepared also for change. Or, if you don't care for change, be prepared for regular maintenance requiring a good pair of gumboots.

All wetland plants prefer full sun—even the ferns commonly found in swamps, such as carrier tangle fern (*Gleichenia microphylla*), the neat and tidy *Hypolepis distans*, the very common swamp fern (*Blechnum minus*), the tall and spacey water fern (*Histiopteris incisa*) or the rather scruffy and coarsely stiff, scented ring fern (*Paesia scaberula*), although they may grow just as well in partial shade. Only when a dense shrubland has developed are you likely to get the shade-loving species that don't mind wet ground and that are infill at ground level—the hook grasses (*Uncinia* spp.) are particularly useful in these circumstances.

Constructed dune ponds

Shallow ponds in duneland are prone to overheating and subsequent clogging with undesirable algal growth. This doesn't seem to occur too often in the wild, as shallow ponds would normally develop swiftly into a rushland, with the plants helping to aerate the water and to shade it. If, however, the ponds are made by bulldozer rather than nature, there are several ways in which to overcome this problem. The first, obviously, is to plant the pond immediately with rushes and sedges, with the expectation that it will progress fairly quickly into a swamp. This is a good strategy as swamps support more species and soon attract insects and birdlife. The second approach is to start with a deeper pond. If it is more than 2 m deep, there is a better chance of cooler water, but you should still expect summertime algal blooms or, at the very least, an abundance of the floating native red water fern (*Azolla filiculoides*). Whatever you do, prevent fertiliser or enriched runoff from entering any static pond—the

Water fern (TOP) and red pondweed (*Potamogeton cheesemanii*) (ABOVE) both enjoy stagnant water, but if temperatures and nutrient levels are too high they are soon joined by algal growth, which can deoxygenate the water and build up to toxic levels.

107

results will be smellier than you desire. Try not to shade the entire waterbody. This approach works well for flowing streams, helping to cool the water for fish life, but in the static duneland pond, the best results are gained from rushland growth, and that requires full sun.

Sandy bays

Whereas the dunelands we have been exploring are formed by sand driven onshore by waves and then wind, there are numerous sandy shores where dunes aren't necessarily forming. They may be places where sand that was migrating along the coast has become trapped between headlands. Or perhaps it gets trapped on shallow underwater 'bridges' known as tombolos between islands and the mainland (such as Mahia Peninsula, or Lyall Bay in Wellington), building up until it forms dry land. It may have its primary source from streams bringing fine sediment into a bay from which it is not readily flushed.

Northland and Hauraki Gulf, East Cape, Coromandel Peninsula—these picturesque coastlines are peppered with sandy bays protected by rocky headlands that provide relatively benign conditions for humans and plants alike. Generally there will be a foredune on the beach, a damp swale behind it, and sometimes a rear dune, but rarely much more. Perhaps sand has been blasted some way up the footslopes or cliffs behind the beach, as a veneer of sand over rock.

The main difference between sandy bays and extensive dunelands is that sand in the former is more fertile. Seaweed growing on the rocky points blows and drifts in to decompose on the strand line. This, along with plankton foam and blown leaves from forests that can grow so much closer to the coast in sheltered bays, provides dune plants a great head start in life.

This is the perfect setting for one of our other sand-binders—shore spurge (*Euphorbia glauca*, bottom left)—to dominate. Although it works as well as spinifex and pingao to stabilise the young dunes, sending its sappy stems horizontally through the surface of the sand, it requires a lot more shelter to thrive than most open duneland beaches can offer (as you can tell by its large and less specialised leaves). It also needs a lot more nutrition.

In general, although everything written about dunelands is relevant in this setting too, you can expect foredunes in sandy bays to support denser, stronger growth. The 'matrix' is greatly compressed, and you could reasonably expect woody shrub and tree growth within metres of a sheltered sandy beach.

You also tend to get more level terraces of sand within a bay—formed by the action of streams—or level terraces built up by storm surges. These provide a habitat without the competition of spinifex and pingao, which prefer moving sand. Here, the stable sand herbs such as shore spurge, shore bindweed, New Zealand spinach, sand piripiri and sand lobelia (*Lobelia arenaria*) thrive, along with grasses such as sand brome (*Bromus arenarius*) and sand wind grass, and the larger toetoe (*Austroderia splendens* or *A. toetoe*). It is often all knitted together with small-leaved pohuehue.

In close association will be the plants of swales and brackish water where seepages and streams meet the beach. If a beach terrace is built up, swamps will be formed behind it. Plants such as oioi, sea rush (*Juncus kraussii* var. *australiensis*), sand sedge and three-square (*Schoenoplectus pungens*) are very much part of the bay scene, perhaps even with watercress (*Nasturtium officinale*) and celery (*Apium prostratum*). So many of our bays have been developed, often with roading right to the edge of the sand, that the nuances of

dunes, terraces and back swales have long been lost, but remembrance is something gardeners embrace, and bringing former character back into the modern setting is a valuable contribution.

Sandy bay gardens

Snug little bays will have housing on the surrounding banks; large bays are likely to have housing on the central sand flats also. It is the sense of enclosure that ensures the character of the place is a seamless integration between shoreline and hillslope vegetation. Compared with duneland sites, there is more scope in a bay setting for those plants that enjoy shade or semi-shade, as well as the sun-lovers.

Bays are places of retreat and rest for seabirds. Strand lines of broken shell are picked over at leisure by birds and humans alike. What better way to combine all these sensual aspects than with exposed shell aggregate walls, steps, seats . . . anything that invites repose and relaxation? Even just reflecting the sinuous strand lines or the coarse sand grains will resonate with both contemporary and traditional designs. Inevitably there will be a stream issuing into the bay, and the patterns created as it makes its way to the sea are part of the character of these shorelines—perhaps sharp collapsing terrace edges; plaited strands of water wending through dry sand; or rills of fast flushing water taking a direct route.

Tauhinu, often scattered sparsely through duneland, can grow more

TOP Tauhinu. ABOVE Sand coprosma and *Pimelea*. RIGHT This garden truly celebrates the intensity of planting possible in sheltered, relatively fertile sandy sites, combining small-leaved pohuehue, sand coprosma, shore spurge and *Brachyglottis bidwillii* in ways that are almost, but not quite, random.

Bays are all about enclosure and framed views. This garden is sensitive to both.

densely around the bay edges because it appreciates the increased nutrient levels. It so happens that this plant looks great with shelly aggregates and crushed shell mulches. Keep it pruned back after flowering or it will get quite leggy, and simply rub off or break off the old dry stems around the base before they build up into a scruffy fire hazard. A suitable companion plant to use as a ground-cover with tauhinu would be sand daphne (as long as it does not get too shaded), as the similarity in colour and texture makes a pretty continuum. In the photograph at far left, the *Pimelea* used is a species from shingle shorelines, but the effect of using *Pimelea villosa* from sandy coasts will be the same.

The curse of the fertile bay sand is African import kikuyu grass. The lengthy spreading stolons are extremely invasive, and although many people deliberately plant this tough, thick-leaved, mat-forming coastal grass, it is causing huge problems by creeping into places it

is not wanted. That may be your neighbour's garden or it may be a natural site. Pulling it out is not always the answer as it readily sprouts from small pieces of underground rhizome left behind. Spraying or, if you are cunning, feeding the runners into a plastic bag filled with herbicide, which will be translocated around the rest of the plant, is the best solution.

Within bays, the sandy patches and the rocky headlands or clay hillsides are so integrated within the view that gardeners will often draw on both habitats for inspiration. The transition from low-level dune plants to taller shrubs and trees is naturally achieved in gardens, but it is important to give the sand-dwelling plants in particular the essentials of their habitat—sun, drainage and only a modicum of fertility.

CHAPTER 4

Rocky shores

Punishing winds, destructive salt encrustation—and hard ground. It's a recipe for stress no matter what form of life is attempting to grow in the severe salt edge, but so many plant species have adapted to these conditions that gardeners are really spoilt for choice. Not that too many of us live in this, the harshest of rocky coastal zones, but we look at it, draw inspiration from it and are often building micro-environments on our properties that replicate the astonishing array of micro-environments found along the shoreline. If one word were to sum up the character of the rocky coast, it must surely be complexity.

It's a sensible approach in gardening when we start afresh, on disturbed land, to mimic the harshest of natural environments to get the best results. Many of us, therefore, are choosing to adapt what we see close to the splash zone to create interesting gardens, even though we live somewhat more distantly.

The richness of rock

What do we need to know about this environment? One of the myths of the rocky coast is that conditions are infertile. Certainly we have, in the last 200 years, lost one of the major inputs of nutrient from our coast. Once, huge flocks of seabirds roosting and nesting on the coastal cliffs and rock stacks added enormous amounts of guano to what little soil there was. Only recently have we realised just how many coastal herbs were feeding off these highly fertile sites. Many of the coastal species on the threatened lists are plants—some seemingly too lushly herbaceous to be truly coastal—

that depended upon the birds that egg-raiding predators have subsequently eradicated from the mainland. Cook's scurvy grass (*Lepidium oleraceum*), the bushy coastal herb used by the explorer as a salad green on his voyages, is one of the plants that made the most of this source of nutrition—and provided humans with nutrition in turn—until it was browsed almost to extinction.

Yet other sources of nutrient remain. Rocky coasts are where seaweeds grow, and when they die and rot on the beaches, they generate a chain-gang of nutrition-seeking organisms that support an even wider range of coastal biota, not just plants. Plus, plankton is sprayed ashore with the foaming waves, providing a further source of nutrient, albeit not as rich as algae. One of our now-familiar garden species, shore spurge, thrives in the accumulated detritus of seaweed and driftwood flung high up the beach by storms. Its rhizomes creep through the jumble of decaying material, pushing down roots at intervals to support the next flush of growth. The rocks themselves constantly release nutrient through weathering by chemical and water action—a slow but steady supply that is conveniently trapped in cracks and crevices for plant roots to benefit from. Fresh water also collects in those cracks and crevices, providing a source of sustenance for plant life.

As Northland dwellers know, not all rocky shores are necessarily harsh places, and the more indented the coastline and the more sheltered the coastal bluffs, the greater the variety of plant forms possible—even tall trees. The following section explores this diversity, from the meanest of the rocky shores through to the more benign.

Survival tactics in the 'severe salt zone'

While the roots of coastal plants may be catered for, it's their topknots that need to address the tough conditions, especially where the rocky shore is a windy one. The severe salt edge close to the sea can be a place of both physical and chemical hardship, where the abrasive force of the wind combined with the burn of salt forces plants as well as people to batten down the hatches. Unlike sand beaches, where scorching sun and sometimes frost play a part in dictating plant life, there is a wider diversity of plant form possible here—it just has to be cunningly suited to micro-environments. Also, unlike dunelands, many rocky shores are shady for

OPPOSITE BOTTOM Veined with resilient quartz but shattered by faulting, greywacke provides sculptural interest around the shores of Kapiti Island and Cook Strait.
ABOVE Seaweeds support a food chain even after death.

113

part of the day. This offers yet another micro-environment, whether it be the cool of south-facing bluffs or intermittent shade behind large rock stacks.

For plants, it pays to be succulent. If you can't be succulent, be flexuous. If you aren't flexuous, moving freely with the wind so you don't split and fracture, then the flatter you can lie to the rock, the safer you are.

Succulence

On the rocky coast, plants with succulent foliage include ground-creeping species like the native iceplant, with pretty little pink flowers and leaves that are much smaller than the rather brutish South African import so common now around our coastline. As it creeps, it sends little roots into the tiniest of crevices.

The native climbing spinach (*Tetragonia implexicoma*) is useful for trailing. The flowers are not particularly conspicuous, but in a good fruiting year the bright-red berries are an attraction. This adaptable plant becomes more succulent the more exposed the conditions get and its stems become increasingly red. It is a very similar plant to New Zealand spinach, which is more likely to be found among the driftwood and boulders on the beach; its little red fruits have hard horns on them.

There are a number of ground ferns with succulent fronds, in particular the shore hard fern (*Blechnum blechnoides*), which has very evenly arranged, round pinnae (looking like a coastal version of the forest fern *B. fluviatile*) and coastal spleenwort (*Asplenium appendiculatum* subsp. *maritimum*), whose thick fronds can rebuff most coastal winds and which

TOP **Native climbing spinach.** ABOVE **New Zealand iceplant.** RIGHT **The plump fronds of** *Blechnum durum*. FAR RIGHT **Coastal spleenwort.**

can tuck into tiny crevices so that often it is the only plant brazen enough to enjoy the sea views. The leather-leaf fern (*Pyrrosia eleagnifolia*) will sprawl happily in and out of rocks and driftwood, seemingly oblivious of sun or salt-burn. It may seem to be shrivelling with stress some days, but the slightest rainfall will see it pick up again.

Damp perches on cliffs may become home to *Blechnum durum*, which, as its name suggests, is durable in these conditions. Although not always as succulent as the ferns just mentioned, it is able to build up a spongy base of dead fronds quite quickly, which must help it survive drought periods. The little hard fern (*Blechnum penna-marina*), with its diminutive perky fronds, may join it.

The rock-perching succulent herb peperomia (*Peperomia urvilleana*) is found through the North Island and Marlborough, and can grow in sun or in shade (which makes it a fuller, taller plant). The spires of seeds held stiffly erect are one of the endearing properties of this tough little plant, but also its fresh, plump, lettuce-green foliage makes it an eye-catcher.

TOP Leather-leaf fern. ABOVE Peperomia. LEFT Where salty spray constantly keeps surfaces moist, ferns may become more rampant. Two *Blechnum* species sprawl across these west coast rocks amidst the wind-tolerant wh_arariki.

TOP Oioi is mostly a wetland rush; one of the stranger coastal sights is surely the oioi that grows in the seepages of vertical cliffs in north Taranaki. There is no better illustration of the advantages of the flexuous form.

ABOVE Movement is emphasised where dynamic plants are silhouetted against a static background.

Flexuous forms

Synonymous with 'flexuous and coastal' is flax. It's on the rocky coast that we get to know wharariki (*Phormium cookianum*). The smaller cousin of harakeke (*Phormium tenax*), wharariki is the more resilient of the two species to extreme conditions and is the one found hanging off cliff faces, perched on rock ledges, tucked into coastal crevices or into smothering hillsides that have previously been burnt by wildfires.

Wharariki flowers are greenish yellowish (in contrast to the red flowers of harakeke), and a distinguishing feature is that when the seed pods wither, they dangle, twisted and spent; those of harakeke remain stiffly upright. Wharariki seeds, thin flakes blown readily by the wind, seem perfectly suited to settling into rock cracks, and the stringy but succulent roots also seem perfectly adapted to life exploring crevices.

The strength of a flax leaf cannot be underestimated, and even when shredded by the force of the wind, the leaf can still function. While it can take a thrashing from the weather, this does not necessarily make it a great choice for coastal gardens as, first, the shredding of its leaves can make it unsightly and, second, the whipping of its leaves can inhibit any other less robust plant within range. Perhaps the best solution is to mimic the common coastal sight of individual flax bushes poking through a dense 'canopy' of springy divaricating shrubs that move very little in the wind, acting as a support for the flax and limiting its movement. Flaxes are, however, very useful for difficult steep banks, and they are certainly a lure to bellbirds and tui during spring and summer months.

Grasses and lilies tend to enter the rocky coast scene only where there are pockets of loess (wind-blown silts) or where rock is weathering to clay. The polka-dotting of bluffs with erect tussocks, very rarely in abundance, is a characteristic look. Silver tussock (*Poa cita*) is especially common around Cook Strait and Otago Pensinsula, although it is shaded out as surrounding shrubs encroach, but the small toetoe *Austroderia fulvida* can hold its own within the coastal shrubland.

One of the most amazing coastal grasses of rocky coasts is one of the most restricted in its range—*Chionochloa bromoides*, found only around the Bay of Islands and a number of offshore islands in Northland. It appears to be able to break the general rule that fibrous-rooted plants fare poorly in rocky places. This endemic grass seems to be able to defy gravity. It gives itself a sporting chance of avoiding desiccation by securing itself mostly to shady cliffs, but it is also slow to lose its dead leaves, which build up a spongy fibrous 'nest' and no doubt retain moisture. *Chionochloa beddiei* fulfils the same role in Cook Strait. Most chionochloas are high-altitude snow tussocks, but these two, plus the garden favourite *C. flavicans*, have conquered the coast. *Chionochloa flavicans* almost fills a gap in the distribution of the genus around the North Island, occurring naturally between Coromandel and Hawke's Bay.

Astelia and *Collospermum* are suited to exposed rocky coasts but, because they also tolerate semi-shade, can be found associated with coastal forest as well as on rocky outcrops and cliffs. They are mostly northern New Zealand occurrences, apart from the infamous *Astelia chathamica* from the Chatham Islands. Coastal astelia or shore kowharawhara (*Astelia banksii*) is the most commonly occurring coastal astelia, often perching on steep cliffs or rock stacks where only passing insects and birds get to admire the pretty clusters of magenta berries it produces. It is restricted to the northern half of the North Island.

Along sheltered coastlines, where coastal forest extends practically to the water's edge, you may find the larger, finer-leaved kauri grass (*Astelia trinervia*). The only South Island locations for this astelia are in northwest Nelson, where it likes the dappled light of open kanuka canopies; otherwise, it is found in the northern half of the North Island. Kaiwharawhara or perching lily (*A. solandri*) is also found in coastal situations at times—most noticeably on the lava fields of Rangitoto—but its usual habitat is perching on trees within the dappled light of coastal forest.

Astelia chathamica, coming as it does from a rather cool island, is cold-hardy but not frost-hardy. Unlike

TOP Silver tussock.
ABOVE *Chionochloa bromoides* clings to the rocks at the Mokohinau Islands in Northland. These old plants are almost self-sufficient, gaining moisture and probably nutrients from their accumulated dead leaves—and hopefully attracting the odd perching seabird as a bonus. Their flowerheads dangle attractively and their foliage always seems to look fresh, no matter how stormy the location.

Other than *Astelia chathamica*, astelias tend to be associated with the more northern rocky coasts, pairing well with pohutukawa, which, renowned for drawing any available soil moisture away from other plants, limit their companions to plants that have excellent moisture-storing adaptations.

Laying low

You don't get to lie much lower than a lichen—the first plant to colonise new sites. Even within the lichen world there are flat (crustose) lichens and erect (fruticose) lichens, and not surprisingly, the former are more common on rough coasts. Given that lichens consist of a mutually beneficial fungal–algal blend, this seems a perfectly appropriate habitat.

Rocky shores have little pockets of damp ground or brackish ponds where you can find the succulent, mat-forming herbs. Often growing so intermeshed that they can't be distinguished from each other are shore stonecrop (*Crassula moschata*), with its succulent red stems; the starry-eyed shore primrose (*Samolus repens*); perhaps the wee sand buttercup (*Ranunculus acaulis*) with its podgy succulent leaves and, of course, the ubiquitous glasswort.

It is the way these bright green mats fill the spaces between large grey outcrops, as though poured in like syrup, that creates such vivid imagery. The lowest-growing woody shrubs may be here too— *Muehlenbeckia axillaris*, in particular, can sprawl great distances. It does, however, lack the showiness

the previously described astelias, it will not appreciate being dried out as it has evolved in a moist climate. However, aside from having fleshy, water-storing roots, astelias also create their own mats of absorbent organic material around their bases, which helps them survive drying winds. This aspect should carry through to gardening with all astelias—the less they are 'tidied up', the hardier they will be. The bases of the leaves as well as the roots have adaptations to both prevent evaporation and to absorb readily any moisture that is available. The roots are useful both for seeking out cracks in the rocks for anchoring and also for growing close to the expanding stems, where they can absorb minerals and water gleaned by the leaves themselves.

ABOVE Kauri grass is readily recognised by the sheer length of its skinny leaves.
OPPOSITE 1. Shore stonecrop. 2. Remuremu. 3. Shore primrose. 4. It may look like turf, but the green syrup oozing through the limestone comprises *Selliera*, *Samolus* and *Crassula*. 5. *Muehlenbeckia axillaris* and glasswort. 6. *Leptinella potentilla* (feathery), remuremu and stonecrop (tiny grey leaves).

of the other mat-forming herbs, whether it be their ruddy stems or their spangling of small flowers. These densely packed communities where tiny ground-cover species intermingle is a theme to carry through into the garden.

Springy and prostrate ground-covers

Resilience also comes in the form of shrubs that, while stiff and therefore theoretically vulnerable to storm damage, defy the elements by having a multiplicity of small branchlets, often to the extent of being divaricate (with branchlets at right angles or more to the main stems), and small leaves. The plants can be shaped and shorn by the salt winds without losing their overall vitality. The plasticity of form and the springiness of their structure helps them dominate the windiest of coastal shrubland environments.

Around Cook Strait and Taranaki, we find an extreme case of springiness: shrubs of *Coprosma propinqua* densely intertwined with scrambling pohuehue vines (*Muehlenbeckia complexa* or *M. australis*) create an impenetrable mat. Wellingtonian children will tell you that a common local name for *C. propinqua* is 'the mattress plant' for good reason. Admittedly, part of the shaping process is undertaken by browsing possums, but even without their grazing, the plant will form a very bouncy mattress indeed.

The ground-hugging forms of shrubs and trailing plants play an enormously important role on rocky shores. Rooted into the base of rocks where rainwater gathers, and with firm anchorage in strong winds, they will seek to spread across the sunny sides of rocks preferentially, benefiting from the warmth radiated off the rocks. Warmth also attracts the geckos and skinks that will eat their tiny fruit and distribute seeds. Although we tend to think of lizards basking on warm rocks, it is the close-knit miniature canopy of coastal shrubs that creates their preferred habitat, meaning most are quietly invisible to the casual beach stroller.

The tightly interwoven branchlets of divaricating species such as thick-leaved mahoe (*Melicytus crassifolius*), *M. obovatus* or *Coprosma propinqua* create a trap for blowing leaf litter (including that from the plants themselves), which in turn provides the sustenance and seed-beds as well as shelter for coastal herbs such as New Zealand linen (*Linum*

monogynum), shore groundsel, fire weed (*Haloragis erecta*), ground ferns, or the vine that seems to get involved at any opportunity, small-leaved pohuehue.

Shore lobelia (*Lobelia anceps*) puts up a brave show on rocky coasts by sprouting out of the most unlikely cracks in rocks, but this straggly, weedy-looking herb also benefits from the protection of prostrate shrubs. Its dainty, lopsided flowers are a mauve version of the more familiar white-flowered remuremu (*Selliera radicans*).

You will often find the coastal *Clematis forsteri* winding its way through the root-shading mat of prostrate shrubs. Like most clematis species, it will want to have its roots in cool, shady soil while its stems seek the light.

Even in parts of New Zealand where divaricating shrubs are less common, this prostrate habitat is still a feature of windswept rocky headlands and bluffs. Down south in the Catlins, for example, there are headlands where cushions of Lindsay's daisy (*Celmisia lindsayi*) take the brunt of the salty winds. It is not common to find Celmisia species at the coast, and this one is pretty specific about its needs: shady, south-facing and rocky sites only. There is an equally fussy Celmisia in Northland—*C. major*—which doesn't form the same dense mats but is commonly found on damp cliff faces.

Between Northland and Greymouth, the fantasti-

OPPOSITE TOP Plants like *Coprosma propinqua*, which can hug the warm north faces of rock stacks, will provide a haven for lizards, butterflies and bees. OPPOSITE CENTRE Not only lizards benefit from coastal shrublands. Here, kereru gorge themselves on coprosma berries. OPPOSITE BOTTOM Where crevices collect wind-blown silt and rainwater, roots will benefit, in this case those of thick-leaved mahoe. ABOVE *Clematis forsteri*. LEFT Taupata roots have levered a slab of rock clean off the cliff face.

121

cally plastic taupata (*Coprosma repens*) displays an extraordinary ability to bend and twist and clutch at rocks and boulders in the saltiest and windiest of sites, almost to the water's edge. Look at the roots though—inevitably they are seeking fresh water at the base of large rock faces or cracks in rock faces, and the branches wind themselves into the sunniest position possible.

Taupata is not the only tree to adapt to a more lowly life form in order to cope with wind-blown cliffs. From an interesting stretch of coastal cliff on ultramafic rocks in Northland come a number of prostrate forms, including coastal five finger (*Pseudopanax lessonii*), growing as a dense bush, and *Pittosporum serpentinum* (whose closest relative is a small Northland tree). From offshore northern islands comes a prostrate form of ngaio (previously known as *Myoporum decumbens* but now taxonomically lumped in with *Myoporum laetum*, the common ngaio), long popular in gardens because of its creeping, low growth.

A semi-prostrate kowhai can be found gracing our steep headlands along the Cook Strait–Wairarapa coasts and islands. This bushy kowhai, *Sophora molloyi*, tends to hide its flowers among the foliage but has nevertheless become popular as a garden plant, sold as 'Dragon's Gold'.

Some woody coastal shrubs are simply remarkable. What do their roots find to clutch onto? Marlborough rock daisy (*Pachystegia insignis*) attempts the seemingly impossible Spiderman technique and usually succeeds. So finely tuned is this plant to dry, exposed rocky sites that it can readily rot in humid garden situations and certainly dislikes root disturbance. The woody structure of the shrub is stiff rather than flexuous and it generally keeps a low profile against the rock, but its seedheads benefit from their exposure to the wind, and wind-blown seed will no doubt settle in some tiny crevice and persevere like its parents did.

Of the 80 or so species in the *Veronica* (=*Hebe*) genus, a small portion have found themselves a niche at the seaside. These generally prefer rocky coasts rather than sand, as fertility is greater and they are unlikely to be shaded out by taller species. They have developed thick, fleshy leaves to suit the conditions. The stand-outs are the smaller shore hebe (*Veronica elliptica*), *V. chathamica* (from the Chatham Islands), *V. stricta* var. *macroura* with large leaves and fairly prostrate form, *V. obtusata* (found only in some Northland sites), and in relatively sheltered locations the taller *V. pubescens* (from the Coromandel) and napuka (*V. speciosa*) with its flashy magenta flowers and red-edged succulent leaves. As it turns out, napuka has been a garden favourite for hundreds of years: genetic studies are showing us that coastal populations previously understood to be isolated relicts are likely to have been planted by people prior to European settlement, and the species' 'natural' distribution is actually very limited indeed. *Veronica chathamica*, a very prostrate form, is proving a useful sand-binder in cultivation, although its natural habitat is somewhat stonier.

Similar in looks to hebes are the shrubby pimeleas. Most of the coastal species have prostrate forms, and there are several that are also adept at dangling off banks and cliff edges. *Pimelea carnosa* has a particularly attractive form.

Banking on good roots

Banks with accumulations of clays and silts, either blown in or weathering on site, are suited to a number of plants that have succulent roots and grasses that have bulky fibrous roots not suited to restrictive rock crevices. The later section in this book on weathered clay substrates (pages 166–73) explores more of these, but commonly found in salt-sprayed areas are some curious large herbs whose roots are one of the keys to their survival.

Soft speargrass (*Aciphylla dieffenbachii*) comes from the Chatham Islands, and although its former habitat has been greatly shrunk by grazing, its preference for ledges and slopes on south-facing cliffs, in association with grasses, is clear. The stout, swollen root requires at least 200 mm soil depth to reach maturity. The feathery foliage also has a hidden secret. It may not look suitably adapted to the wilds of salty storms, but its stems contain latex, a complex chemical brew that coagulates on exposure, thus healing the plant after damage. It has generally been supposed to be a defence against insect browse, but it may also act as the ambulance at the foot of gale-ridden cliffs!

Taramea (*Aciphylla squarrosa*) is a much more widespread coastal speargrass, also needing the ability to enlarge its roots freely. Common on rocky coasts, it does nevertheless tend to be confined to shingle scree or loess-clad ledges. Not affected by browse the way its soft-leaved cousin is, it makes an eyecatching display when its golden flowerheads—as nastily spiky as the parent plant—are in bloom.

OPPOSITE TOP Prostrate ngaio hugs the rugged cliffs on the remote Mokohinau Islands in Northland. OPPOSITE CENTRE Marlborough rock daisy. OPPOSITE BOTTOM *Veronica chathamica* (foreground). TOP *Pimelea carnosa*. ABOVE Soft speargrass.

TOP Chatham Islands forget-me-not.
ABOVE Rengarenga.

Far more benign is the rengarenga lily (*Arthropodium cirratum*), whose starchy roots provided sustenance for early Maori and hence has often been found associated with coastal kainga (villages). It is also seen festooning steep bluffs on western rocky coasts and offshore islands.

The Chatham Island forget-me-not (*Myosotidium hortensia*) is another giant herb we have become familiar with in gardens, so much so that we mostly overlook the fact that its natural habitat is the rocky shore. Because it relies on year-round soil moisture and high fertility, it is not surprising to find it growing naturally just above the strand line, sometimes in damp peaty hollows, or taking advantage of any pockets of organic soil further up the bank. Its root is fat and fleshy, and with age the stem becomes rather woody. It may also have grown in damp back dunes but has been lost from these habitats. Like rengarenga, it tends to grow in clusters, perhaps because its seeds, although winged, are quite heavy and don't travel far. They both tolerate semi-shade so may be found on the fringes of coastal forest.

The Poor Knights lily (*Xeronema callistemon*) is finely tuned for coastal life, with succulent leaves that have fibrous, sponge-like skirts, but its stand-out feature is its thick, rhizomatous roots. For some reason, the more restricted the roots are by tight crevices, the better the plant flowers.

Exposed coastal forest

Moving inland from the herbfields and shrublands of the immediate rocky shore, we find a zone where small trees can grow—or in the case of Northland and Coromandel, where pohutukawa reigns supreme. Just how close this zone is to the shore depends on the degree of shelter from salt-laden spray and wind, as well as the ability of tree roots to find enough soil to live off.

To survive here, plants still need protective adaptations. Their leaves are generally wrinkly and leathery, or furry, or perhaps very waxy—all methods of preventing excessive evaporation in the wind and salt accumulation on sensitive surfaces. Some, like ngaio, have oil glands dotted through their leaves, which probably works partially as a protection against salt drying the leaves out and partly as a store of energy reserves when the going gets tough.

This is a fringing forest with character and contains plants that transfer well to new sections, gardens and hedges, because not only are they generally drought- and wind-resistant, but their root systems are

accustomed to uncompromisingly awkward situations. Some of them are also beautiful in intimate settings where rough or papery bark becomes a tactile as well as a visual delight.

In the Marlborough Sounds photo (above), the typically dominant coastal trees can be picked out: the pale crowns of akiraho, dense mid-green pittosporums, dark glossy crowns of broadleaf (*Griselinia littoralis*) and taupata, and deep olive-green kanuka.

In other parts of the country there may also be akeake, mapau or ngaio. Kaikomako (*Pennantia corymbosa*) adds its weight to the floral displays over summer. Kowhai is often present as it favours the broken canopies of steep banks and dry slip faces: *Sophora chathamica* and *S. fulvida* in Northland; *S. microphylla* south of Northland, including the South Island; and *S. tetraptera* along the eastern coast of the North Island.

This jumbled mixed bag of trees is very characteristic of rocky-shore forest. It is generally a single-tier forest (with little undergrowth), and all the trees jostling for space are equally well adapted to these conditions. It is only when you step back and look at the wider landscape that a pattern starts to become obvious, and the key to the pattern is moisture. Both the spurs and the gullies receive the same rainfall, but which has the moisture-retentive

TOP RIGHT Kaikomako's floral display is typical of coastal forest trees. Perhaps it is a reliance on wind for polliation or seed dispersal that concentrates plants with mass terminal flowering on these sites. ABOVE *Sophora chathamica*.

soils and where does the rain drain to? On hard spurs, dry and exposed to the wind, a dense, low forest contains the species we have just met—tough, small-leaved and often with terminal flowering so that seeds are wind-distributed. But in the gully alongside, where soils are forming in the moisture of a sheltered catchment, a flush of green broadleaf forest has established.

North of the Bay of Plenty and Kawhia, pohutukawa is a dominant coastal tree on exposed coasts—indeed, often it is the only tree. Although its preferred habitat is clay substrates, this large tree's roots do find surprising ways of dealing with rocky faces.

The *Olearia* genus deserves special mention, as although no single species grows naturally throughout the length of New Zealand's coastal vegetation, when you link a number of species together, olearias are ubiquitous along our coast. Up north, it is akepiro (*O. furfuracea*), *O. albida* and the scarce *O. angulata*; the now-endangered *O. pachyphylla* occurs across Bay of Plenty; akiraho (*O. paniculata*) is found predominantly through Cook Strait and down to Banks Peninsula; mountain akeake (*O. avicenniifolia*) occurs through the South Island and Stewart Island; and *O. angustifolia* flourishes around Foveaux Strait. The Chatham Islands have *O. traversiorum*, which grows into a venerable old tree, but mostly on old dunes rather than rocky coasts.

As we can see, overall the rocky shore is a curiosity shop of different habitats, nooks and crannies, shady sites and hot. In many places the vegetation is windshorn compared to the comparative shelter of fjords and harbours. It is because most rocky shores are frost-free, thanks to the air movement down the steep headlands and hillsides they extend from, that we find so many large-leaved herbaceous plants. There are, of course, rocky coasts within areas of frosty climates such

as Golden Bay and Tasman Bay, but often the frost lies just on the flat sandy beaches between the headlands, or on the only flat surfaces exposed to the sky—jetties and wharves. It can be a very fine line at times.

What species are knocked out of the rocky coastal vegetation by frosts? Of the tree species, pohutukawa and ngaio, the flimsy-leaved whau, karaka and puka, even the seemingly hardy taupata—all are susceptible to frost. If any of these species are found south of Christchurch, you would suspect they had been planted or are naturalising from introduced specimens. Their roles are filled instead by hardy olearias, pittosporums, mapau, native brooms, kaikomako or broadleaf,

TOP Kanuka clearly needs little rooting depth and minimal soil to survive.
LEFT AND ABOVE Akiraho. Olearias often dominate coastal forest edges.
OPPOSITE They may not grow huge on these hard rock headlands, but pohutukawa will try anyway. Roots will work their way into crevices and get meagre nutrients and water there, but probably not enough to support a fully grown tree.

although none of these would naturally grow as close to the splash zone as pohutukawa or taupata are able to. As might be expected, some of the flimsier herbs such as lobelia are not frost-hardy.

Hard-rock harbours

What differences are there between the coastal vegetation of the exposed rocky shore and that found within harbours? The main difference is not so much the range of species we might expect but that in these calmer, less erodable conditions, coastal shrubland and even forest may grow to the water's edge, creating an aesthetic missing from the outer coasts. The gradation through splash zone or severe salt edge to shrubland, then coastal forest and nikau belt is highly compressed.

The inner Marlborough Sounds or Fiordland, and intimate harbours such as Whanganui in northwest Nelson or Whangaroa in Northland, have the least severe salt edge of all, and delightful scenes result where vegetation overhangs the water. These are picturesque cameos that lend themselves well to steep gardens in equally sheltered locations, and plants are shown off to best effect on banks and ledges.

There is often a fringe of grasses or monocotyledons such as astelias or flaxes that can tolerate the drought-prone existence of life on the edge—a very distinct band. Rock faces, black shadows and horizontal layering is the inner-harbour aesthetic (and readily translated into garden settings).

A genus of shrubs that shows a predilection towards rocky bluffs is *Dracophyllum*. Through the Marlborough Sounds and northwest Nelson, the needle-leaved *Dracophyllum urvilleanum* clings to coastal cliffs, in places adding a curiously sci-fi feel to the vegetation where it catches the light, at other times so soft and fluffy that it almost becomes invisible.

OPPOSITE TOP Whanganui Inlet, northwest Nelson. OPPOSITE BOTTOM Above the fringing wharariki is inaka, the white-flowering shrub *Pimelea longifolium*, the climbing rata *Metrosideros perforata* and a fine-leaved kohuhu (*Pittosporum tenuifolium*).
LEFT *Dracophyllum urvilleanum*.
BELOW LEFT Winter-flowering *Metrosideros fulgens*. BELOW RIGHT The fringing base is *Muehlenbeckia axillaris*, the two flowering ratas share the space with taupata and shining spleenwort. The tree-fern trunks used for fencing locate the concept in forest and the species used locate the concept within coastal forest.

The 'nikau belt'

We are on the west coast. As we move further inland from the rocky shore or into sheltered moist gullies, away from the worst of the salt spray but where it is still mild and relatively warm, we find ourselves in the lushest environment of all. This is where the prevailing wind's energy abates, allowing windborne silt to settle. Here, fed by groundwater draining from the hills and by constant humidity, life is good, growth is fast, nutrient recycling is efficient and nikau (*Rhopalostylis sapida*) thrive. This zone may be close to the coast in high-rainfall areas or it may be more distant.

Nikau is the most conspicuous component of this type of forest, but kohekohe, wharangi, broadleaf, mahoe and kawakawa ensure a fresh-green canopy, flush with ferns and climbers. Towards the southern end of the North Island, some of these trees drop out with the cold, leaving kohekohe as a major component. This is a vigorous tree, withstanding storm and stock damage, but the one thing it can't withstand is possum browse and, sadly, entire groves of dead and dying kohekohe litter the valleys around Wellington and the Marlborough Sounds.

This forest association can grow almost to the shore in the shelter of the inner Marlborough Sounds, but even along more open coastlines, as soon as that combination of conditions occurs (mildness, shelter and moisture), these species can dominate. In Taranaki they may be joined by rain-loving whau (*Entelea arborescens*) or further north by karaka (*Corynocarpus laevigatus*). Most of the South Island is too cold for these species and the east coasts of both islands (south of the Coromandel Peninsula) too dry.

Although the nikau belt is not influenced directly by salt, it is usually in view of the coast, sometimes very close indeed—just a steep ridge between the salt winds and a moist valley may be all the protection needed, as in the Taranaki photograph (opposite, right). There is scope here for some lush undergrowth, such as parataniwha (*Elatostema rugosum*) in the company of king fern (*Ptisana* (=*Marattia*) *salicina*) and spleenwort ferns of all kinds.

LEFT Whau. RIGHT Parataniwha and king fern in a damp gully near the coast at Urenui.
OPPOSITE LEFT Mahoe and kawakawa team up with nikau at Punakaiki, where the wet but mild climate allows this lush growth only 100 m from the coastal cliffs. OPPOSITE RIGHT At Urenui, on Taranaki's fierce west coast, one sheltering ridge is all that is required to enable nikau to thrive.

Coastal weathering literally takes the edge off freshly eroded rock, so to harmonise, use weathered rock in the garden.

Rocky gardens

I'm sure we all gravitate to rock outcrops as a feature to be climbed, enjoy views from, feel superior on top of. It's part of our makeup. With modern machinery, it's no great problem introducing outcrops to places where no outcrops currently exist, but doing it well is extremely difficult.

Having considered the natural plant life of rocky coastlines, let's not overlook the rock itself. One need not fear sheer rock. It may be fun to start with just the raw ingredients—time will then be the master. If lichen latches onto the rock, so be it. In the meantime, it is water that shares its elemental status with rock, so a celebration of the interaction between the two is a valid formula in the garden as well.

But, first, what rock to choose? Using local rock is so important to avoid artifice and to blend seamlessly with the environment you are part of. The next best thing is to use rock that echoes the landforms in the distance.

Large rocks are best bedded well into the ground—they look ridiculous perched on the surface unless you really are wanting to re-create the ambience of a quarry. They also look best placed in clusters. Get your plants ready for planting at the same time that the rock work is being undertaken, before the surrounding ground is tamped down. Successful growth in the wild occurs where roots are tapping down to the base of large rocks, which collect and direct cool fresh water (and the reflected heat from the rocks is beneficial for flowering and fruiting). Rocky-coast plants need both cool root-runs and enjoy the reflected heat of rock—a challenging combination of conditions to be met, which is why tiny seedlings often fail. Planting rocks and plants together will give the rock garden a great head start.

Bear in mind also that clean rock makes light seem harsh—and playing with shadows imparts a design detail into a garden that is well suited to the rocky coast, so choosing plants that are more stem than leaf or have stiff, slender foliage that casts crisp shadows can provide interesting detail.

Pacific rock oysters encrust any inanimate material in Northland—rock, concrete, hulls of boats. The dizzying patterns of oysters are sensational but hard to mimic and nastily sharp when fresh. Perhaps it is best to collect the wave-worn shells for ornamental paths and leave nature to decorate our coastlines with her frilly petticoats. The broad banding of encrusted white rock, dark seaweed-blackened rock and, higher still perhaps, colourful lichen-encrusted dry rocks within the splash zone lends itself to mimicking with hard landscaping in a garden. Perhaps materials such as fine shingles, dark timbers, exposed aggregate, asphalt, or even crushed glass can be used in ways that mimic the natural zonation.

Most rocky shores are repositories for driftwood and washed-up kelp that dries into queer crackling. Bull kelp proliferates in the deep south, growing at a fantastic rate, and promises to provide a lucrative harvest (as it does in other countries) for industries needing thickening substances. Perhaps there could be a sideline in garden ornaments!

Lichens

One day I hope we'll be able to purchase colourful lichens in nurseries along with vascular plants, to 'seed' our coastal gardens and achieve the fabulous colour schemes and textures of the lichens we find in the wild. Applying yoghurt to rocks and pots and hoping something will become established may be the next best thing.

Lichens will in time encrust timber, concrete, stone—don't be afraid to allow them to spread, as this ageing process is what blends your garden in with the wider environment texturally. If lichens have colonised any garden surfaces and you have a dominant colour (they are likely to be either strong yellows or mottled whites and greys), it can be echoed, or contrasted, in the flowers or leaves of the plants nearby. Some very lovely and very striking effects can be achieved, and certainly it would be a shame to waste the opportunity for some colour play.

Similarly, it makes perfect sense to team up a lichen-encrusted feature with some highly textural plants. So instead of combining the sharp, glossy green slashes of Poor Knights lily with your crusty rocks, perhaps encourage leather-leaf fern to crawl across the surface, or find some niches for the felty, curled leaves of *Craspedia* amid the foliose lichens.

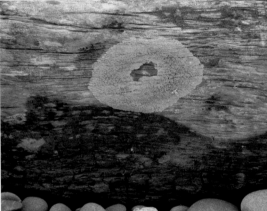

TOP The zen-like quality of stillness, light and shadow are achieved in this garden by using a very stiff plant—shrubby tororaro—to create sunny-day magic.
CENTRE AND BOTTOM Lichens rarely take centre stage in inland gardens, but coastal lichens tend to be attention-grabbers.

Rock-hopping and creeping

The plants that tuck into nooks and crannies along the rocky shore are rarely domineering; usually the rock is the prominent feature. A garden where creeping, perching ferns, herbs and trailing plants are used sparingly and casually reflects this opportunistic aspect.

As a rule, creeping succulent plants have very small root systems and can be used to great effect in rock walls, rock gardens, roof gardens, and difficult nooks and crannies. This allows them to achieve the other beneficial coastal format—prostration. Keeping your head down is all-important for these plants, except at flowering time, when taking advantage of the wind when setting seed is a good idea, and many creeping herbs are quite spectacular through summer flowering months.

OPPOSITE TOP LEFT Climbing native spinach can be used to trail as well as climb. This is best achieved in a sheltered spot where wind will not whip it around, but it does provide fast cover for plain corners. OPPOSITE TOP RIGHT AND BOTTOM LEFT New Zealand iceplant. OPPOSITE BOTTOM RIGHT Not so spectacular as flowering herbs perhaps, but interesting when used in combination with beachy materials, are the prostrate woody shrubs. Two different coprosma varieties create a firm, reliable cover in this garden.

LEFT TOP A bit more patience is required to establish the creeping herb mats so typical of damp hollows and seepages, but this combination of glasswort and shore primrose makes an attractive filler. LEFT BOTTOM The sleek, controlled look of the pond, on the other hand, makes sure the crassula is the centre of attention, with the overall design perfectly suited to a crisp, rocky landscape.

ABOVE The prostrate shrub combination here shows how often combinations of the same genus make for some wonderful textural interaction. *Melicytus crassifolius* (with the smaller leaves) has a stiffly rigid form, but teamed up with the laxer *M. obovatus*, they seem to haunt each other.

Capturing the haphazard character of the place

Perhaps on a rocky shore more than any other type of coastline we are aware of opportunists grabbing hold of some micro-habitat that suits their needs. Whether their seed has blown there or their fruit has been conveyed by birds and lizards, the result is a conspicuous feature in the otherwise severe rockscapes. Gardeners who think hard about the micro as well as the macro will soon find there is great pleasure to be had in inventing tiny niches for their treasures, and nurturing the unexpected arrivals that turn up when our backs are turned. Using the cracks and crannies between large rocks is the essence of a good rock garden. The planting is haphazard, so it is important that the overall structure has clarity and purpose. Coastal shrubs such as mingimingi will thrive when planted *with* the rock, and being forced to hug it both looks natural and offers great wildlife habitat.

The haphazard nature of the rocky-shore vegetation, reinterpreted by garden design, can result in a happy, shambolic floral mix. If you have an eclectic mix of plant types (herbs, scramblers, ferns and shrubs), you have discovered the essence of the rocky shore. Rengarenga looks fabulous teamed up with native broom, with both plants having the fleshy foliage (or stems in the case of native broom, whose foliage is almost non-existent) needed to withstand desiccation. With such algal forms, there is no question that the rocky shore is being invoked. The combination of lax rengarenga with the erect Poor Knights lily is also a witty juxtaposition of form that makes a natural pairing, with both plants suited to the same substrates and conditions.

Actually a bushy vine rather than a shrub, small-leaved pohuehue, usually an integral component in rocky-shore shrublands, is frequently used as a major player in garden designs as its hazy softness lends itself to both merging with similarly rounded, soft forms or

BELOW LEFT Silver tussock turns a lichen-encrusted stone wall into a gallery. This effect of grasses cascading down rock walls could also be achieved with the larger tussocks of *Chionochloa beddiei* or *C. bromoides*. BELOW RIGHT Small-leaved pohuehue.
OPPOSITE Creating the nooks and crannies for haphazard arrangements is the essence of a coastal rock garden.

contrasting with rigid construction. Some gardeners avoid using it, claiming it will overtake the garden and invade where not intended. It pays to understand that in the wild it survives on a very minimal diet. In the garden, frequently overindulged with fertile soils, it will, of course, respond accordingly.

Once you move away from the splash zone to where dense shrubland dominates, another character emerges that is highly suitable for suburban gardens in windy sites. It is the continuum of shrubs of even height, packed together yet always interwoven with more delicate surprises like clematis or ferns. This concept is rarely used in modern gardens, which is odd, given the common desire for a 'low-maintenance' garden. Most often it is applied to thin hedge lines.

Capturing the motion

The few flexuous species along the rocky coast—tall grasses such as silver tussock or toetoe and wharariki—certainly lend a dynamism to an otherwise uncompromisingly resilient coastal shrubland. The grasses really only dominate where they can root into loess or clay and are often tucked into a tightly knitted weave of shrubs, but where they are free to flow in the wind, they certainly speak volumes about the weather! If they are positioned in a garden setting to catch the wind and have a static backdrop, your eye will be drawn to the movement so much more readily than if they are lost within a mass of vegetation.

One grass managing to break the rule about needing silts or soils to root into appears to be buggar grass (*Austrostipa stipoides*), which on the one hand grows happily in estuary muds but also makes a cameo appearance on Rangitoto Island in the Hauraki Gulf, our youngest volcano. Here it perches on lava flows with seemingly no soil at all (although the crevices must be collecting wind-blown dirt). The stiffness

LEFT Massed grasses are not generally a characteristic of rocky coasts—but used in a hard-edged setting that is sympathetic of a rocky landscape, they can certainly be dramatic. This garden simply uses two species: *Chionochloa flavicans* (distant) and silver tussock. RIGHT Buggar grass.

of buggar grass is perfectly attuned to its static rocky habitat; you would optimise its effectiveness in the garden by locating it where it is backlit by sunlight.

Rock-solid coastal forest

The forms of small coastal trees—usually multi-trunked with a multi-branched, spreading crown—lend themselves to the role of the specimen garden tree. Let them steal the show. Akeake, akiraho and kanuka will hold their own even in windswept conditions. They are rarely given breathing space in the wild—or in gardens for that matter—but with some foresight and planning, they can fulfil their potential. These are undemanding trees, needing neither fertiliser nor special attention. They all share the stringy, ragged bark so typical of coastal species, which contributes to their visual attraction as well as to the welfare of the insect kingdom.

Coastal cameos

There are some 'set pieces' in the wild where certain combinations of plants are found over and over again. A garden is one place you can get away with plagiarism. Refine the cliché to fit the space and it will become either part of the place or a witty commentary on it. Either way, make sure the physical circumstances are right first.

ABOVE Letting akeake mature without pruning rewards you with a glamorous character tree, which really comes to life with backlighting. RIGHT Taupata and its prostrate form from Poor Knights Islands blend together; above them, *Coprosma macrocarpa*, the northern coastal coprosma, takes on the geometry of the built structures.

TOP King fern (left) and ponga (right).
ABOVE Shore spleenwort.

If you are in the north, the combinations that you often find on rocky islets are well suited to gardens. You could either take the silvery-leathery approach or the fresh lush-green approach; both are perfectly 'real'. The first would probably involve pohutukawa, necklaced with leather-leaf ferns that flap their underfelt like white flippers, and studded with perching lily and collospermums, and all underlain with ground astelias and rengarenga lilies. The second might involve the glossy greens of taupata or its prostrate cousin, combined with prostrate ngaio, over a scrambling ground-cover of New Zealand spinach and *Selliera radicans*, and with some judiciously placed shore spleenwort ferns.

Lush and fresh

Are you lucky enough to live in the nikau belt—that band of humid, frost-free, relatively salt-free and richly fertile ground where kohekohe forest thrives? Along much of the west coast (all the North Island and the top of the South Island), it might occur kilometres from the shore, but in very sheltered bays, such as within the Marlborough Sounds, in the northern stretch of the South Island where humidity is very high but the climate still relatively warm, or in the relatively sheltered east coast of Northland and Coromandel, the so-called nikau belt can be very close to shore.

With the right combination of warmth, humidity, absence of frost and good soils, it shouldn't be too hard to reconstitute this vegetation (although nikau grows so slowly, you've got a long wait ahead to have mature trees on your doorstep). Even without space for the larger trees, the shady spots can become home to characteristic ferns. Green is of the essence. The fresher the better. *Asplenium* reigns supreme!

If there is room for larger trees, there is none better than kohekohe, especially in combination with wharangi, mahoe and kawakawa. Kohekohe is particularly rewarding in a garden as its cascading floral displays are less likely to be scoffed by marauding possums. Bellbirds and tui are greatly reliant on its winter flowering for sustenance during scant times. The flowering is from branches, so the mature tree lends itself to having the garden seat located beneath its bowers to help you admire the blossom.

Do use climbers with abandon in these gardens. *Clematis* (primarily *C. forsteri*), New Zealand passionvine, New Zealand jasmine and climbing spinach are all at home here—even supplejack (*Ripogonum scandens*) for

the brave-hearted (easily raised from seed). The creeping ferns *Blechnum filiforme* and hound's-tongue will also become established readily in the shade of trees and will seek to climb them.

Mahoe is often underrated—another victim of 'common as muck' plant snobbery—but apart from its less-than-endearing habit of dropping its mauve-staining fruit on the freshly hung washing, a well-tamed mahoe provides that fast-growing lushness, perfumed flowers and prunable form that makes it a useful garden addition. If, instead of pruning it as it grows (to create compact foliage or a low crown), you allow the branches to spread, you will in due course be able to show off the ghostly arms and trunks that inspired its colonial nickname whiteywood. Rub off the young side shoots and enjoy the unadorned white structure of the tree. Mahoe will grow stunted and browned where salt burns—keep it tucked into sheltered corners and coves.

ABOVE LEFT Kohekohe.
ABOVE RIGHT Fragrant fern and kiokio grace these garden terraces. The strength of the palette in this environment is in the yellow-greens and creamy yellows.

ABOVE In defiance of its prosaic title, grey scrub contains a magical assemblage of the weird and wonderful, and the pretty and peculiar.
OPPOSITE 1. Tauhinu. 2. Coastal shrub daisy. 3. *Brachyglottis greyii*. 4. *Sophora molloyi*. 5 & 6. *Clematis afoliata*.

Grey scrub

Grey scrub is a name given to a vegetation type that is widespread well beyond the coast. It grows in response to dry, thin soil conditions generally found on greywacke hilly coastlines or in the eastern rain-shadow of the Southern Alps.

We live in a country where uplift of mountain ranges is so rapid that parts of our coastline comprise the jumbled scree slopes of material eroding off steep faces; this is grey-scrub territory. The southern Wairarapa–Palliser Bay area is quintessential grey-scrub country, as are the shingle beaches of Canterbury. It does not appear simply as reversion scrub recolonising burnt-over or grazed land; this is a vegetation association that can sustain itself for decades.

Tauhinu contributes the most grey to the grey-scrub palette. It seems to have a preference for the freshly eroded sites or accumulated clays, presumably because it has a higher demand for nutrient than many of its fellow shrubs. Coastal shrub daisy is so similar to tauhinu that it is easy to confuse the two. When they are flowering, tauhinu's flowerheads are at the tips of the stems, whereas those of coastal shrub daisy are along the full length of the branchlet. You also will often see an orange tinge to the stems on coastal shrub daisy.

Manuka and kanuka are also to be expected here, and together with tauhinu create a very cheerful flowering through summer. Along the scrub fringes there might also be splashes of bright yellow daisy heads—the compact bushes of *Brachyglottis greyii* can be found from halfway down the Wairarapa Coast and around into Cook Strait. Another splash of yellow, albeit less conspicuous, is found through Cook Strait in the semi-prostrate kowhai *Sophora molloyi*.

ABOVE This is quintessential grey shrubland—a fine-leaved delicacy that casts a spell over the visitor—quite unique and perfectly suited to an intimate garden. The species illustrated include manuka, native broom, *Coprosma crassifolia*, fine-leaved New Zealand jasmine, *Clematis forsteri* and small-leaved pohuehue.

Small-leaved, shrubby coprosmas proliferate in this dry, windy environment; expect to find *Coprosma crassifolia*, *C. virescens*, thin-leaved coprosma (*C. areolata*) and *C. propinqua*. These are all divaricating shrubs with very fine leaves—shadowy in the sense that they are difficult to distinguish from one another in the scrub and lack definition; collectively they help create an entrancing vegetation. Shrubby tororaro (*Muehlenbeckia astonii*) and the fearsome matagouri (*Discaria toumatou*) may join in the mix until they get overshadowed.

More than any other coastal vegetation type, this scrub has a magical elfin feeling when you are in it (one that belies the somewhat bleak external appearance). It is enhanced by some unusual plants. Native broom is in its element and provides both sculptural elegance and an other-wordly feeling. But it is surely not as weird as the leafless bush lawyer (*Rubus squarrosus*), which scrambles itself into loose, billowing, impenetrable messes like a poorly bundled and surprisingly prickly fishing net. This is but one of a number of interesting climbers found in grey scrub. Shrubs are interwoven with the fine-leaved New Zealand jasmine, which favours the drought-prone conditions (more so than the broader-leaved jasmine *Parsonsia heterophylla*). There may be climbing bindweed (*Calystegia tuguriorum*), which, unlike the shore bindweed, with its dainty pink flowers, has large white flowers. Two clematis are common: like the bush lawyer without its leaves, there is a leafless clematis (*Clematis afoliata*), which grows in a similar style but is smothered in dainty little creamy-white flowers in spring. The common coastal *C. forsteri* will be there, too, winding in and out of scrub and rocks alike.

The plants that make this environment so curious also make for superb gardening. Those sturdy, divaricating coprosmas cry out for plucking and tweaking to show off their wire-mesh structure to perfection. Billows of leafless clematis and bush lawyer will provide plenty of intrigue for visitors unaccustomed to our more bizarre native plant forms.

If you were using the polished trunks of native broom or *Coprosma crassifolia* as focal points, you would want the afternoon light to side-light them for greatest impact, and the bared trunks of mature manuka need little more than simply to be seen.

Shingle beds

Shingle beaches generally have more to do with rivers than with the sea. As you scrunch, scrunch your way along a desolate beach ridge, it is worn fragments of mountains that rub their smoothed surfaces together

TOP The spare, dry shrubland feel is conveyed perfectly in this simple pathway.
RIGHT Makaka with (top left) the fine-leaved native jasmine *Parsonsia capsularis*, whose foliage seems to become finer with increasing aridity.

underfoot. They've had a long journey, and only the hardest rocks survived. Rivers moved them to the coast, and huge currents and pounding waves pushed them back on to dry land.

You can also scrunch, scrunch your way across extensive flats of fine, ragged shingles that have taken a more direct route, spilling out of gorges and off scree slopes of steep coastal cliffs to create a finer, siltier shingle.

There is the old axiom, 'where it is possible for there to be life, there will be', but it is hard to comprehend how life could get a purchase in the rounded and often mobile beach shingles. Clearly, the finer the material to root into and the more wind-blown silt it can trap, the faster vegetation can take hold. Look closely. There are amazing patterns and processes at work in this, the bleakest of all coastal environments.

One advantage of shingle is the easily penetrable and cool root-run it offers. The disadvantage is how water and nutrients leach away so quickly. Succulents can fill this arid niche, but even for these plants, it's hard work and it takes a very long time for them to start trapping enough organic material to spread very far. Beaches where the onshore winds carry lots of nutritious debris with them—the odd scrap of seaweed, the foam of dead plankton—will support denser plant growth. Any piece of driftwood will attract plant life—for the protection it offers and the slow release of well-rotted nutrients.

Sand tussock is associated with dune habitats, but given enough fines to feed its large root mass, it can be found on shingle bars. Accumulations of finer material are perfect habitat for two almost inseparable genera: *Raoulia* and *Pimelea*. Numerous *Raoulia* species

The most successful colonisers of shingle beaches are the most succulent herbs, for good reason.

colonise gritty, fine, shingly habitats such as volcanic scree fields and braided rivers as well as beaches, but on the shingly coast the most common species will be *R. hookeri*, *R. albosericea* (which used to be grouped under *R. hookeri*) and *R. australis*, which are very difficult to tell apart.

Also difficult to tell apart are the range of pimeleas growing along the coast, as this is a naturally variable genus with many similar species. Two, pinatoro (*Pimelea prostrata*) and *P. urvilleana*, have a number of subspecies each and, along with *P. carnosa*, they are all prostrate, ground-hugging, rock-hugging grey-green plants that get smothered in tiny white flowers in summer.

These raoulias and pimeleas, however, grow very differently. *Raoulia* has an astonishingly huge but shallow, spreading root system that sprawls far further than the foliage in its quest for moisture. Roots will be sent down at intervals along stems so that a surface mat is formed. Pinatoro, on the other hand, is a woody shrub with a single trunk that simply has a very prostrate form—incredibly prostrate.

Among plants dealing with seemingly impossible conditions, it is little wonder that some 'new' forms develop. *Muehlenbeckia* species in less extreme conditions include resilient, wiry shrubs and creepers, but here on the boulder banks they become more specialised still. Leafless pohuehue forms untidy mats on the older beach ridges and may look unsightly here, but brought into a garden environment where its

TOP The *Pimelea prostrata* illustrated here is like a cartoon character run over by a bus, with an overall height measured in millimetres. BOTTOM An intriguing sight is the beautiful ripples of *Raoulia hookeri* created on a very windy beach where the leading edge of the plant keeps dying back, in so doing creating little ridges. It is common to see raoulia and pinatoro polka-dotting across gravel flats.

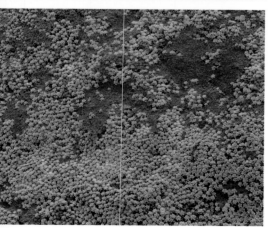

unusual form can be shown off to best effect, it can be used to fascinate and intrigue.

The shingle patch

Which brings us to shingle gardens. A flat site, a desire to sell the lawnmower: what better starting point for a shingle garden? And yet, such gardens can be a menace, as if there are fertile soils underlying a layer of shingle, weed growth is encouraged. Every seed blown in on the wind seems to want to germinate in this perfect nursery. When designing a shingle garden, minimise future effort by ensuring really deep beds of shingle. Mix in enough fine grits or sand so that the more interesting plants can cope but try to avoid anything resembling orthodox soil.

The native iceplant makes a brilliant lawn, especially when flowering. The moister the climate, the denser it will grow, and you will avoid those dead patches where it dries off—but then those dead bits are perfectly natural, too, and simply evocative of the wild beach. Growing mat plants is also rather challenging for the perfectionists among us, as inevitably there are areas of dieback. There are two possible ways around this problem: one is to combine a *Raoulia* with another mat plant such as a *Scleranthus*, which can fill any gaps created; another is to polka-dot the individual plants, as occurs in nature, making it a bit easier to prune away dieback without disturbing any overall design.

Gardens of prostrate and mat plants work best where there is a lot of wide-open space available. The more space there is, the more sparing the planting can be, which mimics the natural world. If the plants are cramped into small pockets around buildings, it may be a good idea to create some height, so that the contrast between Lilliputian plantings and gigantean housing is ameliorated. Tall pots, taller plants (such as knobby clubrush) and sculptures will all help to create better linkages between garden and surrounds. When plants are scattered rather than cramped together, we have a better chance of enjoying their unique structure and personalities. Here is a chance to show off the delicacy of plant forms usually overlooked.

What of our urban gravel beaches? They contain such interesting relics of human construction—worn brick fragments, pebbles of glass, a veritable miscellany of objects all treated with similar disrespect by the forces of

the ocean. They do make for some interesting design references. Acknowledging our intrusion into the natural world is really what gardens are all about, so we may as well be honest about it in our garden landscaping.

Succession processes are always evident along gravel beaches. Once the hardy colonisers have gained a foothold, then trapped more dust and leaf litter to provide slightly better living, more and more species can take advantage of the improved conditions. Conditions become feasible for more ground-covering herbs, including upright species like epilobiums and harebells, and for more coastal grasses. Gardens can offer the perfect micro-environments for herbs, so we can take advantage of this by finding intimate niches for the more delicate gravel-habitat species. Epilobiums come into their own when they produce seed pods that split open into long, wispy wands, and harebells enchant us with their dainty mauve flowers. It takes a discerning eye to weed among our weedy-looking native herbs—but it's worth it.

OPPOSITE TOP **Leafless pohuehue.** OPPOSITE CENTRE AND BOTTOM *Raoulia* species. TOP LEFT **Epilobium.** RIGHT TOP TO BOTTOM **The more space there is, the more sparing the planting can be, which mimics the natural world.**

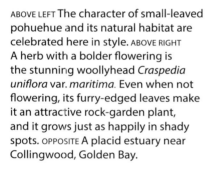

ABOVE LEFT The character of small-leaved pohuehue and its natural habitat are celebrated here in style. ABOVE RIGHT A herb with a bolder flowering is the stunning woollyhead *Craspedia uniflora* var. *maritima*. Even when not flowering, its furry-edged leaves make it an attractive rock-garden plant, and it grows just as happily in shady spots. OPPOSITE A placid estuary near Collingwood, Golden Bay.

Kaitorete Spit runs southwest from Banks Peninsula for 25 km, effectively forming Lake Ellesmere behind its stony barrier. This long pile-up of shingle is home to some scarce species. Shrubby tororaro is one of them, and if this shrub can survive on the minimal rainfall and soils associated with the spit, then it clearly makes for a no-fuss garden plant that will probably thrive on neglect. Its deciduousness is no doubt one of its important survival strategies, but losing its foliage doesn't make this plant any less attractive. Indeed, the purplish-red stems look stunning through winter. Although its flowers are tiny when it fruits, the abundance of the little white fleshy baubles can be astonishing. If you have any interest in stick insects, then plant this shrub—the insects seem to be attracted to it and are certainly perfectly camouflaged within its stiff zigzag branchlets.

CHAPTER 5

Estuaries, sand flats and their surrounds

Estuaries

The notion of estuaries being the lungs of the land is not so strange. If the hard coastline is the skin that defends the land, repelling the constant advances of storm and ocean swell, it is easy to visualise the slow, passive inhaling and exhaling of saline waters that occurs so regularly within an estuary as the very breathing of the land. Passive, calm, but rich with the food sources that sustain our lives, the fingers of tidal water penetrate up the tiny creeks and swamps that multiply the effective volume of the estuary like bronchioles. These breeding grounds for fish, crabs, shellfish, wading birds and shorebirds have helped sustain humans in New Zealand for hundreds of years, playing a significant role in our cultural history.

Once we no longer depended on estuaries for food—or European settlers purchased the land that embraces estuaries from the people who did need them—we developed a love–hate relationship with these waterbodies, especially those somewhat smelly mangrove-fringed ones up north. Bulldozers provided the means to eradicate the mud, to bury the dumped refuse and push roads across tidal flats,

and the incredible volumes of sediment being flushed down off denuded hillsides did permanent damage to the wildlife within the estuaries. Nevertheless, with our insatiable thirst for views of calm water, the new New Zealanders have continued the traditions of living around estuaries, but for different reasons.

Estuaries occur on all scales but in essence they are all internal harbours, silted up with the outwash from

A mass of a few species sharing similar circumstances is the dominant feature of estuarine vegetation, whether saltmarsh or rushland.

streams or rivers, and shallow enough to have deep fringes of vegetation that tolerates saline inundation twice a day. The flushing effect of the sea is constrained by a narrow entrance, perhaps blocked by shingle or sand bars, which also protect the estuary waters from wind-driven wave action.

Some estuaries merge into sand flats once the fines have settled out to leave coarser sediments, so this chapter looks at both habitats—although they do differ considerably in their nature—and therefore how they might influence our gardening thoughts. The muddy flats are places of slow water movement, where soupy-coloured sea water leaves its silty grey-brown residues at low tide; the sand flats have swifter water movement so the low tide reveals ripples and glistening ponds as the sea retracts.

Above all, estuaries are places where pattern dominates. The duality of fresh and saline flushing is what creates the patterns of vegetation—that and the depth to which individual species can cope with being inundated. It certainly is a limited palette of species. Of all the rushes and reeds that can grow in water, only a small subset can tolerate saline water. And of all the plants that can tolerate inundation, even fewer appreciate being regularly dried out again. However, this ability actually makes estuarine species quite adaptable to garden situations, and in recent years we've seen an influx of some of the key estuarine players into commercial nurseries.

The obvious feature of estuarine vegetation is its zonation: the massing of one or two species that are suited to a particular water depth and salinity strength, creating great swathes of uninterrupted colour and texture. These rules can be broken in gardens to a degree, but in order to understand the landscape of the estuary, here is what nature determines.

In the tide

That green, seaweed-like, strappy plant that forms large patches on tidal flats, exposed only at low tide, is the aquatic (marine) eelgrass (*Zostera muelleri* subsp. *novazelandica*). Even though it has ready contact with the great oceans, the species is found only within New Zealand waters. Auckland Harbour mudflats were once a stronghold for it but disease killed it off.

The astringently green alga sea lettuce (*Ulva lactuca*) is also common in estuaries, especially ones enriched with nutrients flushing down the streams and stormwater culverts. Washed up, it rapidly bleaches to a rather unappetising toilet-papery look.

Mangroves

In northern areas mangrove (*Avicennia marina* subsp. *australiasica*) dominates and shades out the rushes that would otherwise be dwelling within the intertidal parts of the estuary. This amazing plant is of more curiosity value than aesthetic, it has to be said, as its bronze-green dullness is accentuated by its formless appearance. But up close, it never ceases to fascinate as one of the weirdest trees on the planet. Those erect fingers in the mud are its breathing apparatus, and the seedlings emerging from the water have been dropped as pre-germinated seeds from the parent and allowed to bob about before getting waterlogged and sinking into their new muddy home.

In modern times mangrove has become a tree to be argued over. The great influxes of mud into estuaries have resulted in more mangrove growth, which captures more mud, of course, which creates more habitat for more mangroves—and so on. In addition, it is thought an increase in temperature (or at least a reduction in spring frosts) in recent years has resulted in further spreading of mangrove over mudflats. You'd have to say we get what we deserve!

In general, mangrove growth is a positive thing. On each high tide, baby fish invade to feed on the incredible richness of encrusting shellfish, snails and weed. At low tide the birds have their turn hunting for crabs and snails. As efficient silt collectors, mangroves keep the outer mudflats cleaner, assisting a flourishing food chain involving cockles, pipi, snapper and trevally. In future years, no doubt humans will also benefit from this buffer between rising sea-level and their coastal properties.

One of the mesmerising attributes of mangrove trees is the way they become visual tide gauge helping us measure the daily fluctuation—in the morning a

tree; in the evening a tethered raft of foliage.

Where the waters are not warm enough to support mangrove growth, tall sedges and rushes take its place, especially sea rush. As the fresh-water influence becomes stronger, closer to land or closer to stream mouths, oioi dominates, often growing in great patches of female or male plants, which turn different colours as they come 'into season'.

Photos do little to convey the soundtrack of mangroves: the constant popping of crab holes and snapping shrimps; the mechanical barking of kingfishers; and the cooing of kereru feeding on mangrove fruits.

Sea meadows

If, however, there are expanses of very shallow mudflats that are dry for longer than they are wet, we can also find salt meadows, which are dominated not by tall rushes but by short, tufted sedges and sprawling, succulent herbs. Sea blite (*Suaeda novae-zelandiae*), glasswort, shore primrose and remuremu—the latter easily distinguished by its lopsided, half-star-like white flowers and dense carpeting—create mats that are ideal for birds to rest on in between tidal courses. In turn, the birds' droppings may well be an important source of nutrient for the plants, a self-perpetuating relationship (faltering perhaps now that fewer flocks of birds are resident in our estuaries).

Sea blite, innocuous though it usually looks, can turn a striking purple, adding an unexpected richness to the scheme. If there is bachelor's button (*Cotula coronopifolia*) growing here, too, then summertime will be a joyous sight, with the bright yellow, button-head flowers spangling the sea meadow.

The turf of the saltmarsh meadow is provided by mats of the miniature grass-like herb *Triglochin striata*, the segmented leaves of *Lilaeopsis novae-zelandiae* or the finely leaved, bright green slender clubrush, distinguished by holding its black seedhead 'at arm's length' at the tip of each delicate stem.

It's not too difficult to re-create mats of sea-meadow plants in a garden, as long as it is flat, periodically damp (as on consolidated sand that pools the rain—perhaps a version of a rain-garden integrated into the stormwater system) and you don't mind some exacting weeding.

Fringing shrubland

Around the drier fringes of the estuary, but where groundwater is brackish, saltmarsh ribbonwood (*Plagianthus divaricatus*) and, to a lesser extent, coastal shrub daisy thrive. Saltmarsh ribbonwood is a rather hysterical-looking hippy of a plant, with a stiff Afro hairdo and the inevitable tissue-like spiderwebs tucked haphazardly into the mop. The shrubs turn quite purple in winter when they lose their leaves. Sometimes you will find them

TOP Shore primrose.
CENTRE AND BOTTOM Bachelor's button.

intertwined with pohuehue (either *Muehlenbeckia complexa* or *M. australis*), but the leafless wintery combination makes it hard to distinguish each plant, and the tangle of stems presents a peculiar web that any playful kitten would be proud of.

Although the saline edge is their natural habitat, these plants grow perfectly well in fresh-water-saturated soils in gardens. In the wild they seem to crowd each other, growing shoulder to shoulder, and this is a useful characteristic to mimic in those permanently boggy bits of the garden (or where your garden rolls down to the water's edge). In autumn they can be absolutely festooned with small, pale fruits, which must provide geckos, and the few birds small enough to penetrate the tangled bushes, with ample feeds.

The drier fringes, with only periodic soil saturation (and generally with fresh water), support a zone of manuka, cabbage trees and harakeke. The zones are very distinct. This banding can be carried through into gardens with the simplest of design tools: the hedge—the leisurely hedge, that is, following the contours and blending in to the subtle shape of the landform. Manuka, kanuka, saltmarsh ribbonwood, *Coprosma propinqua* or coastal shrub daisy— naturally occurring, small-leaved and somewhat delicate-looking plants rather than the traditional hefty broadleaf hedges—will give adequate shelter and provide flowering or fruiting interest as well.

Estuarine garden design

The essence of estuarine vegetation, then, is its simplicity, layering, subtle colour shifts and generally earthy tones. There are no knockout highlights or attention-seeking focal points in this environment; all is serene and mesmerisingly calm. Even the colourful fields of bachelor's button, if present, seem

TOP *Coprosma propinqua* and cabbage trees fringe the estuary on dry land.
ABOVE Saltmarsh ribbonwood.

155

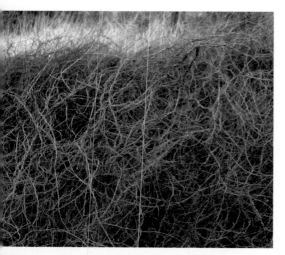

TOP The winter leafless tangle of small-leaved pohuehue.
ABOVE Even the conspicuous banding of fringing estuarine vegetation is soft-edged and curvaceous.

to merge into the overall blur of colours—a painterly haze created using pointillism techniques or subtle washes rather than with pen or brazen brush-strokes.

But overall, too tawny? Dull? Too drab to be inspiring? If you like the idea of extending the estuarine view into your place, how would you lift it, lighten it, make it interesting? Even the water colour in estuaries is inevitably 'muddy', with its high clay content.

I can suggest several approaches. First, there's the mangrove-free estuary (we'll investigate mangroves a little later).

There are actually quite striking seasonal colour shifts, especially within the herbfields of the mudflats, as well as within the swathes of oioi and saltmarsh ribbonwood fringing the estuary. The intense coloration is largely due to stress. Even though these are plants coping with tidal conditions, there is no reason not to introduce them into the garden, but you do actually want to stress them to extract their full colour, so don't plant them in a fertile soil—make it hard for them. Don't allow them to become shaded. Bachelor's button is probably the least-suited herb for gardens as it does require a constantly moist rooting medium, but if you have water, try planting it along the edges.

To really intensify the garden palette, make sure to have the richest-coloured plants in close proximity to the lightest colours (probably your paths or walls). Substitutes for the dark purple clumps of saltmarsh ribbonwood in drier conditions might include the dark-foliaged and red-flowering manuka cultivars, which grow in suitably smooth-crowned, lumpy forms.

There are many coastal environments where straight lines and sharp angles are de rigueur, but estuaries are not one of those. There are no straight lines to be found in the curvaceous scenery of estuaries, and angular, rigid garden structures will inevitably feel awkward and foreign.

What else happens out there in the estuary? As the tide recedes, mudflats are incised by dark, deep channels. There is a strongly sculptural visual element here not found in any other coastal environment. What better excuse can there be to introduce similarly sculptural elements into the garden design? Even the wildlife of the mudflats makes a design statement in its own unique way with sprinklings of polka-dot burrows everywhere.

When the tide returns, expanses of mud shrink as silvery-blue rivers

ooze and push their way across the flats, reflecting the light and contrasting starkly with the browns and greys. This tidal flow is, in reality, the visual focus of the estuary—the vegetation providing the backdrop or stage across which the reality show of tides is displayed.

Transferring this concept into a garden setting probably means creating high-contrast, sinuous paths or walls separating 'islands' of simple, low-diversity, low-stature plantings of those earthy fawns, orangey browns and dull purples. These 'paths' would be following the contours of the land, not slicing across them, and need not be of regular width.

Using a highly reflective 'pick-me-up' pathing material such as crushed glass or crushed shell, or shell-rich concrete evocative of scattered light on water perhaps, will enliven the palette. Shingle or

pebbles would be entirely out of keeping with the silty environment, but if they are to be used, ensure they are the same colour palette as the dominant estuarine materials.

Clearly, there aren't going to be many gardens actually within the saltmarsh or rushland estuarine environment, but there will certainly be quite a number where housing has usurped the natural fringing shrubland and where that merges into taller treeland further inland. Keeping the tightly interwoven, dense shrubland look going works really well in these circumstances, and even where a range of species is used, the overall effect will be in context.

In the many estuaries around Tasman Bay at the top of the South Island and in Northland estuaries, one plant stands alone, often literally, as a local identity. Known variously as buggar grass or estuary needle grass, *Austrostipa stipoides* is one of the few grasses tolerant of saline conditions at high tide. It also grows very well in drier places, such as the volcanic rubble of Rangitoto Island, so it adapts successfully to gardens. Its erect, stiff growth form makes it a very attractive proposition and, as in its natural habitat, it is best shown off by planting it amid creeping ground-cover.

Gardening near mangroves

Remember these lyrics penned in 1944 by Johnny Mercer – 'You've got to accentuate the positive, eliminate the negative . . .'? They always come to mind when I'm around mangroves and wishing they weren't quite so . . . well, so dull. It seems the best way to stay sympathetic to a mangrove estuary is to both merge in with it and, like the song suggests, accentuate the positive. I find that the natural bushy verges around mangrove swamps, the deep greens we are so familiar with, can actually clash horribly with the colours of estuarine plants, especially the olive-greens of mangroves, and I wonder whether this has further disenchanted people about mangrove estuary environments.

It would be far preferable to at least manage the view from your own garden so that it is 'at one' with the mangroves in the distance. If you study the colourways of the mangrove, there are the muted, dark olive-bronze greens of upper leaves, muted greys of the leaf undersides, silvery- or brown-greys of the stems, often decorated with whispy grey lichen, and surprisingly strong hints of orange in the leaf stems and veins. All fall within the yellow to yellow-green spectrum. When the tide is in, the darkness of the water beneath the trees offers another colour—black—although when the tide is out, that soon turns to a blue-black or brown muddiness.

Thanks to the muted yellow fruits and orange petioles of mangroves, they look very good teamed up with yellow-flowering species (as estuaries infested with gorse and wattles attest), which will pick up the highlights without falling outside the range of compatible colours.

The 'merging colour' species that partner mangroves naturally include glasswort, sea blite and, best of all, the stiff buggar grass, which seems to include so many of the mangrove's colours within a single tussock clump. These are plants that do equally well wedged between rocks or in open ground, but they do need full sunlight. There are coastal plants with bronze foliage that can blend well with mangrove even though they come from different environments, such as sand coprosma. If you take this approach, be sure to provide these plants with the soil characteristics they are best suited to.

Saltmarsh ribbonwood, although a constant estuary-edge companion, is not helpful in the gardening sense, being far too purple in winter,

OPPOSITE FAR LEFT, TOP This garden does an excellent job of reflecting its views of an estuary, albeit using different species. The rocks, while unusual in estuaries, do actually occur locally. The shingle mimics the texture of the shell-dimpled mudflats at low tide. The garden has captured the essence of its environment simply, with colour and form. OPPOSITE CENTRE AND BOTTOM Buggar grass. OPPOSITE LEFT The photo of this garden near the Pauatahanui Inlet offers an example where the smoothed low shrubland, backed by cabbage trees, provides a visual continuum to the estuary, reiterating the placid calm of its fringing vegetation.

which further deadens the overall look when they are adjacent to mangroves. Backdrops of neutral grey (choose carefully; it needs to be a slightly brown grey) help to enhance the greys within the mangrove trees—so perhaps if your view to the swamp is across grey paving or a plastered grey balustrade, this may lighten the overall aspect without clashing tonally.

Ironically, accentuating the highlights might actually involve accentuating the recessive black shadows (perhaps achieved by using black fencing or black roofing; black house walls look fantastic beside mangrove swamps) or simply working with the highlight colours of orange or yellow-green. When you look around the bushy edges of a mangrove estuary, most of the *dark* greens do nothing to assist cheering up the mangroves, but the occasional fresh yellow-green foliage of hangehange (*Geniostoma ligustrifolium*) works surprisingly well. Limited amounts of broadleaf can achieve the same effect. Oioi, when it is at its most orange tinge, fits the bill, although too much of the greyer male plant and the scene is a bit flat.

Shrubs that can offer a supportive tonal role in mangrove estuaries include akepiro, which has the bonus of conspicuous daisy-florets. Closely related is akiraho, which has tighter, wrinkly-edged leaves and less conspicuous flowering.

Golden tainui or kumarahou (*Pomaderris kumeraho*) grows on clay banks throughout Northland and makes an ideal garden plant where the view is of mangroves. For a brief few weeks in spring it is smothered in yellow flowers, and for much of the rest of the year the prematurely formed buds that decorate

OPPOSITE TOP LEFT AND RIGHT Mangrove.
OPPOSITE BOTTOM LEFT Buggar grass.
OPPOSITE BOTTOM RIGHT Golden tainui.

the shrubs echo the muted greys of the swamp but with more textural interest.

Is there room for totara? Or mapau? Or the enchanting mangaeo (*Listea calicaris*), which especially enjoys limestone clays and turns positively purple out in the sun? Of all the trees that grow around estuaries, these are the ones that look best, picking up the bronze coloration of mangroves. None will like wet feet, and so we think about their role around estuaries on dry clay soils (pages 172–3).

Of all the coastal environments, mangrove estuaries demand the most disciplined gardening to complement and reveal their positive qualities. With most native species either clashing in colour and texture, or, alternatively, creating a dangerously drab effect, do be strict with plant choice, and rely if you must on hard landscaping to furnish the necessary ingredients.

Sand flats

It makes sense to visit tidal sand flats in the same breath as estuaries as they often merge into each other and share the relentless tidal rhythm so accentuated by shallow coasts. The tidal flats around Golden and Tasman bays are particularly exciting as the tides are so large there and the changes so dramatic.

Sandy flats are also full of wildlife, whether beds of cockles and pipis, eelgrass meadows seething with bustling hermit crabs and shellfish, or the ebb and flow of oystercatchers, rails, herons and stilts to pace the curling edge of water. It is not uncommon to see humans joining in the hunt for cockles as the tide recedes.

Cockles are a formidable cleansing force in estuaries and sand flats, filtering each tidal flow. Shell banks of cockles and pipi are found at many estuary mouths and are very much part of the repertoire of symbols that can be expressed in coastal gardens.

Sandy flats inevitably indicate the shallow, offshore sandy waters attractive to scallops. Who hasn't reached down to scrape the sand off a perfectly formed scallop shell and secreted it into bag, pocket or car boot to find a purpose to put it to later? So, OK, it's hard to be original with scallop shells, but they can undertake any number of roles in our gardens. Crushed into concrete for a pink-tinged paving . . . adhered to walls and steps . . . suspended in perfect empathy with kawakawa leaves.

The edges of sand flats are not as conducive to rushes as mudflats, presumably because the extremes of drainage are just too great compared to mud, which can retain moisture for longer between tides. You will certainly find succulents such as glasswort and sea blite, but the rushes are likely to be in pockets around the edges where there is a fresh-water influence from springs or creeks. *Juncus* species such as *J. baumea* dominate, or three-square, commonly seen at sluggish stream mouths.

Sand flats are wonderfully picturesque at low tide as the sand remains standing in ripples in the most incredible variety of patterns. Repetitive chaos seems an apt description. Trying to replicate these patterns seems

RIGHT Sand flats can be summed up in a few words: elegant, placid, rhythmic. OPPOSITE As the tide recedes across sand flats, a rich scrapbook for landscaping ideas is revealed.

a bit too obvious and clichéd somehow, but the idea of subtle texture that is both rhythmic and chaotic is an idea to explore in the garden's hard landscaping, perhaps in concrete, or by shaping plaster. There are pressed metals that use the 'sand ripples' patterns, and reflective materials are certainly going to express the effect of sunlight on retreating waters.

Another kind of chaos is frequently found at the

The gentle wave action of shallow flats offers more entire, uncrushed shell than might be expected elsewhere.

river mouths in smaller estuaries, where piles of small-scale woody fragments accumulate at the high-tide mark. This is just drift—not the great flood-borne logs of the open coastlines but the pick-up-sticks collections of gentler tidal washes. What a marvellous mulch this would make and a far more suitable

Choosing just one idea from sand flats and concentrating on that can provide enduring interest in a garden.

material than shingle or overly reflective shell, which can do more damage than good in very hot climates.

Shell is highly reflective. It should be used with circumspection, as even the hardiest plants, if planted into a shell bed, could suffer heat stroke when young. The use of shell endures, especially in places where shell banks bar the estuarine waters and the supply of broken shell seems unlimited. Is it the way it reflects the clouds of a summer day that makes it so appealing? Or the tactile scrunching underfoot, or the placid neutral nature of bands of white, or the contrast it can provide that gives a garden that extra lift? Yes, shell endures.

Overlooking the flats

The hills overlooking estuaries are where most people choose to live, and there comes a point where the garden relates not so much to the detail and textures of the estuarine or sand-flat environment but to the way it can frame the view of the entire scene of hills dropping down into these sheltered, flooded valley basins. More often than not, the surrounding hill slopes are deeply weathered clays—the material that is feeding the estuarine system to begin with.

TOP AND ABOVE Shell banks often found at estuary mouths are a shared resource.
RIGHT A shell path leads to the cockle beds of Rangitoto Island.
OPPOSITE TOP AND CENTRE While you may not relish the challenges of a clay-based garden, the colours of clays can be shown off to great effect.
OPPOSITE BOTTOM A thin veneer of humic topsoil containing roots.

Clay

Not all clays are made equal, but they all share attributes important for gardeners to understand, whether they are derived from greywacke (much of Cook Strait), from limestone (common along the east coast of the North Island), from volcanics (many parts of Northland, Coromandel and Otago), or from granites (such as Golden and Tasman bays). Clay is probably the most common garden substrate, as weathered slopes offer the easiest excavation and piling substrates for housing.

What are clays? They started as rock that has been exposed to the weather so long that rain and air have rusted and corroded the mineral structures, forcing them to decay into new mineral structures that have finer particles and fewer bonds holding them together. The rock softens and then releases (albeit very slowly) its minerals, often in a form that is nutritious to plants. Sometimes clays will have formed from the weathering of ash layers. So far so good. But the downside, as gardeners know only too well, is that clay-rich soils dry out, shrink, turn to 'concrete' then, when wetted again, the soil pores get clogged with clay particles (which are finer than sand or silt) and become saturated—or water doesn't even penetrate because the 'concrete' surface has become unreceptive. Having said most clays are fertile, some parent rocks, such as the Separation Point granites, are so lacking in useful minerals that the clays created are also infertile.

The trick of working with clays has traditionally been to apply lime (which not only breaks up heavy clods of clay, but also makes their nutrient chemically available to plant roots) to prevent them getting too wet (through drainage or heavy mulching) and to add large particulate material such as sand to the uppermost soil horizon to increase oxygenation. That all sounds like a lot of work. Some people also put their effort into terracing sloping clay banks, adding a tier of imported topsoil and hoping the problem goes away. Sooner or later, though, plant roots will strike the underlying clay. The problem hasn't gone away—it has just been veneered over. This happens in the wild also, and you can often see a thin veneer of humic topsoil revealed in road cuttings and slips, with relatively few roots penetrating to lower soil horizons.

When clay hillslopes are cleared of their native forest cover, it is no wonder that regeneration is very slow, especially on dry spurs. Not only is it very hard ground to colonise, but it is also likely that the thin cover of humic soil has disappeared and the starting point is an undeveloped clay soil horizon. For some species—a very few—this is fine. Manuka and kanuka are by far the most pervasive scrub species across regenerating clay hillsides. With manuka living 40–50 years and kanuka living at least 70–90, some previously cleared areas will already be clad in the *next* phase of regeneration: the broadleaved trees that were able to grow up within the kanuka or manuka canopy as the old trees became senescent, dying back and letting more light in.

It can take many decades to get beyond the manuka–kanuka stage, so let's look at its character more closely, as this is what so many of us buy into. We then wonder how to work with it or develop it.

Never underrate kanuka scrub. It represents a hive of industry for bird and insect life. The rich insect life (they just love that paper-shaving bark)

attracts birds, but so do the honey-bearing flowers, small though they are. Geckos are often found hanging out in manuka scrub—possibly attracted to the sooty-mold-forming sugar secretions of the scale insects, as well as the insects themselves, and certainly to the shrubs that bear tiny juicy fruits that are almost always found alongside manuka and kanuka.

It is not always clear why some clays support manuka, some kanuka and others a mixture of both. Both species can tolerate low fertility and low pH, but manuka has the added ability to cope with saturated or low-porosity soils. Sometimes it relates right back to the state of the land when regeneration started. There is a tendency, for example, for manuka to follow stock as it seems to cope with compacted, poorly oxygenated soils better than kanuka. And harking back to the Australian origins of manuka, fires cause it to release seed from the hard capsules, giving it a head start as a coloniser following burn-offs. Kanuka, on the other hand, tends to occur on the silt-based soils, such as wind-blown loess that has weathered into a clay-rich soil and therefore has a naturally higher porosity than the really stiff clays. And as we have already seen, it responds on excessively drained sandy soils better than manuka.

Companion planting

There are several shrubs known as mingimingi that cope—or even thrive—on arid clay soils. Prickly mingimingi (*Leptecophylla* (=*Cyathodes*) *juniperina*) and tall mingimingi (*Leucopogon fasciculatus*) look like close cousins, and not only of each other; they are frequently confused with manuka and kanuka. They are really showy in their own rather private way. Because they have a preference for semi-shade, they are often tucked into bush edges, but that makes them perfect for shady clearings made for house platforms or driveways. Their foliage becomes yellowed out in the open. Their fruiting, which is the highlight of prickly mingimingi in particular, can be either red or white, even in plants growing alongside each other. Inexplicable but very cheerful!

There is another clay scrubland companion—inconspicuous amidst these larger shrubs—with even smaller leaves, and that is *Pomaderris amoena*, another species known commonly as tauhinu. It seems to take pleasure in the hard, bony spines of coastal headlands. Massed up, it makes a useful garden ground-cover in the sun-parched clays, although it is difficult to raise from seed or cuttings (cuttings seem to root best in untreated sawdust).

A mosaic of these shrubby species—one that displays a subtle variation in foliage colour and texture but with such similarities that the eye confuses the brain—can be a great way to smother a difficult clay bank. One thing all these plants—manuka, kanuka, both mingimingi species and tauhinu—share is a dislike of root disturbance. From rooted cutting or seedling through to garden planting, their roots must have the same soil around them and suffer minimal moisture shock.

It is the 'getting things going' that is always the hardest in clays. Even the thinnest of leaf duff layers is important for seedling establishment in the wild. Critical, too, is some shelter from the sun, which allows moisture to linger a little bit longer each day. Never underestimate the need to start slowly with the right plants and patiently wait until those colonisers have created suitable conditions for a more diverse range of species. These really 'hard' sites are often the ones that surprise us the most with their magic moments of delicacy. Mossfields can be found on the shady side of clay spurs that rival the misty fens and *Sphagnum* peats of inland areas.

Climbers can play a big role, especially in scrub that has been protected from animal browse (whether domestic stock or wild possums). Clematis species can put on terrific displays (just ensure their roots are in a shady pocket of moisture-retentive humus), and the spectacular scrambling climbing clubmoss (*Lycopodium volubile*) will sprawl across bare ground and drape itself down banks, in sun or shade.

A couple of sedges and lilies come into their own on clay soils, especially *Gahnia*, hook grasses (*Uncinia* spp.) and the dainty turutu (*Dianella nigra*). Gahnias rate as one of the most elegant sedges in New Zealand, with *G. setifolia*, in particular, creating spectacular performances on banks and outcrops with its graceful, drooping flowerheads. You would certainly want to give it room to show off. Gahnias are reputed to be difficult to raise and do not like being transplanted, so that sounds like an interesting and rewarding challenge for a keen gardener to take on.

Turutu growing vigorously could easily be mistaken for a small coastal flax—until spring arrives and the flowerheads emerge. If it is named after Diana, goddess of woodlands, it would come as no surprise, as

Prickly mingimingi.

169

TOP Clematis festoons this clay shrubland in Elliot Bay, Northland. CENTRE *Lycopodium volubile*. ABOVE Turutu.

the dappled shade of a light canopy and open-ground characteristic of clay habitats is the idealised native woodland. This dainty companion of manuka, kanuka and mingimingi is an essential plant of coastal clay gardens. It is tolerant of salt spray, is a great gap-filler in both shade and semi-shade, and provides a lovely spray of deep blue-purple fruits through summer. To maximise the show of berries that are held on to the plant so tenuously, ensure a sheltered location.

Orchids abound in undisturbed sunny clay soils. Some may fool you into thinking a new grass has arrived on the scene—until the hooded flowerhead appears or a stalk spangled with tiny flowers emerges. They aren't going to produce showy or colourful blooms, but this is their favourite haunt, so they definitely deserve some undisturbed ground.

As for ground ferns, not many enjoy the parched conditions of clay, but leather-leaf fern and hound's-tongue are usually present, and scented ring fern is found in the open. Up north, the hardy and colourful rasp fern (*Blechnum parrisiae*) or other close relatives are common. Tree ferns may well appear later on once leaf litter has built up under kanuka, so in moister, shadier sites you may find ponga (the most drought resilient of our tree ferns) and possibly mamaku establishing in damp gullies.

One important shared characteristic of clay-soil vegetation in dry-summer climates is its flammability. It seems a terrible shame not to nestle a house within a tall stand of mature kanuka, which filters the strong sunlight and attracts birds right to the window ledges, but it is increasingly a condition of subdivision that there must be either separation or a fringe of more fire-resistant species close to the dwelling. The flammable species are generally the small-leaved, rough-barked, oil-storing plants that are there in the first place because these are the very adaptations plants such as manuka, kanuka, akeake, mingimingi and mapau need to colonise dry coastal sites. So the concept of replacing them with less suited species means, theoretically, that you will be creating the right conditions for the *second* wave of regeneration—the greener broadleaved species that, in time, will grow up through the flammable colonisers to create a coastal broadleaf forest. However, they aren't going to do this without shade and without adequate humus in the soil, so if you are going to concentrate 'greener' species around your dwelling, you need to provide them with those prerequisites.

What are some of the existing components of clay-soil scrub that could be pressed into service? Regenerating scrub may well include common native broom, but you might also consider gardening with the offshore island–East Cape (and strictly coastal) *Carmichaelia williamsii*—its curious strappy growth form won't detract aesthetically from other drought-tolerant plants around. The great benefit of *C. williamsii* is that it provides winter flowering, bearing quite large creamy-yellow flowers; the downside is that it is short-lived.

Kohuhu is likely to be found and presents less of a risk than, say, the oil-gland-filled leaves of its ally mapou. At ground level turutu will be a friend and can be bulked up to great effect along with the green ground-hugging ferns such as fragrant fern.

Otherwise, the greener, larger broadleaved species that will be useful include *Coprosma lucida*—not only a common component of coastal bush but a much more handsome shrub than the more commonly supplied karamu (*C. robusta*). Try also broadleaf, five finger or, in the north, houpara (*Pseudopanax lessonii*). These will certainly pull in the birds, including bellbirds and silvereyes. Hangehange is a very common undergrowth shrub but does need shade; however, this makes it useful for filling in open spaces if you need privacy.

Although hebes do not withstand drought conditions very well, the lookalike pimeleas do. They offer a very useful shrub-sized garden plant, especially in the semi-shade of fringing vegetation, and would provide some fire protection. Pimeleas share the strict pairs of opposite leaves so characteristic of hebes but their flowers are always at the very tips of branchlets, whereas those of hebes emanate from the leaf axils. *Pimelea longifolia* would team up beautifully with mingimingi to provide a spangled white snowdrift effect.

Golden tainui is recommended for tough clay sites in the north. It also thrives in dappled shade and, if planted at the same time as manuka or kanuka, will not mind their shading later on. In true pioneering fashion, however, it is a short-lived species. Yet another *Pomaderris* from northern New Zealand comes into its own on clay coastal sites, but this species has become endangered. *Pomaderris phylicifolia* grows as a compact shrub, with the same grey-green tint to its leaves as its relatives; its flowers, although not showy, are certainly abundant.

TOP Leather-leaf fern.
ABOVE Giant-flowering broom.

171

TOP *Pimelea longifolia*. ABOVE *Pomaderris phylicifolia*.

Probably the most iconic clay hillside combination, repeated throughout Northland, Coromandel and Porirua Harbour (near Wellington), involves kowhai, kanuka, totara and, if frost-free, ngaio. Often these will also be spangled with puawananga (*Clematis paniculata*), which briefly smothers their crowns in white blossom in early spring. A large garden would be required to do justice to these trees, but even a careful combination can distill the essence of

this teamwork. They are sometimes joined by rimu (*Dacrydium cupressinum*) or tanekaha (*Phyllodadus trichomanoides*; in the north) and always have the understorey of mingimingi.

Clearly, the clay substrates—dry but fertile, hard yet nurturing some of our daintiest plants—create a discrete and unique environment. This is a world of tiny leaves, subtle white or yellow flowers, dappled light and unyielding surfaces. Yet there is one outstanding exception to the rule, and one that imbues Aotearoa with a personality shared by no other country: pohutukawa—the New Zealand Christmas tree.

Most New Zealanders equate pohutukawa with sandy beaches or rocky headlands, but they need to look more closely. Pohutukawa are hungry and thirsty. Sand alone will not sustain them, but sand may well blow up over the clays and loams that do. Some pohutukawa may perch like parrots on rocky headlands, their roots finding crevices of rainwater and weathering rock, but these are far outnumbered by the ones rooting into the clays that overlay the rock, sometimes their own hefty roots causing the collapse and erosion of the clay banks and benches that once nurtured them, making it look as though they began their life on rocky outcrops.

Pohutukawa occur naturally north of East Cape in forests and as lonely sentinels in a changed landscape. Even then they come complete with a loyal community of plants: perching astelia and collospermum; leather-leaf fern; ground companions of shore astelia or kauri grass, rengarenga and hook grass. It seems odd to find a pohutukawa with its friends absent.

In gardens, pohutukawa are often deemed problematical, unable to share their ground space with other plants (sucking the soil dry), but the plants that keep pohutukawa company in the wild are those that have adaptations to drought. The lilies are adept at water storage. Rengarenga, astelias, leather-leaf fern and hound's-tongue fern all enjoy semi-shade and their shallow rooting does not compete with the thirsty roots of pohutukawa.

One of the regeneration patterns we frequently see on coastal clay hillsides is the conversion of paddock to kanuka scrub and then the development of a carpet of tree ferns beneath the canopy. The ferns have time, as kanuka matures, to become quite dense, making an attractive 'woodland' with a Kiwi twist.

The tree ferns most commonly found on these drier sites are ponga (*Cyathea dealbata*, our silver fern) and sometimes mamaku (*C. medullaris*) in the gullies. If these have had a head start over broadleaf tree species, their heavy frond litter might suppress seedlings. A fernland will survive for as long as the kanuka persists overhead, perhaps continuing even after the kanuka has grown old and died.

One of the keys to enjoying tree ferns in the garden is, if at all possible, to look down onto them from above. This way you get the full rhythmic whirl of fronds to look at. The house itself is probably providing the shelter they require (no tree fern will tolerate salt winds; they need shelter and moisture-retentive soils).

A mature coastal forest on clay is, like forest on old dunes, most likely to be dominated by drought-hardy, small-leaved trees like totara, beech (in the South Island), matai, kowhai and akeake. With added soil fertility available, you might also expect more broadleaved species: kowhai, karaka, mahoe, five finger, rewarewa and lancewood (*Pseudopanax crassifolius*).

Shore astelia is is well suited to life out in the open, or on the edges of shading bush.

PART THREE

Design scrapbook

CHAPTER 6
Your garden, your story

Gardens tell a story. No matter what the circumstances, the scale or the environment, a good garden reads like a good novel. There's a plot, with intrigue, tension, undiluted passions, climax and resolution. Unfolding through the story are the lives of the central characters. Whether villains or saints, they take centre stage and all action revolves around their needs and wants. But where would they be without the supporting cast of friends and family, colleagues and underlings?

It is important to pay special attention to *all* the characters that make up a thrilling plot. No good story is without its creeps, crawlers and social climbers, for starters. Even at the coast, there are plants that creep across the ground, almost unnoticed but essential. We may resent the weeding they force upon us, but creeps give us the opportunity to contrast their needy character with the stars of the garden. Tough ones, like raoulia, also provide us with options to replace paving with vegetation, at least in a visual sense.

Crawlers . . . well they get under our skin, intertwining themselves inextricably in our lives; every garden should have the crawlers that bind characters of any social level together. Some of the less showy clematis species achieve this role—*Clematis forsteri*, in particular; the native jasmine, and the *Muehlenbeckia* clan, when held in check, also bind communities together.

Often overlooked as a garden component are crawling ferns, partly because we intuitively believe ferns are not suited to coastal environments. There are several that are, however, and they are useful for filling the space underneath shady bushes or trees where few other coastal species will thrive. Fragrant fern is common, as is leather-leaf fern.

It pays to capture the audience from the very first page. Welcome to story-time.

Leptinella dioica (TOP) and *Acaena pallida* (ABOVE) rate as two of the classic coastal garden creeps.
RIGHT Hound's-tongue fern.

Taking the spotlight are the social climbers. In sheltered bushy areas, supplejack can be planted to provide a spectacular fruiting display for long periods right through the year. It needs moist soil, and trees to help it ascend, but is really well suited to low coastal forest where the vines need not grow too far to reach the sunlight. Although a plant maligned by our bush-bashing and pioneering legacy, supplejack is also a fabulous food source for kereru and rather fun in a sculptural sense.

Less well distributed through New Zealand (it truly is a subtropical species), *Tecomanthe speciosa* is a social climber extraordinaire. Incredibly vigorous and with bold foliage, it's proving to be one of the few climbers we have that can match the built environment on its own terms. Do remember that it needs constant watering, however.

OPPOSITE ABOVE Two social climbers steal the show here: *Tecomanthe speciosa*, the offshore-island climber, and lancewood. OPPOSITE BOTTOM LEFT White rata gains height by crawling over materials that support its many rooting stems. The reward when height is gained is prolific flowering that attracts bees in abundance. OPPOSITE BOTTOM RIGHT A favourite crawler, *Clematis forsteri* rarely reaches great heights but knits the low-lying coastal vegetation together.

How often do we overlook this motley assortment of characters in a garden, and yet what natural drama is complete without them?

The craft of the storyteller is to create a story that displays integrity from beginning to end; it has a shape to it that becomes clear as we move through its pages. But how to structure this story? What is its setting?

Treat the following pages as a scrapbook of ideas. No garden is simply a collection of plants, as there are inevitably paths, walls, buildings, lighting and ornaments to consider. The beauty is in the detail and in the juxtaposition of raw, artificial and vegetative materials.

Some of these ideas are based strictly on place and suggest how we might draw upon its essential natural characteristics. Some are simply an exploration of colour and texture. Others are a celebration of the human activity that has helped shape the coastline character over decades.

ABOVE Puawhananga (*Clematis paniculata*) has a short spring-flowering season but graces sheltered coastal bush, especially through Northland.

RIGHT Creeping fuchsia (*Fuschia procumbens*) will never reach the dizzy heights of the climber *Tecomanthe* but creates a neutral foil for it on this trellis by creeping its way through gaps in the foliage without fighting for attention. Fuchsia always rewards close scrutiny, nevertheless, with its jewel-like flowers and lolly-like fruits.

Colourful stage sets

We could start with the most colourful coastal places of all: fishing settlements and working ports. Paint, whether bright or weathered; plastics; rusting metals; weeds and opportunist plants that clutch at the meanest of locations for survival—instinctively, you expect to have fun in an industrial garden.

THIS PAGE Enhance the intensity of the colours of rusting steel and weathering paint with vibrant foliage.
OPPOSITE Shimmering water can be reflected in both foliage and metallic finishes.

Silver and blue are omnipresent at the beach, particularly in calm, reflective harbours, but blue occurs as fragments on sandy beaches too. Rarely are there deep navy blues in the coastal scenery, but muted powder blues, silvery blues, green-blues and sky blues abound.

White, also, is ubiquitous along the coast. Bleached shell, bleached bones, flowers, foam and boat hulls all contribute to the flash of white, the streaks of white, the banks of shelly white that provide highlights on all types of shores. Rather than overdo it with this prominent, forthright colour, apply it as it occurs in nature for best effect—in narrow, sinuous bands that mimic the shell banks and strand lines, or scattered and disseminated through a darker matrix. Many of New Zealand's flowers are 'white', but that actually encompasses a range from tawny off-whites and creams to crisp white. Try not to mix the various shades of white in the same space as they do each other no favours.

At the strictly white end of the spectrum, coastal flowering offerings include pimeleas and hebes, manuka, Marlborough rock daisy, New Zealand linen, a number of creeping herbs including cresses and *Lobelia angulata*; the lilies *Libertia* and rengarenga; and olearias (although their subsequent seedheads are a lot duller).

CLOCKWISE FROM TOP LEFT *Lobelia angulata*; rengarenga; *Pachystegia minor*; shore primrose with glasswort.
OPPOSITE TOP RIGHT *Pimelea prostrata*.
OPPOSITE BOTTOM LEFT *Brachyglottis greyii*.

If you prefer the softer, creamier version of white, look to the flowers of *Tecomanthe speciosa,* most coastal clematis species, *Carmichaelia williamsii,* toetoe, rangiora (*Brachyglottis repanda*), perhaps in combination with foliage that flaps like white underwear in the breeze, such as *Coprosma crassifolia* and *Helichrysum lanceolatum* (which also sports fluffy creamy flowers).

CLOCKWISE FROM TOP LEFT *Acaena anserinifolia;* cabbage tree; giant-flowered broom; golden tainui in bud.

CLOCKWISE FROM TOP LEFT *Chionochloa flavicans*; *Clematis afoliata*; tauhinu; *Chionochloa flavicans* (rear) and silver tussock.

In the same way that there is a wide range of whites to draw on for ornament, so too, surprisingly, there is a spectrum of browns, from the almost iridescent seaweed browns to the dull mud browns of estuaries. The best way to show off browns is to team them up either with dark, dark browns and blacks, or with whites and creams. You will often see rock benches along the shoreline of mottled and fractured sandstone that translates well into worn brickwork, perhaps peppered with plants.

It's just a small step from browns to oranges, of which we have a generous supply in coastal environments. This entire range is totally compatible and is at the heart of the natural character of estuaries and dunelands, in particular.

OPPOSITE CENTRE LEFT Sand iris. OPPOSITE BOTTOM LEFT *Coprosma acerosa* cultivars. OPPOSITE BOTTOM RIGHT Trip-me-up. BELOW LEFT Red flax cultivar with trip-me-up. BOTTOM RIGHT Purple form of *Haloragis erecta* with sand coprosma.

Much of New Zealand's foliage is in the yellow-green spectrum, so it is boosted by being teamed up with yellows. Our fresh greens also pair up fabulously with the creamy yellows that are found in some flowers. A really kinky look occurs where black and vivid lime green mix, which is surprisingly common on rocky coastlines. Whether it be the blackness of mussel spat or dried seaweed and the sharp green of sea lettuce or algal slime on rocks, or simply the stark contrast of shiny green leaves of salt-tolerant plants against dark rock, it's a stunning look to carry through into a garden setting.

Fresh greens serve their greatest impact when used in bulk, with consistency. You will also show them off to best advantage with backlighting. Those who live in the nikau belt of moist, mild bays or along the west coast beyond the worst of the salt wind should be thinking of little else but lush, luxurious, flashy greenness.

TOP LEFT *Brachyglottis greyii* in front of puka. TOP RIGHT *Craspedia uniflora* var. *maritima*. CENTRE *Metrosideros excelsa* 'Aurea'. LEFT Kowhai blossom. ABOVE Poor Knights lily. OPPOSITE 1. *Phormium* 'Emerald Gold'. 2. Pukanui. 3. Puka. 4. Hound's-tongue fern. 5. Lemonwood. 6. Kohuhu. 7. Taupata.

Somewhat out of left field for the coast, and indeed for the New Zealand flora generally, is the colour pink. Although there is a vast range of pink- and red-flowering manuka or hebes in cultivation, in the wild this colour hardly exists. Treasure it when you find it. It may be small geranium flowers or the blush of misty gossamer grass. It's not the easiest part of the rainbow to deal with in a garden when the rest of the palette is generally in the green-yellow part of the spectrum, but our soft pinks work beautifully with materials such as concrete and crushed shell.

Darker pink shades verging on mauve, indigo and purple are perhaps more common, whether they be the winter foliage of estuarine shrubs, mangaeo leaves in the north or horopito (*Pseudowintera colorata*) in the deep south, or the berries of turutu. Hebes are the queen of frothy violet, whereas shy harebells take a more subtle approach.

LEFT CENTRE New Zealand iceplant.
LEFT *Leptospermum scoparium* 'Keatleyii'.
ABOVE *Geranium brevicaule*.

OPPOSITE CLOCKWISE FROM TOP LEFT Karo; red manuka cultivar; pohutukawa; Poor Knights lily.

190

Dramatic tension

Having applied colour to help create the theme for the coastal garden, some of the theatrical tension of the storyline can be derived from the interaction of textures. This does not just have to involve outright conflict—it could be more subtle. Sometimes playing two *similar* characters off against each other can work (without reducing both of them to mediocrity and invisibility in the process).

It's not enough for a garden simply to rely on contrasts and whimsical mismatchings for interest. That would be like producing a comic strip rather than a novel—lacking depth and a *raison d'être*. But let's be honest—it can be fun! The photograph opposite, top right, of *Craspedia uniflora* var. *maritima* set against a backdrop of *Melicytus crassifolius* shows a combination that is certainly unusual, held together only by the white edges of the *Craspedia* leaves echoing the white branchlets of the *Melicytus*. If the radical pairings do have some common feature, whether texture, colour or pattern, then that will strengthen their bond.

192

Resolution

Perhaps, though, in the end, the best gardens are ones not contrived by humans for humans but the ones where the human intervention is minimal but meaningful. How often do we have the grace to acknowledge that we are privileged to share in something already created over a greater period of time than most can imagine—a natural garden that is the way it is because of a give and take between the physical and the biological forces of that particular place, with these particular ingredients? If no bulldozer has yet visited the site, and no browsing animal has insisted on grass growth, then 'relax and enjoy' is probably the best advice a gardener can receive.

ABOVE LEFT Poor Knights lily and nikau. ABOVE RIGHT *Craspedia* with *Melicytus crassifolius*.
OPPOSITE TOP LEFT Fierce lancewood and shrubby tororaro.
OPPOSITE BOTTOM LEFT Taramea and *Scleranthus uniflorus*.
OPPOSITE LEFT Taraire (*Beilschmiedia taraire*) and gully tree fern (*Cyathea cunninghamii*).

Structure

If our garden story were a play, it would need skilled workmanship to create a convincing set, but so often at the beach the set is right there around us and we need only to 'borrow' a few objects or materials to complete the illusion. It's been evident right through this book that shapes, materials and textures are as important, if not more important, than plants to get the right feel or sense of place.

LEFT A rocky coastline or industrial harbour deserves sharp, crisp angles and lines for the hard landscaping, but that does not necessarily imply rectilinear regularity. It can always come with a twist.

OPPOSITE TOP AND CENTRE In shingle environments (either shingle flats or raised beach ridges), it is often more a question of containment. When you confine or frame elements, it concentrates attention on their innate beauty and the patterns their shapes create. But without that containment, masses of stones become an undefined blur very quickly and their potential is lost.

BELOW AND OPPOSITE BOTTOM Generally it is along the wild rocky coastlines with shingle beaches where driftwood abounds and timber becomes an important ingredient in the garden. Driftwood is by nature chaotic but can be tamed by human workmanship, often without losing its intrinsic spirit.

In the placid estuarine environment, keep thinking about relaxing and concentrate on horizontal surfaces and clean, leisurely lines. Life has a slow rhythm to it here, and humans should be encouraged to let it permeate their lives also. Similarly, if the coastal geology is sedimentary, built up from layer after layer of deposited material as it is so strikingly around Auckland, let this be your lead for the built structure also. Used cleverly, the sense of layering, colourways and visual features translated into a built environment need not be boring. Look to the colours of sand-flat and estuary shells for inspiration too.

Dunes are where things loosen up with a somewhat haphazard, chaotic, organic 'freedom of speech'. Curves are broad and sensuous. Timber takes on a weathered, sand-blasted persona. The texture of sand can be translated into a number of materials—gritty concrete or ground glass, for example.

ABOVE LEFT Our artist is keenly aware of how shells rest on a wet beach.
ABOVE CENTRE AND ABOVE RIGHT Bays with sheltered bush and gentle spaces can be respected by utilising the timbers that made them such attractive places.
OPPOSITE Layering and gentle, sweeping curves are well suited to estuaries and areas of horizontal rock strata.

Sensitivity to the landscape becomes almost a social responsibility when paths are formed in places that many people see. A little bit of forethought can alter a potentially brutal intrusion of hard and sharp edges into something more akin to a work of art.

197

A head above the others

One of the greatest anxieties coastal gardeners seem to suffer from is the challenge of creating the height they would like. If you can't plant trees (perhaps you are on young sands, or too close to the salt wind, or the ground is too hard or, heaven forbid, the water table is too high), you need to rely on climbers or built structures. Fortunately, there are some very hardy vines growing in coastal environments that we might encourage to even greater heights.

The star of them all is *Tecomanthe speciosa*, the endemic climber discovered on the Three Kings Islands when it was down to the last surviving plant! It was found growing amid low-canopy coastal forest that also supported seabird roosts, so the ground was fertile, sunlight was guaranteed, and the thick, shiny cuticle on the leaves offered protection from salt-burn. Hidden away inside the vine, presumably handy for lizards and small birds to pollinate away from strong winds, are spectacular creamy-white flowers. A pergola is an ideal way to show off these hidden blossoms.

Far more surprising is the height that creeping fuchsia (*Fuchsia procumbens*) can reach. In the wild we know it as a scrambler weaving through ground-level shrubland in the dunes. Given adequate support, this pretty plant can show off its red fruits and multicoloured flowers to far better advantage.

Similarly, it is only relatively recently that gardeners have recognised that small-leaved pohuehue, common enough along both sandy and rocky coasts as a sprawling cushion, will extend several metres vertically quite happily. Because it grows so densely, it supports itself more ably than other climbers and so needs minimal built structure unless it is likely to be whipped around by the wind.

If all else fails, you can rely on sculptural elements to provide the scale you are seeking!

LEFT Using pots to gain height, these gardens also create a rhythm that helps to draw the eye away from ground level.

OPPOSITE Ideally, structures should be in keeping with their coastal surroundings or, at the very least, able to be camouflaged by the plants they support!

TOP Mercury Bay weed.

ABOVE Although it is not strictly a coastal bidibidi, this use of *Acaena caesiiglauca* near the coast shows what is possible. It will grow well in fine shingles and full sun.

OPPOSITE 1. *Acaena anserinifolia*. 2. *Acaena inermis* 'Purpurea'. 3. *Pimelea prostrata*. 4. *Coprosma* 'Hawera' has a distinctive prostrate growth form and is green rather than orange-tinted like its sand cousins. 5. This meadow uses silver tussock to blur the edges of the severe concrete wall. 6. Iceplant will thrive in sunny shingles. 7. *Leptinella pusilla* creates ground-cover in a sunny rock garden.

Native lawns

There are enough native herbs, scramblers, ground ferns and grasses to create the lawn equivalent—it just rarely happens in our gardens because of the constant, relentless pressure from invasive exotic species. But even a small space given over to such plants can be a success, and less gruelling to weed; what is needed is attention to sun, shade and drainage.

There are several 'lawn-suited' plant growth forms that lend themselves to creating mass beds: the succulent herbs and ferns that creep across the stony ground, putting down roots intermittently but generally surviving on shallow substrates and storing water and nutrient within their leaves; and the mat plants that have astonishingly widespread and deep-rooting systems, seeking out ground moisture at depth. Combining the two would be ideal, of course, if the mosaic look appeals.

Many suitable species have already been discussed in the shingle chapter or the sand-flat section, and useful ideas can be gleaned from the natural 'salt turf' areas that can occur on sand flats, on fine shingle swales or even along the edges of cliffs where exposure to salt and wind makes life difficult for competing exotic species. These are species such as sand daphne, New Zealand iceplant, *Selliera rotundifolia* and the raoulias. They demand full sunlight but little else; certainly they do not seek fertility in their soils. There is a hardy endemic grass that is knee-high to a grasshopper called *Zoysia minima*. It grows naturally in dense swathes on well-drained flats, where it might be mixed in with remuremu or other diminutive succulent herbs. It is very robust, with thick, fleshy leaves, and, usefully for establishing a large area of it, it roots readily from cuttings.

There are further options, however, using coastal ground-covers with a higher tolerance of shade or semi-shade. Mercury Bay weed (*Dichondra repens*) is well known already as a lawn plant, but few people realise it is a native species. It grows naturally in dappled shade where moisture is retained a bit longer than in the open.

Living roofs

The living-roof concept is similar to a native lawn, but high evapo-transpiration rates and all-day sun mean the rooftop vegetation is more likely to dry out.

Traditionally (and let's not forget that the idea of growing plants on roofs goes back as far as civilisation does), there are two broad types of living roof: extensive living roofs and intensive living roofs, the latter sometimes known as wind gardens. Extensive roofs are grown on a shallow substrate—usually 20–150 mm deep—using grasses, succulents or other shallow-rooting, wind- and sun-tolerant plants. Semi-intensive and intensive living roofs have deeper substrates—150–1500 mm for fully intensive roofs—and they are often in deep planters, allowing a far greater range of plants, including woody species.

There is one very good reason for considering a *native* living roof. Overseas, the effect is usually achieved using *Sedum* species (stonecrops). In New Zealand, these creeping succulents are serious environmental weeds and we urgently need to find alternatives before living roofs really take off as a mainstream architectural option. Already there are cities around the world that require all new commercial buildings to have living roofs, so although the technology is rapidly advancing, the choice of plants in New Zealand is still experimental.

Understanding what plants would withstand roof conditions isn't so hard when you compare a natural environment with the rooftop environment. The rooftop will probably be exposed to full sun, wind (so expect drought) and intermittent rain; could suffer frosts; and may have a gradually increasing load of wind-blown sand and silt. There is generally a very shallow rooting depth available and this, combined with a high evaporation rate caused by wind and sun, narrows the species options considerably. Analogous habitats might include shingle or coarse sand beaches, shingle riverbeds, scoria fields, rocky cliffs, disturbed lands or alpine screes.

It is unlikely that fine sand would be used as a growing medium as it could blow away in the windy conditions of most roofs, so a substrate with enough structure but with the capacity for good drainage is required (to avoid too much weight loading when fully saturated with water). Many roofs use a lightweight artificial granular material (a mix of pumice, zeolite, coconut fibre and bark fines, along with a small proportion

LEFT No roof is too small to contribute to neighbourhood greening; in summer, this New Zealand iris living-roof garden will be spangled with white flowers, then in autumn with orange seed capsules.
OPPOSITE This arrangement of *Astelia* within a bed of *Pimelea* mimics the natural process of colonisation of shingle beds.

of soil). This is laid over a geotextile root-barrier fabric, which in turn overlays a drainage mat sitting over the impermeable membrane that waterproofs the roof structure. Irrigation is often helpful for plant establishment and, particularly during dry conditions over summer, to ensure the success of native species. Root irrigation systems with capillary action can be placed within the growing medium. There are a number of good sources of information available in New Zealand for structural, substrate and irrigation advice, including Landcare Research.

So it seems that a combination of dry-dune plants and shingle-beach or rocky coastal-cliff plants would do the trick. The second factor to consider is that you probably need the plants to spread quickly and effectively. Planting large areas of roof with individual plants that don't bulk up will be expensive, and enough will already have been spent on the infrastructure. The principle of using sprawling and creeping ground-cover plants to achieve stability and root-cooling cover applies perfectly to the living-roof situation.

Clearly, succulents are going to offer most resilience to the rooftop conditions, which is why stonecrops have been so popular. Native candidates are the New Zealand iceplant, *Crassula sieberiana* and peperomia (although this spreads relatively slowly), but they will not do well where there are heavy frosts. Frost damage not only has a direct hit, but it can also make plants that survive in a damaged state susceptible to fungal disease.

Then there are the tough ground-cover herbs such as sand piripiri and shore bindweed. If the roof is shaded or is in an area of evenly spread annual rainfall, you could also try Mercury Bay weed, remuremu, shore primrose and *Mazus pumilio*. These are likely to die back seasonally if not protected from direct sun, either by shading or taller plants. But seasonal dieback isn't a bad thing; it won't matter if the roof substrate is exposed for a period.

Raoulia species look ideal but you need to bear in mind that their root systems, although shallow, are often extremely extensive, and they may compete with other plants or their roots may become too heated during summer.

Creeping shrubs that don't require too much rooting depth include creeping fuchsia for frost-free places and where the roof is in shade, sand daphne, dwarf mingimingi (*Cyathodes fraseri*), small-leaved pohuehue and leafless pohuehue.

Grasses are surprisingly successful on living roofs, and coastal grasses such as *Lachnogrostis* species may survive the best. An alternative way of achieving the taller grass-like effect might be to use sand iris. Cox's fescue (*Festuca coxii*) has been used successfully; over time, the dead-leaf mat builds up to create very useful microenvironments and help maintain moisture content.

The Waitakere City Council building in Auckland was one of the first extensive urban living roofs in New Zealand, using only native plant species.

Ferns are generally poorly suited to these conditions, but leather-leaf fern (which spreads well), the curious, upright, clumped *Cheilanthes* or coastal spleenwort would be the most likely to cope, although they would prefer shady parts of the roof.

One interesting duneland living roof uses pingao as the dominant plant cover; since sand was constantly blowing onto the roof, it seemed logical to plant the sand-binding sedge. After some years, however, it seemed that the idea was failing, perhaps because pingao usually uses long taproots to seek cool moisture and its inability to do this on the roof was inhibiting its progress.

If the building is designed from the start to carry the load of a living roof rather than having one retrofitted, a shingle bed that contains lots of fines is a marvellous growing medium, or a scoria bed would be colourful and you could even leave it to self-colonise with local seed.

The challenges of living roofs near the coast might seem too daunting and the advantages less than obvious. The main reasons for having a living roof are to retain rainwater temporarily (especially useful to minimise flash flooding in urban environments), to insulate buildings, to lessen noise and to contribute to light absorption rather than reflection from urban surfaces. In a temperate region such as coastal New Zealand, where winter insulation is not necessarily a priority, one of the human benefits of living roofs might be diminished, but perhaps the benefits should not always be just for humans. I suspect there will be many very happy gulls finding new and safe breeding grounds on living roofs in future, and when that occurs, perhaps it is time to add some of the guano-reliant cresses and leafy coastal herbs to the species list! You will be surprised how many insects establish happily on a living roof, too, although earthworms probably won't as the rooftop is generally a low-humidity environment and, besides, how would they get there? There is no reason not to provide wood or occasional rocks or other forms of insect habitat, as long as they don't blow away in storms.

The living roof pictured opposite, in Waitakere, Auckland, was one of the first in New Zealand on a commercial building to use native plants only and was planted as an experimental landscape that is continually monitored and re-evaluated. Its rainwater retention has been very successful (so important to minimise flash flooding in urban areas), and after several years it has attracted a surprisingly diverse insect population. The substrate contains 30 percent soil mix, 20 percent expanded clay balls and 50 percent pumice granules (a mix of two different sizes). For the kinds of plants that are suited to such extreme environments, this may even be too much organic content. It does now have undersurface irrigation, after one severe summer drought did a lot of damage.

The coastal plants that have grown well here include Cox's fescue, sand daphne, sand coprosma, sand iris, Mercury Bay weed, shore bindweed, *Veronica obfuscata* (planted on a slight mound to allow for better root growth), coastal astelia and *Haloragis erecta*. To everyone's delight, native orchids are self-introduced. *Raoulia hookeri* and *R. parkii*

A mat of iceplant and *Selliera* is forming between woody shrubs such as sand coprosma in this Dunedin roof garden.

are growing well, which suggests that the coastal *R. haastii* would also succeed.

Tips for living roofs include minimising trampling—it can compress the substrate too much—so avoid the need for deadheading or too much weeding. Create some mounds to vary soil depth and therefore increase the range of species possible, and create variable microclimates for plants and insects. Optimise shaded areas with a different range of species; in windy sites (and aren't all roofs?), keep plants as prostrate as possible to avoid the likelihood of plants being rocked. And above all, try to have a living roof where people can see it! The benefits aren't all architectural.

Slow the flow

In this era of increasing storminess, we should be constantly thinking of how we can slow the progress of runoff from roofs and roads to prevent floods and damaging scours. That same runoff is carrying more and more contamination—whether oils off our roads or heavy metals off roofs—and if we can prevent these reaching waterways and estuaries, we are doing the wildlife and aquatic plant life a huge favour. We should never underestimate the role plants play in attenuating rainfall (both by absorbing the energy and absorbing some of the water), and if we can use plants to capture the flow and redirect it underground, there is a greater chance that contaminants will be intercepted by micro-organisms in the soil that help to break them down into less toxic chemicals. Where do we find opportunities to achieve this? Street trees do a great job of intercepting and slowing the downpours but, as we know, growing trees near the coast is not always practicable.

Swales (or living gutters) can slow runoff flow and can be used to capture sediment; in addition, living roofs can also capture the water for use within the building if desired. In an ideal situation, the swale forms one portion of a 'water trail' that leads water through rain-gardens or bioretention wetlands, or into settling ponds. Since water needs to flow along a swale, this needs to be planted with ground-hugging plants that enjoy irregular inundation. Water flowing in riverlets through tussocks or similarly isolated clumps of vegetation may erode the soil between the plants and resuspend sediment rather than trap it. Many designers automatically use stones to prevent scouring, but it does look very odd introducing stones into, say, a sandy environment, and perhaps there are alternative approaches.

In this swale, *Carex* species have been very densely planted to minimise any scouring that might occur in heavy rain.

Traditionally, exotic grasses (regularly mown) have been used for swales. If mown too short, they actually lose their value as water slides too quickly through the swale, but rank grass is extremely effective at capturing silts. Too rank and dense, and water will find an easier route, but a high cut or a high weed-eat should suffice. In a sandy environment any swale will slowly infill with wind-blown sand, and in time the swale may need to be scraped out and replanted. This is another reason not to use stones in duneland! Grass is certainly a cheap and easy option if you are already mowing other verges and lawns nearby.

If you plan on using native grasses and sedges, likely candidates (ideally species that spread rather than clump and are flexible during high flows) include *Microloena*, *Uncinia* and *Festuca* species. The advantage of going native is that these grasses and sedges are short enough not to require mowing. A deep swale that often stays damp could become a host to colourful floral display of yellow-headed bachelor's button.

Where possible, include wider portions of the swale to allow water to pond during big downpours. This might also create slight turbulence, which will help to dissipate energy. On steeper sites it will be important to have a collection point for sediment at the lowest part of the water's journey.

Alongside busy roads and car parks, swales will collect so much sediment, contaminants and litter that they will need stripping and replanting every few years. However, in rural areas or low-use areas, where maintenance disturbance is less likely, it may be feasible to plant trees within the swales. In duneland this concentration of runoff is going to help sustain street-tree growth.

The rain-garden is a more highly designed swale that first slows or collects the water flow. It may be capturing water from your roof or from stormwater drains. Plants are rooted into soil that is deep enough to absorb a lot of the surface water and hold it there, allowing soil micro-organisms to strip out as many contaminants as possible. The soil is underlain by a layer of sand and a lower layer of gravel, and there may even be an impermeable layer below that (although clay subsoils function just as well). So the water draining slowly down through these layers collects in the gravels and is released in a controlled fashion (usually through underground piping) into an area where further treatment can take place, or into a waterway. The longer the 'bath' collecting the runoff, the better the system can 'clean' the water as it

TOP *Carex virgata* and oioi are suited to swales that flood frequently and fast. This also explains why the channel is lined with stones rather than natural ground soil, which could erode.

ABOVE *Carex virgata* and sharp spike sedge (*Eleocharis acuta*) after rain—a rain-garden on a scale that ducks can appreciate.

stays in contact with plant roots and micro-organisms for a greater period of time. Many modern car parks use this system, but there is no reason why it cannot be successful on a residential scale as well.

Plants that grow well in these odd conditions (dry for long periods and erratically wet for long periods) are generally those found around the edges of ponds and estuaries, for example, oioi, marsh clubrush, *Carex*, *Juncus*, *Isolepis*, *Eleocharis* and *Cyperus* species.

The Kiwi rose garden

Wouldn't you like a native rose garden? Yes, we can do this in New Zealand, but it does take a bit of lateral thinking. Think Rosaceae. The local Rosaceae representatives are *Acaena* (piripiri) and *Rubus* (bush lawyer). They haven't completely shed their armoury in New Zealand: bush lawyer is well fortified with prickles. Piripiri uses hooks and barbs, not to defend its seeds so much as to encourage wildlife to carry them away. Both genera have a bad rap in New Zealand as a result of these adaptations, but if they are nurtured and planted in suitable locations, it soon becomes clear that one man's weed can be another man's treasure.

One of the most popular garden bush lawyers—and one that can withstand the rigours of the rocky coast—is actually a hybrid. *Rubus × barkeri* is popular for its bronze-purple foliage, and it can even be used alone as a ground-cover.

TOP Bush lawyer is distinguished by its red prickles.
LEFT AND BELOW Leafless bush lawyer flowering and fruiting.

TOP LEFT *Rubus × barkeri*. TOP RIGHT The leafless bush lawyer is most commonly growing on dry eastern coastlines, so it is well suited to the exposure of a trellis fence; to avoid the fence dominating completely, it has been planted here alongside New Zealand jasmine.

ABOVE Sand piripiri fruiting (left) and flowering (right).

LEFT The concept of a native rose garden really belongs to the potter Rick Rudd, a designer of a 'Garden of National Significance' by the coast in Taranaki.

PART FOUR

Back to nature

CHAPTER 7
Restoration

It is reasonably easy to say what gardening is about. We are selecting plants to put in a place, based on their horticultural or physiological merits, in order to create some manifestation of a human sense of beauty, interest or function. Gardens revolve around us. Rarely do they revolve around the needs of a wider community of wildlife—birds, bees, worms, lizards and so forth—although as a by-product of having any vegetation, there will be a limited source of food and shelter for some of these friends.

Restoration, on the other hand, generally has ecological connectivity and process as its *raison d'être*. Both styles of planting aim to have vegetation that thrives, is diverse and is resilient to seasonal events, but restoration or rehabilitation has the humble aim of learning *from nature* how best to heal, and how to heal as naturally as possible.

A gardener dealing with the seasonally wet–dry yellow clays of Auckland, or the old acidic soils of Northland, could get a broader range of plant growth by changing the pH with lime and counteracting the clays with compost. Not so restoration planters, who get the best deal they can with the existing conditions and seek to match the plants to the site, no matter how difficult the terms of negotiation.

Not surprisingly, given the meddling, interventionist nature of humans, many restoration projects do end up looking more like gardening projects on a massive scale. Gardening techniques can be put to good purpose where there are insurmountable obstacles in the way of restoration, but it is worthwhile teasing out just what is truly required, as a lot of money and effort can be expended if we do not make the effort to learn a few tricks from Mother Nature.

Newly planted pingao is protected from rabbit browse. Once established, the grass species can be sprayed off, giving pingao (a sedge, not a grass) room to spread.

As with any gardening project, restoration requires vision and a purpose. No matter where on the coast you are, the vision should be to return full health to the life cycles and successional processes that were suited to the site, before browsing mammals, fire, invasive weeds, bulldozers, herbicides, pesticides, floods, nutrient enrichment, chainsaws and guns came on the scene. Those life cycles and processes of decay and regeneration meant the place had the ability to revitalise itself after storms or erosion because the spores and the seeds, the pollinators and the soils were present. We know we are going to be getting more storms and larger rain events in future, so we need to anticipate damage. Change was not always as destructive as it can be today; processes were more adaptive. Can we emulate this?

Restoration isn't just about getting mature forest overlooking the estuary again; it is about putting in place all the infrastructure that allowed forest to grow there previously. If the soil subsequently eroded away, then we need to start by growing a new soil—slowly but surely. If the seed sources have long been burnt to ashes, then we need to provide a few seed sources upwind, or the bird corridors to existing seed sources, so that those linkages can be re-established. Removing those detrimental influences listed above has to be the starting point.

Restoration, especially when starting from scratch rather than just freeing up an existing natural environment from pests, is usually more strategic than gardening, especially if scale and isolation make it hard to get the required input of helpers at the right time of year. But perhaps the grander visions are, in reality, unaffordable. Or perhaps you know that five to ten years of 'kick-starting' will be required before natural succession is triggered. A sound strategic plan is an essential ingredient.

Lesson 1: Don't try to take on too much

You may have many willing hands for planting, but will they all be back later for weeding and releasing? Will there be enough water to irrigate young plants? The roll-back model for ridding dunes of marram, whereby you start at the windward edge, killing the marram and planting sedges among the dead grass to minimise risk of sand blowouts, slowly working downwind in this way to minimise marram seed replenishment, is a good example of a softly-softly strategic approach to restoration.

Lesson 2: Take all the time you need

Look at the weed control and ground preparation needed for a planting programme, for example. If you are dealing with blackberry as a dominant weed, then ideally it would take two years before a new plant goes into the ground. The first year is one of spraying. A second season is needed to both spray the regrowth and dig out those key root systems while they are accessible. (Sow grass seed in the interim—this is easily gotten rid of if necessary later on).

Lesson 3: Benefit the native wildlife, not the foreign browsers

Unless you control rabbits, hares, possums and rodents before you start planting, you are simply going to be feeding them and not the lizards, insects and birds you intended. Rabbits adore the fresh, moist roots of nursery-grown stock and the soft new foliage. Come autumn, your seeding plants are feeding rats and mice, and the processes of self-seeding are just a dream. Of course, if you reduce the populations of those pests, you also have to control the mustelids and cats that would have to look to native wildlife as a food substitute. Pest control is a big, ongoing commitment but unquestionably worthwhile. You will see tangible results within a single season.

What is the starting point?

Restoration is human-induced succession. We need to determine the starting point and decide whether to fast-track succession for some particular purpose or simply establish the basis for nature to take over—whichever is the most practical approach.

If you are endeavouring to return pasture to native cover, it is likely that the original soils have been thinned and/or compacted, fertility and pH have been increased over many years of farm management, and the soils now contain only exotic seeds that will keep on germinating for years to come. You need to treat the existing grass cover as the first successional stage (the colonising grasses and herbs that would occur naturally on a slip face, for example) and plant taller shrubs. These will benefit from the shelter of rank grass, then overtop it and gradually shade the grass out. The rank grasses speed up the soil-making processes now that they are not being grazed or mown. The main weeds to concentrate on in this type of planting are the scramblers and vines that may smother hapless new growth. If blackberry or gorse make an appearance, target them swiftly, avoiding having to strip ground bare of all vegetation.

Perhaps you are converting a 'woody weedscape' into a native landscape. Weeds such as lupin, gorse and boneseed are effectively the second successional stage already in place, so a good strategy (if you are not so close to the water's edge that trees are not a feasible option) is to kill the exotic shrubs and, without removing the debris, interplant with tree and other shrub species. The idea is to provide as much shelter for young plants as possible, but also to plant species that will shade out the weed seeds that will soon be germinating. The dead shrubs will also help

Rabbits and hares

Rabbits and hares are dealt with in four ways: repellents, poisons, live trapping or shooting.

- Repellents sprayed on young plants will probably need replenishing, especially after heavy rain or dew. Commonly used repellents include egg white and paint mixes or ox-blood products. Physical protection is another strategy, using sleeves around young plants or the lower trunks of young trees. Be aware of the dangers to young plants of using plastic sleeves that may 'cook' them unintentionally.
- Pindone is the most commonly used pest poison, an anticoagulant in the form of a cereal-based pellet. Remember that it takes a week or so for the poison to take effect, so plan your poisoning and planting accordingly. It will be most effective to introduce poisons when the rabbit's normal food is at a low ebb (such as late summer or midwinter). Secondary poisoning risks exist but the main danger to dogs is if they consume the raw pellet. Fortunately, an antidote (vitamin K) is available. Always let your neighbours know about poison lays.
- Live trapping using a bait such as carrot in a trap box still leaves you with the dilemma of what to do with the captured rabbit. No one else is going to want it. The least humane approach is drowning; shooting or knifing are preferred.
- Do you live in a rural location and have a gun licence? Shooting works! And you may get to become an experienced skin tanner, putting those pelts to good use. Remember, if the rabbit population is high, it may be most effective to shoot the stragglers left following a poisoning programme. It does not take rabbits long to become gun-shy.

In this estuarine urban stream there were no trees for birds to roost in, so one was manufactured—it has been proving popular.

prevent seed germination, as most of these weeds are sun-demanding and their shading of the ground will help inhibit the sprouting of seeds.

If you are dealing with dunes or sites where taller shrubs and trees are not realistic, the 'starting point' is effectively the same but you are substituting similar native plants for the exotic ones. Marram cover can be sprayed off and non-grass species (such as the sedges *Carex* or pingao, or knobby clubrush, or ground shrubs of sand daphne and sand coprosma) can be planted into the dead grassland. If the marram resprouts, Galant (a grass-specific herbicide) can be used to target it. The less bare sand, the better.

The planting stage

Before embarking on the practicalities of planting in different environments, take time to understand some fundamentals.

Be aware that some coastal trees are naturally isolationist. Little grows under ngaio and pohutukawa, for example, so if erosion control is a primary aim of the revegetation, it would be wise to choose other tree species that allow undergrowth so that the ground-cover will help contain runoff and sediment.

Know which species are sun-demanding and which are shade-tolerant. How often is harakeke used where it will shortly be shaded by trees, becoming insipid and diseased, and eventually dying out? It has become the go-to plant for any gardening situation, but not only are flaxes and trees quite an unnatural partnership, it is also a waste of money planting harakeke when the space would be better utilised by a plant that does not mind either sun or shade and will live far longer—such as a coprosma or a mingimingi, or in sheltered localities perhaps kawakawa.

If you want to reintroduce canopy tree species that once would have been present but are no longer in the vicinity, don't forget that many native species are dioecious—male and female flowers are on different trees— so you need to plant groups to ensure long-term productivity. If you can't wait for tall trees to grow to provide roosts for shags or kingfishers, perhaps some dead trees or branches could be brought onto the site in the interim, or even some bird-friendly sculptures introduced, which serve the same function.

How natural is the planting process really?

Fertilisers and potting mix introduce a new aspect to restoration planting. They may be seen as substitutes for the nutrient and humus losses from disturbed soils—they certainly will be giving young plants a healthy start in life—but are the plants you're choosing right for the job anyway, or should you be using plants with low-fertility requirements instead?

In some environments—as we read in the sand chapters—there is a greater issue at stake. In sandy sites not only are plants raised in fertile mixes disadvantaged when they finally make it into the ground, but the great contrast between moisture-retentive and fertile potting mix and the surrounding infertile sand through which water leaches swiftly often means roots fail to extend. Plants become excessively stressed as they encounter the 'real world' of difficult soils compared to their comfortable start in life. In addition, you need to ask whether the addition of litres and litres of potting mix into a sand environment is truly natural restoration.

Propagating dune plants in a sand mix with minimal fertiliser is simply common sense. Growth may be slower but it will be stronger, and the plants will have a better chance of survival in the first several years. If you are raising the plants yourself, a good option is to 'bottom water' by resting the pots on a tray that holds water, allowing capillary action to draw the water upwards through the sandy potting medium. The roots will then grow downwards, seeking that moisture. When the plants are finally transplanted in their position, their roots have already started their journey downwards, where they need to extend in order to seek out ground moisture.

It goes without saying that plants need to be

> ### Planting tips for sand-binders
>
> - If you decide to plant marram, do it only as a short-term strategy and only where no other grass species (such as spinifex or toetoe) are present. The reason? Well, you can also plant knobby clubrush, sprawling native herbs and woody shrubs, and as soon as these are established in the shelter of marram, you can kill off the marram with a grass-specific herbicide without putting your new plants at risk.
> - All the sand-binders can be raised from seed. Spinifex has separate male and female plants, so to ensure longevity in the planted vegetation, you could start with cuttings from known parents to ensure a mix of gender.
> - Remember, pingao and spinifex have long tap roots, so use deep pots (such as milk cartons) for raising seedlings. The raising mix should be largely coarse sand with only minimal potting mix and slow-release fertiliser added.
> - Nursery-raised plants must be hardened off for three months before they are planted out.
> - Eliminate rabbits before planting out, or at least use a repellent on new plants.
> - Adding a light scattering of Magamp slow-release fertiliser pellets (magnesium, ammonium, phosphate) strengthens the growth of spinifex and pingao, but they do not need much more than this. Perhaps some urea applied after several years will continue to boost their growth, but too much fertiliser will encourage marram and other weeds to invade.

hardened off before going into the ground. This means slowly introducing them to a regime of less watering, and more exposure to sun and wind, but in a controlled way over a number of weeks.

The smallest of coastal creeks can support fish and provide spawning grounds, and well-planned revegetation can not only provide the shade and safety for fresh-water life, it can also help trap runoff and phosphate-enriched sediment before it reaches estuaries. One challenge is to prevent invasion by foreign grasses; if regular weeding help is not on tap, weed matting may be required.

Spacing and content

Institutional 'restoration' plantings on a large scale are usually designed around cost efficiencies, so plants are carefully spaced at regular intervals to maximise cover for minimal expenditure. The result is often a recognisable planting that smacks of human intervention rather than natural succession.

Smaller, private undertakings have a better chance at mimicking nature. Some trees are renowned for their prolific seedling nurseries sprouting under their canopies; karaka, kohekohe and kahikatea are examples. Not all the seedlings will necessarily mature, but those that do create a thicket of juveniles. Clustering these species in groups is a natural pattern.

And always keep in mind the full cast of characters. Has the planting got its 'creeps, crawlers and social climbers'? Every vegetation type does, whether coastal, wetland, valley floor or hill country. On the coast, many of these species are sun-demanding participants that are naturally dominant, such as small-leaved pohuehue, *Clematis foetida* and shore bindweed. They can go in right from the start, whereas some of the others would benefit from waiting several years for vegetation to mature enough to shade the ground; New Zealand jasmine, climbing ferns and leafless bush lawyer belong in this category.

It is restoration orthodoxy to stagger planting over two or more years in order to allow a range of sun-demanding and shade-tolerant plants to become established. In all coastal environments we see a new wave of species entering a community once shelter and shade have been provided by the tougher characters. Herbs, scramblers, ground ferns and larger-leaved shrubs can become established—not necessarily underneath sheltering plants but at least surrounded by them, or finding those microclimate sweet spots where their seeds can germinate without being scorched or desiccated. (We can provide those sweet spots, too, in restoration planting, but it will take several years before they exist—Lesson 2, remember?)

Planting that contains grasses or grass-like plants (toetoe, oioi, *Carex*, *Juncus*, etc.) will benefit from a biodegradable weed matting to inhibit the invasion of other grasses. As previously mentioned, this would not be practical for plants such as spinifex, pingao or knobby clubrush, which need to spread in order to expand, but it works well for tussock forms, which require a different approach to keep competitors at bay. Make sure that the spacing between plants is perfect so that as they mature all gaps are filled, and do your homework on anticipated plant sizes.

Dealing with water

Planting wet and riparian areas requires somewhat more rigour in choosing what plants are located where. We need to take into account the effect of open water or groundwater on a plant's root systems and match species to depth as precisely as possible. On page 103 is a diagram identifying the depths at which different species can be planted in and around ponds, to meet their exacting requirements (the diagram is idealised for winter pond depths). Tidal creeks have the additional issues of regular tidal variation and brackish water.

Although some species will be found in both fresh and brackish water environments (for example oioi, kuawa (*Schoenoplectus tabernaemontani*), and *Isolepis*), others are fussier. Raupo and kuta (*Eleocharis sphacelata*) are tolerant only of fresh water, for example. Sea rush, as its name suggests, prefers saline conditions.

manuka, cabbage tree, Coprosma propinqua

saltmarsh ribbonwood, toetoe, swamp coprosma, purei

Cyperus, Juncus spp.

oioi, three-square

sea rush, kuawa

Mean High Water Spring
Mean High Water Neap
Mean Low Water Neap
Mean Low Water Spring

This generalised cross section of a tidal creek illustrates where different species are located with respect to tidal variations.

What are we restoring back to?

That's a hard one to answer. It also explains why many planting programmes are described as rehabilitation (of disrupted, dysfunctional communities) rather than restoration, as restoration implies a known end point. But what do we actually know about what we've lost, or about broken food chains or previous plant–soil relationships, especially in such a dynamic adaptive environment?

Most of us have a grasp of successional processes—starting with colonising species that have adapted to difficult and infertile terrain—as it is obvious that plants that require moisture and fertility cannot dominate until a decent humic topsoil has been formed by those colonisers. And then the forest canopy species—which, perversely, first require shade to establish and subsequently seek the sunlight—need the shady ground-cover of shrubs or small trees, and this can take many years to establish.

The old adage of 'we don't know what we don't know' applies perfectly to vegetation composition. Think of some of these known influences that have created landscapes that now seem familiar and 'natural' to us:

- Maori planted orchards of karaka and in some areas ngaio, titoki, cabbage tree or wharangi, all for utilitarian purposes, sometimes in parts of New Zealand where these species had never grown 'naturally', let alone en masse.
- Northern Maori introduced pohutukawa and napuka, presumably for pure gardening reasons, well beyond their natural range (such as into the Marlborough Sounds and along the Wellington coastline).
- The modern gardener has introduced karo into areas where frost or geographical obstacles would have prevented its establishment, and now it is becoming an invasive weed.
- Colonial demand for firewood saw the felling of nikau as well as more familiar firewood species
- Domination of coastal forest by ngaio, totara and/or kowhai generally reflects long-term grazing by cattle, as these trees are unpalatable or poisonous and will regenerate where more palatable forest juveniles fail. Kohekohe dominates southern North Island west coast forest remnants because of a mix of vigorous resilience to animal browse, and its ability

Be prepared to be successful! The extent to which pingao and spinifex plantings along the shore of Petone has built up the foredune (just as intended) may have taken everyone by surprise. The street sweepers have become a lot busier.

to respond following natural calamities such as storms and earthquake damage to forest.

• Many palatable coastal herbs have been lost not only to introduced browsing animals and humans, but also to munching caterpillers, not to mention the odd botanist determined to gain one last herbarium specimen of a rare plant!

• There has been mass decline of pohutukawa and northern and southern rata from coastal forests due to possum browse.

• Mangroves have spread rapidly through northern estuaries following massive boosts in nutrient-rich runoff and sediment from forest clearance, topdressing and conversion to dairying in their catchments.

Then there are the unknown changes that moa made to coastal vegetation composition—if any. We simply do not know.

Weeds

There are, of course, too many weeds to mention within the coastal environment. Largely due to the open nature of the vegetation, it is only too easy for vigorous foreign species to invade, in some cases changing the character, dynamics and even the topography of the shore completely. After living long enough with a 'mixed bag' of vegetation, people lose sight of what is native and what is introduced. The great danger in this is not recognising a new threat. So many invasions are preventable if action is taken as soon as a newcomer arrives on the scene. So to help the watchdogs, here are some of the most virulent pest plants, bearing in mind, of course, that dominant weeds vary between sites and from one end of the country to the other.

GRASSES AND RUSHES

Ammophila arenaria, marram grass

Listing this widespread plant in a weed section doesn't fairly describe the significant and lucrative role marram has played in New Zealand's economy by stabilising mobile dunes. It was brought to New Zealand in the 1880s, probably from Australia, where it was already being used to stabilise foredunes, and, at the suggestion of the government botanist Leonard Cockayne in 1911, was planted on a grand scale along the North Island's west coast dunelands. *Ammophila* is native to western Europe. In New Zealand it doesn't appear to set seed well, but it spreads vegetatively with great vigour, and fragments of the plants are able to withstand weeks of salt-water immersion, so storms have been instrumental in distributing it widely around our coasts. The plant itself grows over 1.5 m tall in good conditions, spreading by underground rhizomes. As with other sand-binding plants, mobile sand stimulates foliage growth from the rhizome nodes and the plant flourishes in foredune conditions There are only two areas in New Zealand where its presence is minimal: south Westland and Stewart Island/Rakiura.

Marram grass.

Marram is listed here as a weed because by and large its vigorous growth makes it a poor sharer of habitat with less vigorous native dune species. The root mats it creates are unwelcome on erodable beaches, as once uncovered they prevent reconstitution of smooth dune forms. Marram was only introduced on such a grand scale originally for economic reasons, as the research into cultivation had already been undertaken overseas. It was a quick fix.

Controlling it really requires use of a herbicide, as hand-pulling often just gets the old material out, stimulating fragments of young rhizomes to sprout even more rapidly.

Cortaderia jubata and *Cortaderia selloana*, pampas

Pampas flowerheads (compared to the similar toetoe flowerheads) are stiffly upright; in the case of purple pampas (*C. jubata*) they appear in late summer or autumn rather than summer. The dead foliage remains curled at the base of the tussocks like pencil shavings. Most councils require landowners to remove pampas from their properties. To eradicate pampas, first cover all your skin as the leaf edges are very sharp! Then head on in and slash to within 300 mm from the ground. As the regrowth occurs, use herbicide spray at the directed rate. Large infestations should be bulldozed out. Remember, pampas was introduced as stock food and these hardy plants will readily resprout even in grazed paddocks. The reason we take pampas seriously as a weed is that although it shares similar habitat preferences to toetoe (as well as colonising drier sites), it grows more aggressively and will usurp the native species as well as other local native plants. Railway lines have proved to be the perfect conduit for pampas to spread through the countryside, and since the tussocks are a fire hazard, trains and pampas are a poor mix.

Elytrigia repens, couch

This is a highly invasive grass that spreads by underground stolons, which can extend great distances from the main plant. Note that they don't run on top of the ground—this is a distinguishing feature. Couch isn't much of a problem in a lawn situation but can spread aggressively where it isn't cut or grazed. The leaves are long and skinny, harsh and slightly ribbed with a blue-green hue. The flowerheads look rather like ryegrass. Over winter, the plant is dormant and often quite grey. Spot-spray with a glyphosate herbicide during its summer growth period. Make sure each plant already has new leaves as, while the shoot is growing, sugars are moving out of the rhizome into the plant and that will slow up the translocation of the herbicide.

Juncus acutus, sharp rush

There is no question how this rush got its common name—the spikes on the ends of the stems are ferociously sharp. Dark ruddy-brown seedheads are another distinguishing feature of these stiff, large clumps. It is spreading through North Island harbours and estuaries, usurping native rushes as well as invading herbfields and saltmarshes. Probably because few of us are skilled at distinguishing one rush from the next, these plants have often taken a hold right under our noses. Once they are established, we soon discover how nasty they are to handle.

Paspalum dilatatum, paspalum

Very similar to kikuyu grass, this is a subtropical pasture grass with a C_4 photosynthesis pathway, conferring it greater water-use efficiency and the ability to withstand drought. It forms dense mats or flat clumps on moist, fertile soils and has become a pasture grass in the northern half of the North Island. The dark green leaves are very broad (probably the broadest grass in any lawn), sometimes with a crinkled red or purplish margin, but not hairy as they are in kikuyu grass. It spreads by underground stems. The flowerheads are distinctive, with three or four widely spaced racemes branching off the central stalk. Spot-spray with a glyphosate herbicide during its summer growth period.

Paspalum vaginatum, seashore paspalum

This stoloniferous, semi-aquatic North American grass has invaded salt marshes, mangrove swamps and beach fringes throughout the Pacific region, tolerating compacted saline soils and both drought and inundation. It has harsh blue-green leaves that are at odd angles, giving the mass of grass a sparse, messy look. There are usually just two flowerhead

TOP TO BOTTOM Pampas; sharp rush; seashore paspalum.

221

racemes on a central stalk. Its ability to tolerate semi-aquatic habitat, (to mid-tide level) is causing a real headache in estuaries in the upper North Island. The mats it forms can be a metre thick (plus another metre of root mass below ground), so it is not hard to understand what a threat it poses to estuarine shellfish and spawning grounds, as well as to other plants. By inhabiting the intertidal zone, the grass also creates the perfect nursery for mangrove seedlings. Galant and glyphosate herbicides are both effective on seashore paspalum.

TOP Buffalo grass. BOTTOM Kikuyu.

Pennisetum clandestinum, kikuyu

Kikuyu grass is an African species well adapted to poor soils and drought conditions in hot climates. It is a C_4 photosynthesiser, meaning that it transpires at night and uses water and carbon dioxide more efficiently than the more common C_3 grass species. C_4 photosynthesisers can grow in the warmer months and persist on poor land in seasonally water-deficient environments. The Department of Agriculture brought it here in the 1920s and today the Ministry of Primary Industries is still crowing about its virtues, albeit as a way to turn what proved to be a liability into a farming asset with the appropriate controls. So well did it adapt to Northland conditions that it grew out of control, aggressively colonising bare and poor soils. It isn't as easy to farm as other exotic grasses, and Northlanders have had to learn how to control it on their land using grazing and fertility management.

You will be familiar with kikuyu at sandy beaches—the dense mats it forms are bouncy underfoot. Long tillers form at each node along surface stolons, allowing it to quickly engulf everything in its path. The root growth is deep (hence the plant's ability to withstand drought) and fast —up to 3 cm a day. The leaves are hairy and you only rarely see flowerheads (which is one way to distinguish kikuyu from the very similar buffalo grass, which has stiff, broad flowerstalks).

The plant is readily introduced to new areas through seeds in cowpats, cuttings in machinery and tyres, and by its incredible ability to travel long distances underground popping up in neighbours' properties or the other side of roads. It also continues to be introduced to coastal areas to stabilise mobile sand, which is very disappointing.

Kikuyu as a pasture grass is moving south as the climate warms and will inevitably cause similar angst in the farming communities in the Waikato and Bay of Plenty as it did in Northland.

Do not be tempted to plant kikuyu to cover over your problems—it will cause much bigger ones. Get rid of it wherever you can. It is one of the greatest threats to northern natural coastal environments we have.

Stenotaphrum secundatum, buffalo grass

Like kikuyu grass, buffalo grass grows in thick, smothering, bouncy mattresses in coastal places since it is tolerant of salt spray. Stoloniferous grasses such as buffalo grass often spread more through dispersal of fragments of the rooting stolons rather than by seed, which means we need to be extremely tidy in our waste disposal and not just tip garden waste containing this grass somewhere 'out of sight, out of mind'.

The best way to distinguish buffalo grass is by the strap-like leaves and the stiff, upright, flattened flowerheads that emerge from nodes along the tall stalk. This is a dreadfully difficult grass to control, and hard to plant into unless you constantly maintain clear patches around juvenile plants.

SHRUBS

Acacia longifolia, Sydney golden wattle and *Acacia sophorae*, coastal wattle

There are several Australian acacias that have been introduced into sand country (again initially by forestry interests for dune stabilisation and windbreak purposes), but good intentions are often undermined by the voracity of the species, and over time *Acacia* has proven to be a liability and is constantly threatening new parts of the sandy coast. Unfortunately in the meantime, New Zealanders have become used to the idea of it being a useful plant in harsh conditions, so it is difficult to convince landowners that it is a weed that is causing immense harm in the wild.

Acacias can safely be chopped and mulched without fear of branches resprouting and rooting, so although they grow into sizeable trees that would be difficult to cart away, the branch debris need not be removed as it could serve as a useful planting medium.

Lupinus arboreus, tree lupin (yellow-flowering)

Lupin species were deliberately introduced to New Zealand dunelands by forestry and farming bodies needing to stabilise drifting sand or dune blowouts. They were successful! Lupin is here to stay, often forming dense swards across sandy country. It is a nitrogen-fixer, and very efficient at utilising low levels of phosphorus in soils, so was deemed to be a good nursery-crop for plantation forestry in the dunes.

For areas where lupin isn't wanted, however, it is a nightmare: a fire risk in summer, with seeds that stay viable for years in the ground, and a rapid grower and very hard to prevent spreading into wild areas. There are native plants that create similar shrublands in dune country, but those species find it difficult to compete against a nitrogen-fixer like lupin. It may be an effective nursery-crop when it is mulched down to ground level and other species interplanted densely (densely enough to outshade the lupin as it grows back), but that is still experimental.

Periodically, large areas of lupin can suddenly fall victim to a fungal blight (caused by *Colletotrichum gloeosporioides*), and they may disappear for several seasons, but with a large seedbank in the soil they generally return. Similarly, there is a caterpillar that can defoliate the plants, but they inevitably recover.

Although small plants can be pulled by hand, to clear a large area it is possible to cut trunks at their base and split them (to minimise resprouting), and then burn stockpiled and dried branches. On an even larger scale, getting machinery to remove the shrubs and then scraping the topsoil away (to reduce the seed content) is a possibility but carries the risk of wind erosion on the exposed surface before replanting can become established. A costly option is to lay weed matting over the cleared area for one or two years to kill off the seedbank, before replanting.

TOP AND CENTRE Coastal wattle.
BOTTOM Lupin.

223

TOP AND CENTRE Boxthorn.
ABOVE Agapanthus.

Lycium ferocissimum, boxthorn

Equally capable of repelling elephants and humans with its vicious thorns, South African boxthorn fails to repel fruit-eating starlings, which spread this drought-tolerant coastal bush far and wide through open pasture and shrubland (left). The thorns are even known to flatten tractor tyres! Although boxthorn was introduced by farmers seeking its hardiness for shelter belts, now it is a major weed problem. Getting rid of it requires sturdy clothes and often a chainsaw for the older bushes, which, at up to 3 m in height, have sizeable trunks. And you will need a herbicide. The trick is to paint the freshly cut stumps while the sap still oozes. Without herbicide, the stumps coppice and you will be back where you started in a year's time. You will want to get rid of the cut branches as the thorns will remain a danger for years to come on the ground, but the timber makes excellent firewood. Boxthorn hedges have long been a feature of the windswept Taranaki coastal landscape. The only way to deal with these hedges is with bulldozers and fire.

HERBS, LILIES AND CACTI

Agapanthus praecox subsp. *orientalis*, agapanthus

Some garden escapees are benign, but not agapanthus. Often planted initially because it endures hard clay soils and heat where few other plants can, it will rapidly spread and bulk up in both full sun and shade. Its fleshy

root systems are massive and very hard to dig out, and the plant is not easy to poison either. If eradication is proving difficult, the least you can do is chop off the flowerheads before they seed—better in a vase than threatening the local beach.

Carpobrotus edulis, *Carpobrotus chilensis*, South African iceplant

Carpobrotus edulis has yellow flowers and *C. chilensis* has purple flowers, both being bigger than the pink flowers of our native iceplant. Their succulent leaves are far bigger also. These plants will form mats up to 6 m diameter. Keeping them out of natural duneland areas is proving difficult but they do respond to herbicide treatment (Roundup and Galant work well). Leave the mats to wither in the sun and plant into them once the herbicide has decomposed.

There is another self-introduced species found on the Coromandel Peninsula (*C. glaucescens*) that is almost indistinguishable from *C. chilensis* except its leaves have a slightly milky (glaucous) appearance. Although treated as a weed in the past, it is tolerated nowadays.

Gunnera tinctoria, Chilean rhubarb

A garden escapee, this 2 m tall South American monster has turned out to be invasive in wet coastal cliffs, especially in Taranaki's papa country. Frosty weather doesn't faze

OPPOSITE TOP South African iceplants.
OPPOSITE CENTRE LEFT Chilean rhubarb.
OPPOSITE CENTRE RIGHT Formosan lily.
OPPOSITE BOTTOM Pink ragwort.

it—it simply becomes deciduous. It spreads both by horizontal rhizomes that can become the size of tree trunks and by prolific seeding. It is shading out coastal herbs, including threatened species already on the brink of disaster. Part of the problem is that it can inhabit cliff faces where weed eradication is impossible. At present, it is voluntary to rid your garden of Chilean rhubarb, but expect that to change in the future as the problem deepens. It is already illegal to sell it. At the very least, get rid of the flowerheads, but ideally use a glyphosate herbicide to kill the entire plant.

Lilium formosanum, Formosan lily

It is hard to single out any one of the myriad garden escapees that are colonising our shores, but this one is included as an example of how our weakness for prettiness makes us reluctant to remove potential threats as they appear. Formosum lily is popping up in dunelands all around the North Island and changing the nature of the vegetation both ecologically and culturally! It spreads by both seed and bulbil, and is a nuisance overseas as well as here, invading open and degraded sites. Plants are easy to spot—so why don't we pounce on them as soon as one appears?

Senecio glastifolius, pink ragwort, holly-leaved senecio

This South African plant is spreading like wildfire through our dunes. Decorative pink flowers do not redeem it, as this ragwort is incredibly

invasive, perfectly adapted for dry and hot sites, with its daisy seedhead spreading seeds at the puff of a sea breeze. It grows fairly tall, with a slightly woody base to the stems.

The best control is hand weeding, which given the resources available at most beaches, means this is a community-based responsibility. Wear gloves as there is good reason for also being known as holly-leaved senecio. Although it is best to remove it from the beach (especially if the seedheads are ripe), simply leaving the roots to wither in the sun will ensure it dies.

There is another, smaller South African senecio with fleshy leaves and a deep purple flower—purple groundsel (*Senecio elegans*). It is regarded as a weed also, just not quite as rampant, and is most commonly found in duneland growing alongside the yellow-flowered native shore groundsel.

TOP Muehlenbeckia. BOTTOM Pink bindweed.

226

Is it really a weed?

Given that a weed is simply a plant growing in a place or in a way that is not wanted, it is fair to ask whether indigenous species can be weeds that warrant attention also. Several coastal species attract attention to themselves by behaving in a unruly manner, and it is useful to take a closer look at a couple of them, as they are frequently maligned by gardeners.

Pink bindweed is one of many trailing plants in New Zealand that are cursed by gardeners, and it does indeed grow in a weedy fashion. It is indigenous to New Zealand but is also found in numerous countries around the southern hemisphere. It has highly attractive pink-and-white-striped flowers and the characteristic elongated heart-shaped leaves of *Calystegia* species. It can be distinguished from introduced species by its reddish stems and pink flowers. In the wild it has a preference for bush edges, especially the ones skirting estuaries and swamps. It would be perfectly normal to see veils of pink bindweed festooning the interface between tall trees and short rushland, and scrambling through the damp edges of rushland vegetation. There is no need to panic—it is simply doing its thing in its chosen environment. But because it is quick to invade disturbed or young vegetation, it also lends itself to the urban environment and in suburban gardens it can become overwhelming.

Pohuehue and small-leaved pohuehue are frequently found tangled through shrubland and bush edges in all types of coastal environments, with their lianes growing vigorously in frost-free climates. Pohuehue, with the larger leaf, can climb high into the canopy of trees, but like all *Muehlenbeckia* species is sun-demanding, so prefers bush edges or solitary trees for support. Both species flower profusely, attracting innumerable insects to their nectar, and the thick, tangled growth is the perfect safe hideaway for small birds' nests. The way pohuehue winds tightly around its supporting tree's branches can throttle growth and weaken a tree, but it rarely kills it. Small-leaved pohuehue, while sometimes weedy itself, also plays a role in suppressing other weeds such as blackberry, as it rambles over and through whatever stands in its path. These are attractive plants, host to the native copper butterfly, food source for bees and lizards, and ubiquitous throughout New Zealand's vegetation. Small-leaved pohuehue is fast becoming a garden star as its prunability and pretty trailing features make it a versatile plant in tough localities, but it is so tough, and so desired internationally, that it has already become a garden escapee weed in Western Australia.

ABOVE Tauhinu's reputation as an agricultural weed has unnecessarily biased gardeners against using it.

PART FIVE

The inhabitants

CHAPTER 8

Plant portraits

Instead of being an exhaustive list of coastal species, the following portraits contain those plants that are most likely suited to garden situations, and those that the author recommends gardeners become familiar with.

TREES

Alectryon excelsus, titoki

The early English settlers called this tree the New Zealand ash, so 'English' does it seem. Its preferred habitat is well-drained alluvial soils but it will also be found in the mix in old dune forest. Although its stately form lends itself to being a street tree, this is unwise where salty winds blow, and it is best kept in the lee of buildings or other tall trees.

Coprosma macrocarpa subsp. *minor*, coastal karamu

Around the shores of Northland's estuaries and islands, the Northland 'equivalent' of the ubiquitous karamu (*Coprosma robusta*) has somewhat larger, firmer leaves but still has that loose, ungainly appearance of coprosmas in the wild. They are readily tamed, needless to say, into jolly coastal garden inhabitants, especially the female plants, which scream with autumn colour. With even larger, fuller, glossier leaves, the offshore island subspecies, *C. macrocarpa* subsp. *macrocarpa*, is being cultivated widely for mainland gardens.

Coprosma repens, taupata

Maligned by many for being so common and 'weedy', taupata is the mainstay of natural coastline vegetation around Cook Strait and the Wairarapa, as well as being present on most rocky coastlines as far south as Greymouth. It has the same survival tactics as griselinias: fleshy, waxy leaves and springy stems. The natural plasticity of the plant makes it an ideal garden subject. If left to grow in a sheltered location, its branches will eventually become delightfully pendulous. It can be espaliered, trained into arches, trailed over walls or hedged. It will grow 3–4 m in more sheltered conditions or prostrate itself along the ground on really harsh sites. The female plants can be very showy in late summer when the orangey-red berries are ripe.

Taupata grows naturally in rocky or stony areas, and its long roots will

TOP Titoki. BOTTOM Coastal karamu.

229

seek out fissures in rocks for water and minerals. Its ability to grow almost in the splash zone reflects the excellent salt-resilient features of the leaves; even if it were to lose its leaves in particularly harsh, dry salt storms, the plant would recover rapidly.

A prostrate form known from the Poor Knights Islands is sold commercially as *Coprosma* 'Poor Knights'. This can be used to great effect alongside taupata, as long as the height of the larger taupata is managed.

Taupata grows above the Poor Knights form.

Cordyline spp., cabbage trees

Cordyline australis, the cabbage tree or ti kouka, is one of only four trees in New Zealand that can grow in swampy saturated ground. Although that is its preferred habitat, its enlarged rhizomatous root can store enough fluid to keep the tree alive through dry periods but it will not tolerate extended drought. To get the best out of cabbage trees, avoid locating them where drying, salty winds will whip the heads or where ground will dry for longer than a week at a time. Check closely for seepages on hillslopes—even the slightest hint of permanent moisture will be enough to support cabbage trees. An occasional raking of the dead foliage will help to minimise damage to the new leaves by the caterpillar of the cabbage tree moth. Cordylines are geographically distinctive—some areas have trees

that sport finer foliage—so source locally if you can.

At the other end of the scale, dwarf cabbage tree (*Cordyline pumilio*) might be found on coastal clay banks in Northland, where, until it flowers, it is easily confused with *Libertia* or *Dianella* as there is no trunk on this diminutive species. It is an ideal candidate for gardens as it can tolerate both full sun and semi-shade, as well as the poor substrates often associated with new excavations.

'Green Goddess' is a dwarf (2 m) cultivar of *Cordyline kaspar* (now *C. obtecta*) from the Three Kings Islands. Although it is well suited to large pots, be sure not to let drought conditions hamper its growth.

Corynocarpus laevigatus, karaka

The handsome, fast-growing karaka is one of the few plants to have had its natural range extended for cultivation purposes prior to European settlement and can now be found (usually in orchard-like groves) as far south as Banks Peninsula. However, this tree has become 'weedy' in the lower half of the North Island, aggressively dominating native coastal bush remnants and reducing their species diversity. Now that Maori aren't harvesting the crop of orange fruits, there are few constraints on its spread. Bear this in mind, and if you live south of Auckland, resist planting karaka close to native coastal forest for fear of invasion. If karaka does so well south of its natural range, why wasn't it always more widespread? This strictly coastal tree

TOP Cabbage tree. BOTTOM 'Green Goddess', a cultivar of *Cordyline obtecta*.

Karaka flowers (TOP) and fruits.

attracting wasps and smelling awful, but karaka's vigorous growth and resilience to wind and salt make it an ideal amenity tree (especially where street cleaners are regularly at work). It can take hard pruning and can grow in almost any soil, although remember that it does best where its long roots can reach a source of moisture.

Dodonaea viscosa, akeake

We cannot claim this tree as our own (it grows in a number of countries, including Australia), yet its shrubby form helps convey so much of the character of windswept New Zealand coastlines. Just a small tree (6–7 m tall), it can be easily overlooked among other coastal forest species, but when it grows on bush edges or alone, as it can in garden situations, its fabulous form comes into its own.

Tough, linear leaves are held erect on myriad tiny branchlets (sticky, hence its name *viscosa*), and although

is frost-tender and thrives where its deep taproots can reach a source of moisture, so it needed human assistance to overcome the frost and drought barriers of the Manawatu–Horowhenua dunelands in the west and Hawke's Bay in the east. The late summer–autumn drupes (kopi) may attract kereru to the garden, but we don't have enough kereru now to make much of a dent on these prolific fruiters and most seeds sprout beneath the parent tree. If you are thinking of transplanting seedlings, dig deeply as they will already have surprisingly long taproots.

Many local authorities won't plant karaka in public spaces because the fruit ferment on the ground,

ABOVE Akeake trunks. RIGHT TOP Akeake foliage. RIGHT The cultivar *Dodonaea viscosa* 'Purpurea' has winged seed capsules.

growth is upright when young, in time the branches spread laterally, creating a horizontally layered crown. Tough though the leaves are, they appear translucent in the sun, and planting to backlight the tree will not only show it to best effect, but will also create a mottled, dappled shadow.

Bright lime winged seed capsules festoon the branch tips of female plants in late summer. The contrast between the fresh greens of the foliage and capsules and the stringy-barked,

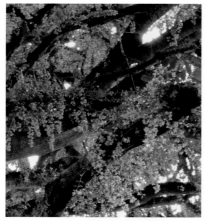

dark orange branches also make you want to expose the trunk or plant in such a way that the branches can be seen. This tree would really lend itself to courtyard plantings, where it can provide light shade under a spreading crown.

Akeake is frost-tender, so although it grows in sandy sites, it will only be found sheltered amidst other trees in the frost-prone duneland areas. It does not grow further south than Banks Peninsula and Greymouth in the wild. One of the ways plants can protect themselves from frost is by storing oils and resins, which also impart colour to leaves. This may partly explain the find in the frosty Wairau River of some akeake with a purple tinge to the leaves. The plants were propagated and thus began a booming market for *Dodonaea viscosa* 'Purpurea'. Unfortunately, this selection has suffered from insect attack and disease more than the parent species.

Dysoxylum spectabile, kohekohe

Although a large tree for gardens, this is a species that would benefit from being grown where possum and rat browse are kept to a minimum. Kohekohe are vigorous and fast-growing trees, but constant browse of their fruits and flowers is limiting their replenishment in the wild. They are beautiful specimen trees for sites that are sheltered, warm and moist (and that is most bays within Northland and a narrow band that extends down

TOP Kohekohe flowers. CENTRE Kohekohe flowers arising directly from the trunk. BOTTOM *Elingamita johnsonii.*

the west coast of New Zealand as far south as northwest Nelson).

What makes these elegant trees particularly special is their winter flowering and the style of flowering, called cauliflory (where flowerstalks protrude directly from the trunk of the tree). The flowers are a crucial winter nectar supply for honey-eating birds. The large compound leaves are a lush, fresh green that partners well with many of the other plants that share their environment, including wharangi, mahoe, hangehange, kawakawa, hound's-tongue fern, *Asplenium* ferns, New Zealand jasmine and New Zealand passionvine.

Elingamita johnsonii

Although this rare stately tree from the Three Kings Islands looks like karaka, botanically it is more closely related to mapau. Dark trunk, horizontal branching and bright glossy leaves make it the perfect specimen tree. Its large red fruits are favoured by kereru.

Entelea arborescens, whau

Although the tropical-looking whau does belong to a subtropical plant family (Tiliaceae), it is endemic to New Zealand. The curious seed capsules ensure this small tree provides interest all year round. Large white flowers offer a lacy display early in summer, swiftly replaced by lime clutches of the bidibidi-like seed capsules that in due course turn brown and persist on the tree for months.

A coastal tree of warm northern areas (also occurring sporadically

south of Raglan and the Bay of Plenty where conditions are warm and sheltered, but rarely reaching south of Taranaki), it grows naturally in frost-free sites, tucked into gullies or in seepages at the base of cliffs, where not only is it protected from the harshest winds and salt-burn, but also receives year-round moisture to feed those large, flimsy leaves. Keep this in mind for the garden: for best results, plant whau in a sheltered corner in a well-drained, organic soil, heavily mulched to maintain soil moisture.

Whau is becoming scarce in the wild, in part because it is very palatable to stock and feral goats. It doesn't live very long—10–15 years—but the seeds sprout readily and will supply replacement plants at will. Early Maori fishermen took advantage of the extreme lightness of the timber, using it for floats for fishing nets and lines—and bobbing toys for small children.

Griselinia littoralis, broadleaf, papauma, kapuka

'*Littoralis*' refers to a coastal habitat, but it is mostly in the South Island that this small tree is coastal; the further north you go, the higher the altitude at which it thrives. Ovate, waxy leaves have quite a yellowish tinge, especially the new growth, and branchlets and leaf stems are strikingly yellow, making this a sprightly foliage plant, even though its flowers and fruit are inconspicuous. Very hardy.

Griselinia lucida, puka, shining broadleaf

'*Lucida*' refers to the shining of the waxy leaf surface. The fairly large leaf is conspicuously lopsided, making it easy to distinguish the plant from broadleaf. Puka are epiphytic in the wild, where you can sometimes see the ridged aerial roots clasping taller trees in coastal forest, but along the

shore it will often perch on rocks or stony places, sending its roots across the outcrop in search of soil.

TOP LEFT Whau with some flowers and unripe capsules. TOP CENTRE Whau with ripe capsules. TOP RIGHT Broadleaf. ABOVE Puka.

233

Kunzea ericoides and *Kunzea robusta*, kanuka
Leptospermum scoparium, manuka

Synonymous with summer, the buzzing of bees, and the chirruping of cicadas, and synonymous also with reverting farmland, these two genera look very similar but have rather different needs and natural habitats. They both fulfil that important function of being pioneering plants, rapidly colonising new ground. Kanuka has recently been re-evaluated by taxonomists, who have formally recognised not one but an astonishing eight species of *Kunzea* on mainland New Zealand. Five of these may be found on the mainland coast. The west coast dunelands are home to the easily wind-sculptured *K. amathicola*, which has stubby, hairy leaves and may be flowering at any time of year, but also to *K. linearis*, which has fine linear leaves and summer-flowering. A weeping form with characteristically hairless branchlets, *K. ericoides* (mostly around northwest Nelson and Marlborough), is also summer-flowering. Tall-growing *K. robusta* is widespread and probably the species most nurseries sell; it flowers throughout the year. *Kunzea toelkenii* is the most unusual of this group, sprawling and suckering within dunes around the Bay of Plenty.

Both manuka and kanuka are naturally variable—and when a species is described as variable, the horticultural industry soon pounces; today there are at least 67 commercial clones and hybrids of manuka alone (mostly based on flower colour, with long flowering season a vital ingredient). The form of *Leptospermum scoparium* in Australia is slightly different and is being crossed (along with other Australian species) with the New Zealand forms for the commercial market. It is surprisingly difficult to buy the pure species commercially. The best source will be from nurseries supplying stock for revegetation programmes.

Both manuka and kanuka are tolerant of low-fertility soils, relying on mycorrhizal fungi to extract the most phosphorus possible, and this might explain why they are temperamental when planted out of nursery pots. Some nurseries provide a fungal selection within their potting mixes, so don't shake soil off the roots. Keep the root mass intact and, better still, visit a site where manuka and kanuka are growing naturally and grab a handful of soil to sprinkle over your own young plantings.

Another reason for failure might be sooty mould. The Australian sucking bug *Eriococcus* (which

TOP Manuka. BOTTOM Kanuka.

'Mean manuka'	'Kindly kanuka'
Leaves relatively broad and large (compared with kanuka) and with a pointed tip. Overall spiky feel and look to branchlets.	Leaves soft and fine, with an overall feathery appearance to branchlets.
Large white flowers borne singly in leaf axils.	Small white flowers borne in clusters at the growing tips.
Seed capsules brown, bulbous and relatively large.	Seed capsules grey, convex and small compared to manuka.
Grows to around 4 m and lives 40–50 years.	Most species grow to a taller 10 m or more and can live for 80–100 years.
Bark grey and flaky with an orange glow to the wood of trunk and branches.	Bark loose and flaky with grey tones to bark and trunk.
Grows in damp and waterlogged sites, dune-lake edges and alluvial flats, clay banks.	Grows in interdune hollows, dry-dune coastal forest, on silty soils.

spreads a blight) was introduced by the agricultural sector to weaken and kill what was deemed to be a nuisance weed—manuka. The insect lives under the bark, making it hard to combat, and the honeydew the insect excretes attracts the sooty mould (manuka blight). The worst-affected plants are generally cultivars rather than pure species and selections, although any plant grown beyond its normal range may suffer. Low-toxicity insecticides containing buprofezin or the fungal pathogen *Myrangium thwaitesi* may offer effective control of the insect.

Manuka is conditioned to cope with soils with low porosity—saturated soils or stiff clays in particular. Kanuka, on the other hand, prefers well-drained and oxygenated soils, so thrives on sandy and silty soils. It lives twice as long as manuka, and most kanuka species grow to almost twice manuka's height.

Manuka can be used as a nursery -crop to fast-track the establishment of canopy species that require shade to start life. Plant these out into a dense stand of manuka that is already several years old. Once broadleaf seedlings are established, the manuka can be thinned (otherwise the dense manuka will 'force' the other species to grow tall quickly) until the young broadleaf species overtop it and shade it out themselves. If you are growing manuka or kanuka from seed, sow when the seed is fresh as it loses viability rapidly.

Litsea calicaris, mangeao

This intensely coloured northern tree brings rare foliage colour to limestone- or lava-dominated forests. Preferring semi-shade, it is a fussy grower so is rarely found in commercial nurseries, but if you can beat gluttonous kereru to the meal-sized drupes, you could raise your own seedlings. Bees are drawn to the clusters of flowers in droves.

Lophomyrtus obcordata, rohutu

This is one of New Zealand's most beautiful trees. Suited to drought-prone, well-drained soils, such as old dunes and the fertile alluvial flats along riverbeds, this is one of our small forest trees that, like akeake,

TOP AND CENTRE Mangeao foliage and flowers. BOTTOM Rohutu fruits.

should be planted on bush edges or garden edges where its spreading 'oriental' form and weathered white bark can be shown off. You'll love the little leaves—they look like hearts. And touch the trunk—it feels cold. Perhaps, prosaically, this is due to its pale colour, but you can't help feeling this is one of the mystic charms of the tree. In summer, the tiny white flowers truly earn the descriptor 'blossom'.

TOP Mature poataniwha.
BOTTOM Poataniwha foliage.

Melicope simplex, poataniwha

This small tree reaches only 4–5 m tall and is common in old dune country as well as on more fertile soils. Its small, somewhat fleshy, oil-rich leaves can withstand coastal conditions and are distinctive, with their crenulated margin and the joint between the leaf and the long, flattened stem that attaches them to the twig. When it is able to mature beyond the bushy shrubby stage, it becomes a tree with intriguing character. Growth is stiff, making this small tree well suited to hedging.

Melicope ternata, wharangi

This small northern tree, 2–6 m tall, is one of our prettiest. The trifoliate leaves are lushly emerald green, slightly wavy and shining, and smell a little lemony when crushed. It was commonly used for ceremonial headdress by Maori, which may explain its distribution around the North Island, with concentrations found close to old settlement areas. It is spangled with glossy black seeds in summer. Wharangi is commonly found growing in the wild with kohekohe and hangehange, and teams up brilliantly with these species for colour, texture and freshness. In its natural habitat it requires shelter, a warm-temperate (frost-free) climate and rich soils that retain moisture.

Melicytus ramiflorus, mahoe, whiteywood

This is one of those trees that is underrated because of its ubiquitous, almost weed-like presence through New Zealand bush and regenerating

TOP Wharangi foliage. CENTRE AND BOTTOM Mahoe foliage, flowers and fruits.

scrub, yet its fast growth, white trunks, and bushy and readily prunable crowns make it a very useful garden backdrop. The flowers are heavily perfumed and are followed by purple fruits (which stain, so beware of planting mahoe above the washing line or parked cars). If the trunk is chopped, the tree coppices. Sometimes the foliage can get an algal infection, manifesting as unsightly blotches that start off orange and turn pale grey. This is probably caused by excessive humidity but can be controlled with copper sprays and rarely harms the tree.

TOP AND ABOVE Pukanui.

Meryta sinclairii, pukanui

The giant leaves of pukanui leave us in no doubt that this is a subtropical species and also that, even with the shine of a waxy coating, they will need protection from harsh conditions to stay in good shape. Many people ask too much of pukanui, planting it in very exposed sites. Although it is a plant for rocky coastlines, tuck it into the lee of the house, or into a protected corner where the salt-laden gales can't reach. It needs full sun but not full exposure. It can be a challenge to blend such a big, bold, brassy tree into a gardenscape, but if there is space, it can be teamed up to great effect with puka and kapuka, or kohekohe, karaka and kawakawa— plants with similarly shiny bravado and coloration.

Metrosideros excelsa, pohutukawa

In my childhood, to see pohutukawa flowering you headed 'up north' in the Christmas holidays, 'up north' being East Cape, the Coromandel Peninsula, Hauraki Gulf or Northland. And you associated the gnarly boughs and drifts of red stamens on the beach with jandals, hot sand and scrambles up headland bluffs. It made 'north' somewhere special. The sweet children's book *The Adventures of Hutu and Kawa*, written in 1955, reinforced the sense of pohutukawa being iconic and Kiwi.

Now, to be frank, with every public park and major coastal development around New Zealand lined with pohutukawa, and with their invasive spread into southern North Island

TOP Pohutukawa. ABOVE The cultivar *Metrosideros excelsa* 'Aurea'.

coastal gullies, I really don't mind if I never see another pohutukawa. Nonetheless, for those who still find them irresistible, here is some growing advice.

Pohutukawa need to be planted in full sun. They flower in December, but only for two weeks and flower abundance varies from year to year. They are a warmth-loving species

Judicious pruning can make smaller pohutukawa just as 'permeable' as these giants.

and it appears that the temperature in early winter determines whether buds set as flowers or as foliage—if it is a mild autumn, look forward to a glorious show at Christmas. You won't get good flowering if you prune pohutukawa heavily, such as for a hedge, unless you prune every second year to allow the growing tips to produce buds.

Pohutukawa are hungry and thirsty, and thus rarely grow in sandy situations naturally. You may well see pohutukawa along the edges of sandy bays, but chances are their roots are in solid ground and the dunes have been driven inland later to surround the trees. Young nursery plants set into sandy gardens may do quite well for one or two years, but once their internal food reserves are used up, they can falter if there is no ongoing supply of nutrient.

The young plants are frost-sensitive, which explains the natural distribution pattern of pohutukawa. The long stretch of frosty coastline south of Taranaki on the west coast or Hawke's Bay on the east coast has acted as a natural barrier to the species. The pockets of very old trees found in Golden Bay and the Marlborough Sounds were introduced by migrating Maori.

Roots utilise the uppermost soil layers and extend well beyond the dripline in search of sustenance. Beware of shallow roots seeking out weeping underground pipes and pushing paving or asphalt out of kilter. And avoid driving over root systems.

Let pohutukawa grow naturally into a large, spreading crown. Although they resprout readily from pruned branches and even cut stumps, this results in an unnatural, densely bushy tree and, when handled poorly, a downright ugly bush. The main advantage of allowing them to grow unfettered is that when you find you need more light or better views through the tree, judicious thinning is both easier and less detrimental to the overall crown shape. A see-through tree that frames rather than blocks the views will result. Don't be too concerned about the danger of falling branches in exposed situations; the timber of pohutukawa is among the strongest in the world and branches will bend under their own weight before they break. However, long splits in trunks or tight forks between competing branches may be sites for rot to set in and should be monitored.

For all its resilience to the forces of nature, this magnificent tree cannot compete with the greed of humans for coastal habitat. Farms and towns have squeezed it into an ever-diminishing coastal strip, possums are capable of killing mature trees, and 30-year-old humans are prone to killing 300-year-old pohutukawa simply to enhance the view of the beach from their lounge suite.

The Kermadec Island pohutukawa (*Metrosideros kermadecensis*) is becoming common in garden centres; this is a smaller-leaved species that can flower almost year-round. Its growth form is bushier and denser than the New Zealand pohutukawa and therefore may be less suited to good neighbourly relations.

The stunningly beautiful yellow-flowering pohutukawa is a clone originating from a sole tree found on Motuiti Island in the Bay of Plenty in 1940. It is known as *Metrosideros excelsa* 'Aurea' ('Moon Maiden').

Another popular selection is 'Maori Princess', which has a lovely dark flower. No one knows the origin of this selection as it derives from a tree planted in New Plymouth in the 1940s. It grows in a more conical shape than most and its upright form makes it well suited to hedging or street trees.

Some of the variation in flower colour we see in commercial plants is due to hybridisation between pohutukawa and either northern or southern rata (with dark red and late-flowering orangey-red flowers, respectively). This hybridising occurs in gardens also and may threaten the sustainability of pure species in the long term, especially now that pohutukawa is being planted in areas that are rata's natural habitat.

Myoporum laetum, ngaio

At 10 m and with a spreading crown, ngaio is one of the largest coastal trees and is widespread in the North Island, though less so in the South Island. It takes a very heavy frost to harm the adult, but take care that very young plants are protected from frost. The oil glands in the leaves help the tree resist salt-burn and insect attack. In fact, you could rub the leaves on your skin as an insect repellent.

Ngaio is easy to establish in most soils and is hardy enough to be grown in isolation. Its spreading, gnarly branches are readily pruned, trained and thinned, and generally accommodate being used 'architecturally' to fill spaces or wrap buildings in their encompassing branches. The corky bark attracts much insect life, although this may be detrimental as weakened branches may be hazardous during

Ngaio.

storms. Keep a constant eye out for disease in the limbs.

Be aware, if you are adjacent to farmland, that ngaio foliage is poisonous to stock.

Don't expect ngaio crowns to hold the compact, dense shape they have when young; the crowns will open with time. To counter this, some decades ago the landscape-design fraternity encouraged the use of Tasmanian ngaio, or boobialla (*M. insulare*), which has a smaller, more compact crown. We know now, too late, that it hybridises with our native ngaio and should not be used. You can tell them apart, even at the seedling stage, by looking at the leaf buds. Native ngaio has a distinctive sticky black growing tip; this is green in the Australian species. In addition, the oil glands are much more common and conspicuous in the thinner leaves of New Zealand ngaio. Hybrids are found around Auckland, Wellington and Kaikoura, in particular.

Myrsine australis, mapau, red matipo

Mapau is ubiquitous along our coast; whether in sandy or rocky habitats, it will be there in the scrub or forest edges, turning its wrinkly leathery leaves to the wind. Red stems and sometimes blotchy leaves impart interest to this tough character. It is a small tree, only 6 m tall, and not confined to the coast. Its wavy-edged leaves are very similar to those of akiraho (*Olearia paniculata*), but mapau is overall a greener, more colourful foliage tree. It is good for dry areas and can be planted in isolation.

Nestegis apetela, coastal maire

Wavy, shiny leaves with an attractive yellow midrib, rather like a cross between coprosma and lemonwood leaves, distinguish this small coastal canopy tree of Northland and Coromandel. It is drought-tolerant and very hardy but becoming scarce because rats just love those red-purple fruits. It is one of those trees easily confused with other species (privet and Canary Island olive, in particular). Plant it for bird food.

TOP Mapau. ABOVE Coastal maire.

TOP *Olearia angulata*. CENTRE *Olearia furfuracea*. BOTTOM *Olearia albida*.

Olearia spp., tree daisies

Terminal florets on these bushy-crowned small trees make for highly showy garden specimens. There are a large number of *Olearia* species in the country; listed here are the ones frequently found along our coastlines. There is a reasonably distinct geographical range for each species, from north to south: *O. angulata* on cliffs and old dune forest from North Cape to King Country; *O. albida* on cliffs from North Cape to Taranaki and East Cape; akepiro (*O. furfuracea*) from North Cape to Wairarapa; akiraho (*O. paniculata*) mostly in the east from East Cape to South Canterbury plus Golden Bay; *O. arborescens* at sea-level in the far south and on Stewart Island; and the two tree daisies on the Chatham Islands, *O. chathamica* and *O. traversiorum*.

It is not easy to tell some of these species apart. The mainland ones listed all have wavy-edged leaves with a white underside, angular grooved branchlets and florets of flowers. Perhaps the most helpful clue is the florets, ranging from relatively spare clusters on akiraho to dense heads smothering *Olearia albida* and akepiro (which has larger leaves than the others).

The *Olearia* trees are most at home in the single-tier coastal forests of very exposed bluffs and rocky shorelines, where wind is crucial to blowing their parachuting seeds around and where their multi-trunked forms are so resilient to stormy conditions. They will, however, also grow in the semi-shade of an open canopy such

ABOVE Kaikomako foliage and flowers.

as tall kanuka. Akiraho is particularly popular in gardens as it prunes easily and, since it comes from dry environments, is very resilient to new garden sites, but its flowering is not as spectacular as the other species.

Pennantia corymbosa, kaikomako

What an overlooked tree this is, and yet what a delight, especially as filiramulate (divaricate) juveniles with their webbed-feet leaves, or as adults in full bloom with perfumed flowers. Although not common in Northland, it grows throughout the rest of the country on fertile soils. It is noticeable on grazed coastal land, where it is often the only surviving tree and frequently smothered in white rata vine. It does, however, require shady sites to re-establish, so a mature garden could support the juveniles along a bush edge perhaps, or on the south side of the house.

Piper (=Macropiper) excelsum, kawakawa, pepper tree

Kawakawa is a shade-tolerant understorey tree in warmer parts of the country; being frost-tender, it rarely grows naturally south of Christchurch. It is often seen today exposed to the salt winds along the coast where the canopy species have been lost. It is surprisingly tenacious, even though the large, flimsy, heart-shaped leaves look vulnerable. They certainly are vulnerable to insect attack, and few are left unmolested

TOP **Kawakawa.** ABOVE *Piper excelsum* subsp. *peltatum*.

by the looper caterpillar of the kawakawa moth (*Cleora scriptaria*).

Kawakawa is reappearing as a food constituent for humans as well (in pepper mixes), as a herbal tonic (essential oil) and as a diuretic (the berries). It earns its name (kawa means bitter; kawakawa means very bitter) from the peppery leaves.

Kawakawa grows best in dappled shade and where it can receive year-round soil moisture (although avoid planting it in waterlogged soils). It responds well to pruning—cut just above one of the conspicuous nodes on the bamboo-like black stems. It teams up naturally with kohekohe, mahoe, wharangi and hangehange, both in looks and in shared natural habitat.

Piper melchior (Three Kings kawakawa) and *P. excelsum* subsp. *delangei* (de Lange's pepper tree) (3 m and 2 m, respectively) are grouped together by virtue of sharing a very select natural habit: the Three Kings Islands. They are both found in the coastal scrub here and make very attractive garden species on account of their deep green and highly glossy foliage, which doesn't seem as prone to insect attack as mainland kawakawa. They both have much larger flowerheads and fruit than the mainland species. Three Kings kawakawa has distinctive crinkling of the leaf (like a heavily stitched duvet) and is less peppery; perhaps this helps explain why it does get some insect attack, whereas the shiny leaves of de Lange's pepper tree (which is very peppery) is almost completely free of holes.

Piper excelsum subsp. *peltatum* is a subspecies from the northern offshore islands; it has wonderfully glossy leaves that are hole-free but lack the deep wrinkling of Three Kings kawakawa. It is grown commercially but often under the name of the Kermadec Island subspecies, *P. excelsum* subsp. *psittacorum*.

Like mainland kawakawa, plant these offshore island subspecies in dappled shade and moist, fertile, well-drained soils for best results.

Pisonia brunoniana, parapara, bird-catcher tree

Birds beware! This subtropical tree from northern New Zealand has you in its sights. A devious means for distributing seeds has been devised; the seed pods exude a sticky glue that traps birds, killing the small and weak, but ensuring the ones that get free take the seeds far and wide. This is a very handsome tree with vigorous, lush green foliage, and the seed pods themselves add interest.

Foliage of parapara.

Pittosporum cornifolium, tawhirikaro

This is such a strikingly handsome plant that it may be one that the cultivar enthusiasts leave alone. Usually epiphytic, either on trees or on rocks, in gardens it will happily grow in soil. Tawhirikaro does prefer moist climates and shelter (such as harbours or banks above estuaries). It does not grow large—perhaps it should be in the shrub section—but its close association with taller trees warrants it being thought of for bushy garden or restoration plantings.

Tawhirikaro.

Pittosporum crassifolium, karo

Karo has become a contentious plant in New Zealand. Its natural range is through Northland and as far south as northern Taranaki and Poverty Bay, and it has a preference for offshore-island habitats. Yet gardeners have spread it much further south and it has become invasive in regions such as Cook Strait. The shiny black fruits are readily spread by birds and rats. Its foliage makes it a perfect match

Karo.

for planting with pohutukawa and korokio, and it is tolerant of being pruned heavily. It is certainly the most salt-hardy pittosporum in the genus. It is difficult to ask for circumspection when thinking about planting karo beyond its natural range, but if you have ever seen the way it is infiltrating and then dominating natural plant associations on the Wairarapa and Wellington coasts, the reasons become clear.

Pittosporum tenuifolium, kohuhu

This is one of the pittosporums the horticultural industry has taken by the horns and from which it has produced myriad cultivars, nevertheless it is still hard to beat the pure species. This fast-growing, wrinkly-leaved plant is well adapted for dry-dune coastal forest conditions although it thrives best with some shelter (as when grown alongside other trees of similar height). It is pruneable, so lends itself to a range of garden situations, including hedging. Regular pruning is required to keep it low and bushy as, like any small tree (it readily grows to 4 m), it will want to form a trunk and grow upright. Although the flowers are insignificant visually, they are distinctively perfumed.

Pittosporum umbellatum, haekaro

Endemic to the Coromandel Peninsula and Northland, this attractive tree shares the spangles of perfumed red flowers of other pittosporums and thrives in shadier coastal forest.

Planchonella costata, tawapou

Northern New Zealand and its offshore islands host this coastal canopy tree, which is fairly unremarkable with the

Kohuhu foliage and flowers.

There is a natural hybrid between *Podocarpus totara* and *P. acutifolius* (from Westland), with pale foliage, that has been commercially cultivated as *P. totara* 'Aurea' or 'Golden Totara'.

Pseudopanax arboreus, five finger

While not specifically a coastal tree, five finger stands up to salt winds extremely well and can often be found on a rocky coastlines in moister sites. The berries are a hit with native birds. It does not naturally occur on the West Coast of the South Island or more southern regions, which is surprising for a plant that prefers moist habitats. The differences between five finger and coastal five finger (*Pseudopanax lessonii*) are that the former's leaves are 5–7-foliate and the leaflets have stalks; coastal five finger leaves are 3–5-foliate and are without stalks.

exception of its glossy, dark red seeds, collected by early Maori for decorative necklace beads. But it is a tough tree for rocky headlands, and in the wild it can be found with pohutukawa, karaka, kowhai, coastal maire and milk tree. The glossy leaves have slightly curled edges and venation that earn it the name '*costata*', meaning ribbed. If the tree has room to develop, you will see its fine structure of upright branching. Because it is drought-tolerant, it does make a hardy street tree, but note that it is frost-sensitive.

Podocarpus totara, totara

Because this is the only native podocarp that can cope with drought conditions, you will find totara near the coast on very old dunes and on the dry weathered-clay hillslopes, especially around estuaries. In both cases it will be far enough from strong salt winds that it will not suffer too badly from salt-burn (especially if offered further protection by surrounding bush), but do not overdo your optimism regarding its role in coastal environments—it does need shelter from salt.

It is one of the few conifers that can be established out in the open, making it very useful in restoration projects. It is tempting to create gardens using only the sprightly attractive juveniles, with the expectation of uprooting them as they grow too large for the site—but could you? They are going to grow into 30 m giants in the fullness of time, so be disciplined! If you need to prune totara, be sure to prune only fresh growth as woody branches will not resprout.

TOP LEFT Tawapou foliage. TOP RIGHT *Podocarpus totara* 'Aurea'. RIGHT Five finger.

TOP Lancewood. CENTRE Fierce lancewood.
BOTTOM Houpara.

Pseudopanax crassifolius, lancewood and Pseudopanax ferox, fierce lancewood

These two very similar species are so well known for their unusual juvenile form that surprisingly few people are familiar with their adult form. After 10–12 years, the downward-pointing spears start to bunch and become shorter and upright, and slowly a lollipop head takes shape. The mature tree maintains this incredible mop-head shape throughout its life, even as the crown expands to form a dark green canopy tree.

The fierce lancewood has knobbly juvenile leaves and a ropey trunk; the common lancewood is more circumspect with its decoration. Both trees are pioneering forest species that get started in life in 'light gaps', perhaps caused by windfalls or slips. This gives them all the attributes for the ideal garden plant—especially having such a compact juvenile stage—so it's no wonder their popularity is booming. The adults are extremely hardy, even in coastal sites.

Pseudopanax lessonii, houpara, coastal five finger

If wharangi is the pretty maiden of the coastal forest, houpara is the courtly lord. It often has trifoliate leaves like wharangi but is more commonly 5-foliate, and its leaves are stiff and dark, glossy green with toothed edges. This northern North Island species is a coastal forest tree so tolerates shade as well as sun, and its resilient leaves are wind- and salt-hardy. As with all northern species,

expect some frost tenderness (that's why they are northern). Birds are attracted to its prolific berries, which are a valuable food source in early winter when little else is available. This has its downside, as in parts of New Zealand where houpara has been planted beyond its natural range it can become an invasive weed.

Houpara has given rise to a number of named hybrids and cultivars (such as *P. adiantifolius*, *P. linearifolius*, *P.* 'Sabre', *P.* 'Cyril Watson'). As will happen, however, with species targeted by birds for their fruit, the hybrids are spreading far and wide, including into natural habitats, and since they are fertile seeds, a weird range of offspring is being introduced into the wild.

Rhopalostylis sapida, nikau

Nikau are the southernmost palm in the world. Fairly common in frost-free inland gullies through the North and upper South islands and Chatham Islands, they are found only near the coast in the most humid and mild of microclimates. Being monocotyledons (without the discrete growth ring directly inside the bark in dicotyledenous trees), they have a great ability to survive damage, so there are many areas in western New Zealand where they can still be seen standing alone long after their harbouring forest has been cleared. Too much wind, however, and their fronds look ragged and dry. Too frosty and they won't survive at all. They are forest trees, requiring a constant supply of soil moisture and rich humus. Occasionally they are

used in urban plantings, but only with irrigation systems and they never look their best in exposed conditions.

Nikau are incredibly slow-growing and require shade for their first few years, then a gentle introduction to more and more light to achieve full growth potential. In the wild, juveniles often cluster in a dense grove beneath the parents, and because they are such slow growers, this look translates perfectly into garden settings, with little change over many years.

Moving a nikau is a gamble; it is best to plant a small specimen and ensure it has a large root ball. You can expect the trees to do well for the first few months, but they are very likely to fail after a year or so without close attention. A common symptom of stress is mealy bug infestation, which can be dealt to with regular applications of summer oil or a systemic insecticide. But it is more logical to grow these beautiful palms only in the sheltered humid locations they are naturally suited to.

Sophora spp., kowhai

New Zealand has a wide range of kowhai and it takes experience to recognise the differences between them, but it is important that gardeners at least know which species is local to their area. It is also useful to know that the Chilean kowhai (*Sophora cassioides*) is common in gardens and often sold by nurseries as *S. microphylla* 'Goldilocks'. Avoid this tree as it hybridises with our endemic species.

Generally, kowhai are sensitive to frost when young (although in the wild they will usually germinate in the shelter of other trees anyway), becoming hardier with maturity.

Sophora chathamica is the most

TOP RIGHT AND CENTRE The classic form of the dark-branched *Sophora chathamica* and its blossom. BOTTOM RIGHT *Sophora molloyi* (right) and *S. prostrata*.

TOP Turepo. CENTRE AND BOTTOM Puriri.

common coastal tree kowhai in Northland, the Hauraki Gulf and Kawhia, thriving on dry clay banks and often seen ringing estuaries. It is also present near Wellington (was this due to Maori translocations?). It has truly yellow flowers and will be found both along sunny edges and in the shade of taller trees (usually totara). The tree has quite a strong form, with upright and spreading branches making it a good choice for a specimen tree.

Sophora fulvida is recognised by its long, fine foliage and is largely restricted to the wild west volcanic coastline of Northland. Neither *S. chathamica* nor *S. fulvida* has a divaricating juvenile form, but *S. microphylla* does. This species is widespread south of Northland, although absent from the very dry eastern coastlines. It is the tallest kowhai, often called weeping kowhai, so requires enough space to show off the mature tree's attractive form. You do have to be patient, however, as flowering does not begin until the plant is 6–10 years old.

Cook Strait has its own distinctive semi-prostrate form of kowhai, common in the grey scrub of rocky coastlines: *Sophora molloyi*. This smaller kowhai is very popular in gardens, even though it tends to hide its flowers inside the bushy mass of foliage.

So what of those dry eastern coastlines? Well, the tall kowhai found there will be *Sophora tetraptera*, which has far larger leaves than other species and also flowers later in spring. In contrast, there is also a prostrate form of kowhai, *S. prostrata*, which, although most common in the dry shingles of Marlborough and North Canterbury braided rivers, can also be found at the coast.

There are several other native kowhai species but they are mostly confined to inland locations. As a rule, coastal kowhai grow on thin clay soils, thriving on sparsely vegetated spurs that most other trees find too dry or infertile. Their natural companions in these places are kanuka, totara, mapau and mingimingi.

Kowhai are sometimes plagued by the kowhai caterpillar, which can strip foliage very effectively. The easiest way to manage this well-camouflaged nuisance is to shake the tree over a ground sheet and collect the caterpillars (they readily drop off as a natural defence mechanism).

Streblus banksii, turepo, milk tree

Although not strictly a coastal tree, this species belongs firmly in the nikau belt, where it grows in forest alongside kohekohe, mahoe, titoki, nikau and totara. It is a tree reminiscent of beech, with small serrated leaves, clearly veined when viewed against the sky. The dense crown is often spangled with strange growths called false watchmen (a fungal infection), which certainly does not detract from the tree nor does it appear to be detrimental to its growth. It really did live up to its common name in early colonial times when settlers who had not yet gained the luxury of a house cow were able to tap the milky sap of this tree instead.

Vitex lucens, puriri

This gorgeous tree is one of the most stately of coastal forest trees. Because its juveniles require warm, moist, fertile sites, it is found naturally only north of Kawhia and Opotiki, reigning supreme on the relatively humid, mild islands of the Hauraki Gulf. Often, now, it stands alone as some proud godfather still determinedly watching over the depleted hillslopes of developed land. It hides its ruby flowers and fruits like jewels among the crinkled folds of its gowns, but the kereru know where to come to find these almost-year-round pickings.

If your garden is northern, humid and fertile, and there is plenty of space, this is probably the one tree to plant for shade—and a glorious canopy.

SHRUBS

Brachyglottis compacta, Castlepoint daisy

This well-named compact shrub belongs in grey scrub habitat and yet is found only around Castlepoint on

the Wairarapa Coast. How strange it is that most of our 'gardenesque' shrubs are highly restricted in their natural range. This shrub generates an electrifying rhythm of its own, so intense is the texturing of its foliage. Good on clay, it also needs full sun.

Brachyglottis greyi

This is a shrub of the southern Wairarapa, where it thrives on tough rocky bluffs and steep hillslopes alongside other grey scrub species. It has long been used in gardens, where it needs full sun and can cope with wind. A regular pruning keeps it from getting lank if it is growing in more fertile soils than it is accustomed to.

Brachyglottis rotundifolia var. ambigua

This statuesque shrub grows only near Westport, but not surprisingly it has become available commercially. It grows within the dense coastal scrub and typifies the terminal flowering and wind-blown seed characteristics of that windy, salty zone where shrubland thrives but taller trees fail.

Carmichaelia appressa, prostrate broom

Although this endemic broom is restricted in the wild to the Kaitorete Spit in the South Island, it is available commercially as well. In the wild it grows on coarse sandy loam and old stabilised dunes amongst other prostrate shrubs and sand-binding plants.

LEFT Castlepoint daisy. RIGHT TOP AND CENTRE *Brachyglottis greyii*. BOTTOM RIGHT *Brachyglottis rotundifolia* var. *ambigua*.

Carmichaelia australis, makaka, whip broom

Of our native brooms, this is the one you are most likely to find within coastal scrub, and its range extends throughout New Zealand (except for the deep south). Although it would prefer to be out in the open, it is often found within an open forest canopy, persisting after being overtaken by taller growth. The flowers (blotched purple) are less memorable than the stunning seed pods, which disintegrate just enough to reveal startling orange seeds suspended within a frame, like an arty Alexander Calder mobile from the 1950s. One of the nitrogen-fixers, this plant needs no assistance nutritionally and is best suited to infertile sites.

Carmichaelia muritai, coastal tree broom

Coastal tree broom comes from coastal cliffs in Marlborough, where it grows tall—up to 6 m—and its weeping lower (and erect upper) branches become festooned with violet flowers in early summer. The bark of the tree is smooth, but there are raised rings at the nodes where it branches. It is one of the tree brooms that is leafless, but the deeply grooved branchlets are so numerous that they form a head of 'foliage' in their own right.

The species requires low humidity and well-drained soils, and will respond well to shelter and make a most unusual specimen tree.

LEFT TOP Prostrate broom.
LEFT CENTRE AND BOTTOM Makaka.

Carmichaelia williamsii, giant-flowered broom

This glamorous broom comes from coastal areas in the Bay of Plenty and East Cape, including the offshore islands. Sadly, it now warrants Nationally Endangered status in the wild, where it grows on cliff faces and slopes among shrubs and low coastal forest. It grows to 3–4 m. All our other broom species have violet or purple flowers, but this one has buttery-cream blooms—and in winter! Its flattened branchlets are wider than those of most brooms. Because it naturally has a short lifespan, a

TOP Coastal tree broom. ABOVE Giant-flowered broom.

248

good tip is to keep propagating from cuttings to ensure an ongoing supply. It grows best in warm climates and free-draining soils, although (given its natural distribution) it is interesting that it does endure frosts. Either full or partial sun is tolerated. It is a most versatile garden plant and can be kept low in stature by pruning.

Coprosma spp.

Coprosma has been an enormously successful genus in New Zealand, with species suited to every environment this diverse country can offer. In the coastal environment there are coprosmas suited to rocky foreshores, dry foredunes, wet swamps and coastal dune forest. Some grow to small tree stature while others sprawl along the ground.

One thing they all have in common is long hairless roots. Alas, they are also loved by rabbits. If you are wanting to undertake a major planting of coprosmas, you simply

Sand coprosma.

must control rabbits first, or protect young plants with plastic or mesh sleeves (repellent sprays rarely last long enough to be effective).

Coprosma acerosa, sand coprosma

This is one of the most important dune plants in New Zealand, establishing on the lee side of foredunes and forming large mats that capture moving sand and assist in stabilising dunes. The rusty-golden glow of sand coprosma across undisturbed wild dunes is one of the memorable sights of coastal New Zealand. It usually grows densely (which supplies lizards with great habitat as well as blue fruit to eat, and ensures the plant sustains itself with a cool root-run and ready supply of organic litter). If buried by drifting sand, it will continue to spread and seek the sunlight.

Curiously, growth is erratic in gardens, and plants from nurseries in particular may not take. It may be that either the potting mix or the receiving soil is too rich. Plants raised from seed in coarse sand and transplanted into sandy gardens (with no potting mixes or compost involved) should do well.

Recent research suggests that *Coprosma acerosa* is a complex that has derived from six lineages, which explains why its form varies slightly around the country. Horticulturalists have taken advantage of some of the most vibrant variations. *Coprosma* 'Red Rocks' and *C.* 'Hawera' are examples of quite localised forms that have been commercialised (they are selections, rather than hybrids or

Coprosma 'Taiko'.

mutations). The selections all vary in colour slightly.

Coprosma 'Hawera', from the clay soils of Taranaki's coastal cliffs, has proven to be a very hardy ground-cover with olive-green foliage and creates a luxuriant undulating mat, while close up the foliage looks somewhat frenzied, giving the plant interesting texture. In contrast, *C.* 'Red Rocks' and its close variant *C.* 'Orange Roughy' are selections that capture the intensity of the stressed wild plants of dunelands. Even the stems are yellow to reddish.

Coprosma 'Taiko' has been a constant garden companion for many years. Its origins are the variation of *C. propinqua* that is found on the Chatham Islands, called *C. propinqua* var. *martinii*, and it is named after a rare petrel that presumably would have fertilised the ground for it. This coprosma has shiny green foliage and sprawls in an undulating fashion with stems stiff enough to cope with wind on garden walls or rooftop gardens. There is a tall-growing form of *C. propinqua* var. *martinii*, but this is rarely grown commercially.

249

Coprosma areolata, thin-leaved coprosma

This tall shrub must rate as one of the most romantic of the coastal forest understorey plants, utterly charming with light playing through the pale, translucent leaves. It could superficially be confused with swamp coprosma but their habitats are completely different, and thin-leaved coprosma has a distinctive 'oriental' layering to its dark branches, which adds to its appeal. It grows throughout the country and, although not confined to them, certainly is an important component of coastal forests and will grow well in garden situations.

Coprosma crassifolia

On the coast, this coprosma is restricted to dry-dune forest, of which there is an incredible scarcity now. At first glance it is an unmemorable plant that doesn't look tolerant of harsh coastal conditions, but its secret weapon is a pale felted underleaf that helps prevent water loss in the wind. It makes a very pretty partner for korokio, or for taller dry-dune forest species such as kowhai, kohuhu, kanuka and rohutu.

Coprosma propinqua

It is curious that for such a widespread shrub, found in almost every environment except dry dunes, this species has never had a common name that has stuck. It is sometimes referred to as mingimingi

LEFT TOP Thin-leaved coprosma.
LEFT CENTRE AND BOTTOM *Coprosma crassifolia*.

(meaning small-leaved) but then so are several other shrubs. *Coprosma propinqua*'s elongated leaves have two conspicuous swollen 'holes' (domatia) on their underside, which helps to distinguish the plant. In the shade the leaves are slightly larger and less dense, but if they are longer

TOP The hybrid between *Coprosma propinqua* and *C. robusta*. BOTTOM Swamp coprosma.

than about 20 mm it is likely the plant is a hybrid between *C. propinqua* and *C. robusta* (see photograph left; this hybrid is very common in the wild). The shrub can be pruned hard, even topiaried, with the interlacing branchlets giving the shrub its 'bounce'.

Coprosma tenuicaulis, swamp coprosma

In terms of coastal habitats, this coprosma is very specifically associated with dune swamps. The leaves distinguish it from the group of interlaced, small-leaved coprosma shrubs: they are heavily veined, often with a pale blotch on each leaf, and the leaf stems are winged.

Corokia cotoneaster, korokio, wire-netting bush

Korokio puts other filiramulate (divaricating) shrubs to shame with its cheery yellow flowers, which smother the bush in summer. The follow-up act is the display of red berries that attract any number of small birds—the ones that can penetrate the tangled branches, that is. This is the quintessential arid-landscape shrub that is one of the survivors, still found in the few remaining duneland forest remnants.

Its equivalent on the Chatham Islands is a larger-leaved cousin, *Corokia macrocarpa* (which also has larger yellow fruits). The third *Corokia* in New Zealand is *C. buddleioides*, which has larger leaves again and black fruit but isn't a coastal species. The combination of these three species has resulted in

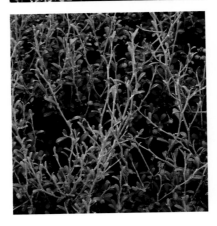

TOP Korokio flowering. CENTRE Korokio fruiting. ABOVE One of the popular hedging cultivars of *Corokia*.

a frenzy of commercial hybridising (triggered by 'natural' hybridising that occurred when these far-flung species were first brought together in cultivation).

It is unclear what the parents of *Corokia* 'cheesemanii' or *Corokia* × *virgata* were—most probably *C. cotoneaster* and *C. buddleioides*—but both are common in plant shops, their upright form making them popular for hedging.

Both of these hybrids and the other species have spawned a range of selections and further crosses for ornamental purposes, and plants are often mislabelled in shops. To recognise the true *Corokia cotoneaster*, look for small leaves, sometimes heart-shaped, with a dark coloration at the stem, and distinctive zigzagging of the branchlets.

Discaria toumatou, matagouri

Generally regarded as the bane of sheep farmers of the South Island high country, matagouri was once also common in the coastal grey

Matagouri.

251

scrub and stable dunes of the North Island. Thorny though it may be, it seems it was either browsed out or the habitat was modified so much it could no longer survive. It is hard to imagine such a ferocious plant becoming a garden favourite, but some folk like to nuture the plant that legends are made of.

Dracophyllum filifolium, inaka

Able to withstand the whistling of gales, inaka can therefore become a sculptural element in the exposed coastal garden. Most inaka are high-altitude plants, but towards the southern extent of the species' range, these shrubs will grow down to sea-level.

Leptecophylla (=Cyathodes) juniperina, prickly mingimingi
Leucopogon fasciculatus, tall mingimingi

Lumped together collectively under the title mingimingi, these two species are incredibly similar, not only to each other but also to young kanuka and manuka. They are rarely, if ever, sold commercially because they are not commercially feasible (slow-growing when young, and few gardeners are familiar with their merits), but are such a staple in the New Zealand landscape that the home gardener should be encouraged to 'give it a go' from seed. Happiest in the semi-shade of bush edges but tolerant of full sun, completely undemanding of soil fertility, and producing a star-studded show of berries, these are versatile and hardy shrubs that are worth the wait.

Melicytus crassifolius and *Melicytus obovatus*

Of these two similar rocky-coast shrubs, *Melicytus obovatus* has a greener appearance, with voluminous little leathery leaves notched at their tips and 'regular'-looking branchlets. *Melicytus crassifolius,* on the other hand, has very sturdy, thick branchlets, a lower stature overall and smaller leaves; the name '*crassifolius*' means thick-leaved. It looks like the tougher cousin and thrives in pretty tough locations, like the

rocky foreshore, shingle or boulder beds. It is commonly called thick-leaved mahoe, but in some ways that distracts from its main feature, the divaricating branchlets. There is something about the plump, motley-coloured berries of these shrubs that is reminiscent of birds' eggs.

Melicytus novae-zelandiae

This compact shrub clings to bluffs on islands through Northland and the Coromandel Peninsula. Like its relatives, the key attraction is the fruiting phase, so it is good to locate it where it will stand out from the crowd, perhaps against a backdrop wall or amid shorter plants.

Muehlenbeckia astonii, shrubby tororaro

A rare presence gracing the grey scrub of Cook Strait and Canterbury, this dense, interlaced shrub is known for its heart-shaped little leaves

Melicytus novae-zelandiae.

Shrubby tororaro divaricating branchlets (TOP), and foliage and fruits (BOTTOM).

and profuse fruiting (on the female plants). Its preferred habitat—scree and shingle—tells us that it likes well-drained, slightly fertile, sunny sites, so make sure it has those conditions in the garden. It will readily grow to 2 m tall and can be pruned to be as dense or as lacy as desired. Translucent fruits with black seeds barely clinging to the fruit are a delight, but you do need an intimate space in which to

appreciate these tiny jewels. Birds, geckos and cleverly camouflaged stick insects are attracted to these shrubs.

Myoporum laetum var. decumbens, prostrate ngaio

This prostrate form of ngaio, from Northland, is now considered part of the *Myoporum laetum* complex, but in shops you will still see the *M. decumbens* label. It can sprawl to cover 2–4 m without getting much beyond waist height and is a very useful hardy garden ground-cover. Like ngaio, it too is frost-tender when very young but then copes well as an adult.

Olearia solandri, coastal shrub daisy

Often confused with tauhinu, this vigorous shrub can be distinguished by its orange stems and very fluffy seedheads. It shows up in both wet and dry habitats, making it a versatile garden addition. It is primarily a plant of rocky shorelines but may be found around swampy edges of dune lakes and in dune swales.

Prostrate ngaio.

Coastal shrub daisy foliage and seedheads.

Ozothamnus leptophyllus, tauhinu

This 'grey' shrub likes open, thin-soiled sites but also enjoys a modicum of fertility, so you often see it colonising fresh slips or bare clay soils. Less commonly it may be found on the lee of infertile dunes. If pruned hard, it stays bushy. If left unpruned, it will grow rangy and the lowermost branches will die off (although these are easily removed for a tidier garden).

Pimelea spp.,
New Zealand daphne

Daphnes are easily confused with hebes when they are not in flower as both have pairs of leaves neatly arranged at right angles along the stems. There the similarities end, as the daphne flowers, which are white, are located at the ends of the stems in clusters of only 4–7. Leaves of the coastal daphnes are softly hairy and have a silvery-grey cast.

There seems to be a habitat distinction between the pimeleas into shingle, rock and sand substrates. This is one of those intrinsically variable genera that keeps taxonomic botanists employed, so it is safest to say that, 'at the time of writing', this is how the coastal species are distinguished:

Pimelea aridula is a threatened Cook Strait species of gravelly sites, which really shows off the quintessential *Pimelea* characteristics of silvery foliage and robust sprawling growth form.

Pimelea longifolia and *Pimelea gnidia* are very pretty, tall, long-leaved pimeleas found through much of New Zealand's rocky coast. *Pimelea longifolia* (illustrated) occurs as far south as Punakaiki, at which stage the very similar, tall *P. gnidia* takes over its role along the coast. They can usually be found tucked into bush edges, perhaps growing on shaded banks around estuaries.

Pinatoro (*Pimelea prostrata*) or Strathmore weed is a creeping, ground-hugging daphne that inhabits fine gravels and coarse sand flats along shingle or rocky beaches. As a garden plant, it seems to be difficult to grow from cuttings and, once in the ground, prefers not to be disturbed.

Pimelea tomentosa is the largest daphne you are likely to find on the coast in the North Island and top of the South Island, especially along coastal cliff-tops. It can grow to 1 m tall and has leaves 25 mm long, although still with the characteristic silky hairs. It is frost-hardy and drought-hardy, and is conspicuous for flowering throughout the year and also for bearing large black fruits. It does well in infertile soils.

Pimelea urvilleana has a handsome presence on the baked clays of Northland, with a compact yet prostrate form.

Sand daphne (*Pimelea villosa*) is a threatened plant in most parts of its distribution, now partly because its dune habitat has been so thoroughly degraded and partly because it has been one of the more palatable herbs

TOP *Pimelea aridula*. ABOVE *Pimelea longifolia*.

CLOCKWISE FROM TOP LEFT *Pimelea prostrata; P. urvilleana; P. villosa; P. tomentosa.*

for browsing stock along the coast. It is one of the first herbs to colonise among the grasses and sedges on the landward side of foredunes and will sprawl through even quite dense dune vegetation.

There are two dominant varieties of *Pimelea villosa*: a northern form that is quite upright and bushy (growing to 50 cm tall), and is the favourite commercial form; and a southern form that is more modest in its size and stature but just as charming. Other wild variants have very localised occurrences, such as *Pimelea* 'Turakina' from the Wanganui cliffs. Both in the wild and in gardens, it forms a stunningly beautiful partnership with the equally silvery spinifex grass.

Southern sand daphne (*Pimelea lyallii*) is the only pimelea to cope with active dunes and is found in the Catlins, Foveaux Strait and on Stewart Island. Perhaps in such harsh climates it is a matter of necessity being the mother of invention! It has slightly longer leaves than pinatoro but most of us would find it hard to distinguish between the two.

Veronica (= Hebe)

There is a broad complex of plants loosely known as *Hebe*, including the genera *Parahebe*, *Chionohebe* and *Heliohebe*, which has permeated every corner of New Zealand's landscape. *Hebe* and its allies evolved from the northern hemisphere *Veronica* complex, and in 2007 botanists undertook a radical renaming of the entire complex in New Zealand to *Veronica*.

For those of us who gained some relief from having different genus names for plants that clearly looked quite different (such as the *Parahebe* species compared to *Hebe* species), this may seem a loss of information, however it more clearly represents the origins of the plants. Hebe as a name will still be around for some time to come as a common descriptor, and it is bound to be retained by the suppliers of industry cultivars.

This is our largest genus, with 120 native and 17 naturalised species. In addition, there are 800 recognised, named cultivars (past and present), reflecting the ease with which hebes hybridise. The 'Wiri' series of cultivars developed by Jack Hobbs since the 1980s continues to dominate the commercial marketplace.

Even with so many species and such diversity, few hebes are adapted to coastal living. They are rarely found in sandy situations; most are best suited to rocky environments where their root systems can seek out moisture from cracks and fissures. Although all hebes require good drainage, they require regular drinks as well and can suffer from fungal

255

infections if stressed. They are all intolerant of shade, preferring full sun.

Veronica chathamica

This ground-hugging hebe is smothered in stubby little pale flowers in summer, resembling a kleptomaniac's collection of thimbles. Although in the wild it grows in fine shingles or scree, it adapts itself well to growing in sand gardens, helping to stabilise blowing sand.

New Zealand lilac.

TOP *Veronica chathamica*. ABOVE Shore hebe.

Veronica elliptica, shore hebe

The only remaining populations of this tough coastal hebe are widely separated: on offshore islands including Stewart Island/Rakiura, near Cook Strait, in Taranaki and along the west coast of the South Island. This resilient shrub has fleshy leaves and is mostly found on open rocky sites or rock with a veneer of wind-blown sand. When able to flourish, it has a compact form, with large, pretty white flowers (for a hebe) and a subtle milkiness to the leaf colour that makes it most attractive.

Veronica (=Heliohebe) hulkeana, New Zealand lilac

Highly attractive sprays of lavender-coloured spring flowers make this plant a stand-out choice for gardens. In the wild it is not confined to the coast (it is found on dry banks throughout Marlborough and North Canterbury) but it has the attributes required for coastal sites. It does not cope with frost but is tolerant of drought. To keep the plant thriving, put it in a well-ventilated location in full sun and prune it back after flowering (or simply pinch out the growing tips) to avoid it turning quite woody and straggly in the long term. It can grow to 1 m.

Veronica macrocarpa var. macrocarpa, coastal koromiko

This large-leaved hebe, common along bush edges around the Auckland area, has large upright flowers, tinged slightly mauve.

Veronica obtusata

Strictly coastal, this hebe is found naturally only on the western coasts near Auckland and Kawhia. However, it is widely grown commercially as its low stature and sprawling growth make it ideal for exposed borders and rockeries.

Veronica salicifolia

Through the South Island and Stewart Island/Rakiura this is the large-leaved hebe most commonly found at the coast. It is very similar to *Veronica stricta* and *V. macrocarpa*, and completes the geographic spread of this group of tall hebes.

Veronica speciosa, napuka

Napuka is of particular interest to us. It formed one of the parents of the first commercial hybrid, in 1845. But long before that it was enjoyed by Maori gardeners for its robust habit and spectacular magenta flowering. It came as a great surprise in 2002, with the benefit of DNA investigatory techniques, to discover that all the supposedly naturally occurring populations of this coastal hebe south of Auckland were probably clones. Only the small Northland populations at Hokianga, Maunganui Bluff and Muriwai are 'natural', and the plant is listed as a threatened species. The outliers have low genetic diversity and are, therefore, very susceptible to inbreeding problems. Whether it was transferred around the coast by Maori gardeners for aesthetic or food purposes is not known, but DNA analysis has shown that the Marlborough Sounds population came from the Hokianga originally—a distance of more

Coastal koromiko.

than 630 km. Another northern plant those early Maori travellers brought with them was pohutukawa, which can still be found in isolated populations in the Marlborough Sounds today.

To distinguish napuka from various cultivars (often sold under the species name), look for a finely hairy pinky-red margin to its leaves and strictly magenta flowers.

Napuka is a sprawling shrub that likes to layer rather than grow erect, and will reach several metres in width and height. It is naturally occurring on coastal cliffs and headlands, needing good drainage and sunny locations. It is ideal for larger coastal gardens, although be careful that the ground it goes into has not been excavated down to impermeable subsoil or rock.

Veronica stricta var. atkinsonii

This tall hebe is a common component of coastal forest in open rocky sites on both sides of Cook Strait. Elsewhere you are likely to

TOP LEFT *Veronica salicifolia.* TOP RIGHT Napuka. ABOVE *Acaena microphylla.*

come across *Veronica stricta* or, in the South Island, *Veronica salicifolia*, in the less dense coastal forest of rocky coasts, although they are certainly not confined to coastal localities.

HERBS

Acaena microphylla

This bidibid grows sporadically throughout New Zealand, but in the deep south it has a preference for coastal sites. Red flowers make it a stunning ground-cover choice for damper gardens.

257

Acaena pallida, sand piripiri

It may give the impression of being 'tough as old boots', thanks to its shiny leathery, foliage and belligerent seedheads, but sand piripiri is no longer as widespread as it would have been before browsing mammals came along. It is more reliable in a garden and especially attractive when the seedheads can be silhouetted in front of a plain background.

Aciphylla dieffenbachii, soft speargrass

This attractive herb grows in damp, shaded rocky locations on the Chatham Islands. The naturalist and medical practitioner Ernst Dieffenbach visited the Chatham Islands during his two years in New Zealand working for the New Zealand Company as they were setting up the new colony in 1840. In the same way that the soft-leaved species does not fit the *Aciphylla* mould of harshly spiky 'spaniards', Ernst himself was something of an anomaly within the New Zealand Company: he was an outspoken critic of many of their colonial practices.

Aciphylla squarrosa, taramea

One of the interesting features of vegetation in Cook Strait is how many coastal genera are also found in montane environments. Taramea is one such plant, and as long as its deep taproot can find a crevice for secure foundation, it seems to cope very well with the salty winds. This is certainly a plant to treat with caution in the garden as it will spear dogs and small children—and perhaps the odd burglar—indiscriminately. Weeding is undertaken at the operator's risk. Think about this in advance and combine it with dense ground-covering herbs that will help to suppress weeds.

Apium prostratum, celery

Our native celery is readily confused with the garden celery gone feral, however there is no reason why we shouldn't replace exotic with native in our diets as the foliage shares the distinctive tangy taste. The native celery is a less vigorous plant and certainly easier to contain.

Celmisia lindsayi, Lindsay's daisy

From the deep south we find an unusual occurrence of celmisia at the coast (the only other strictly coastal celmisias being *Celmisia major* var. *major* around Auckland, Great Barrier and Coromandel islands, and *C. adamsii* var. *rugulosa* around Whangarei Heads from Northland's offshore islands, although there are

LEFT TOP TO BOTTOM Sand piripiri; soft speargrass; taramea.

Celery.

several celmisia species in Fiordland that extend their range down to sea-level). This daisy is very specific in its environmental preferences, being adapted to constantly moist soils in shady locations. Although naturally uncommon in the wild, it propagates readily from seed and provides a distinctive local character to the rocky coast of the Catlins area.

Cotula coronopifolia, bachelor's button

Got a damp, sunny spot that needs cheering up? Bachelor's button has a long flowering season and is synonymous with damp sand flats, estuarine edges, flooding stream flats and roadside ditches.

Craspedia uniflora var. maritima

Strangely, this herb of coastal rock crevices is found both around Cook Strait and way down in Southland. Its perfectly adapted woolly leaves hug the rock, resistant to wind and sun, and it is just the yellow pincushion flowerheads that pop up and face the elements 'head on'. This is an

Lindsay's daisy.

irresistible rock-garden plant that can cope with very salty conditions.

Disphyma australe, New Zealand iceplant

Why people continue to plant South African iceplant when New Zealand has its own native variety is hard to fathom, and sadly the imports are invasive along our shores. This plant is a delight, studded with small pink flowers and with the ability to brave the fiercest salt-spray conditions. It is less common in sand but thrives in full sun on shingles, rock crevices and clay banks.

Eryngium vesiculosum, sea holly

Easy to miss as you wander across pebbly or coarse sandy beaches and shingle bars, but certainly spectacular once your antennae have tuned into it, sea holly is one of the treasures of the coast. It is found mostly on east coast shores and through Cook Strait, and is slowly but surely disappearing altogether, so don't be tempted to remove it from the wild. Being crushed by off-road vehicles is probably its greatest threat.

The rosette plant has the odd distinction of changing its leaf form from a summertime broad and very prickly leaf to an insignificant strap-like leaf in winter. Some of the other *Eryngium* species around the world do the same thing. Strap-like leaves are often an adaptation to inundation by water, and certainly sea holly's

RIGHT TOP TO BOTTOM Bachelor's button; *Craspedia uniflora* var. *maritima*; New Zealand iceplant; sea holly.

259

TOP Shore spurge. CENTRE *Geranium traversii*. BOTTOM The cultivar of *Geranium sessiflorum* (right) has smaller leaves than the cultivar of *G. traversii* (left).

preferred habitat does seem to be close to the edge of water that might flood the plants during winter.

Euphorbia glauca, shore spurge, waiu-atua

Many countries have euphorbias but this is New Zealand's only one, and it is now a threatened species on account of its palatability. Euphorbias have a milky sap that irritates human skin but clearly doesn't affect browsing rabbits, cattle, sheep, pigs and possums. Unlike other euphobias this coastal species has curious red cups arranged around the flowers.

Shore spurge grows in a range of habitats but all have some fertility, such as seaweed-enriched strand lines at the top of shingle beaches in among the driftwood, or in dunes where wind-blown leaf litter and foam have accumulated. It responds very well to garden soils, growing to 800 mm and spreading aggressively by creeping root suckers. You'll be surprised how vigorously it spreads through sandy or stony soils, but it is the root activity that allows this otherwise unlikely beachfront herb to withstand all the action. It was once prolific but is proving difficult to reintroduce to the New Zealand coast because rabbits target it, so garden growth may be the best insurance policy the species has.

Geranium sessiliflorum var. *arenarium* and *Geranium traversii*

Both these geraniums are primarily sand-dwellers, nestling into stable, sheltered places or peaty build-ups in swales, but *Geranium traversii* from the Chatham Islands seems adaptable to rocky environments as well. This has encouraged the horticultural industry to take it on board and many gardeners now have variants of the species or available hybrids, especially ones that exploit the slight purple tinge the leaves sometimes get. Certainly the combination of purple leaves and pink flowers makes it an attractive rock-garden specimen. The plant's preferred sand habitat is a clue that they need good drainage and they adapt well to being pot plants.

Lepidium oleraceum, Cook's scurvy grass

Fame precedes this bushy coastal herb. One of the cress family members, it first attracted scurvy-prone sailors, then introduced browsing animals, then chewing caterpillars, until now it has been eaten almost to extinction in the wild. It is a cheerful addition to the garden—and good in salads.

Linum monogynum, New Zealand linen, rauhuia

New Zealand linen is found throughout the country on rocky coastlines, hugging the cliffs and often inconspicuous until it flowers. The fragility of the flowers seems at odds with these harsh habitats. The form of this plant varies considerably around the country, in some places with sparse, limp foliage and stems, in other places a compact plant, so local seed sourcing is desirable. Plants like this benefit from bulking up in the garden, or at least standing them proud above low-lying ground-

Cook's scurvy grass.

cover. Alternatively, plant them into retaining walls or crevices in rock walls so that we can admire their attributes free from competition.

Lobelia anceps, shore lobelia

One of our 'weedy'-looking coastal herbs, shore lobelia has small lopsided flowers gracing the lank stems. It finds a foothold in rock crevices but does prefer the damper, shadier sites such as seepages at the base of cliffs,

so keep that in mind in the garden and avoid using it where rocks heat up in the sun. Gardeners may be more familiar with *Lobelia (=Pratia) angulata*, a more compact ground-cover, which shares the lopsided white flowers of shore lobelia.

Myosotidium hortensia, Chatham Island forget-me-not

Not only is this glamorous megaherb an iconic species in New Zealand gardens, it also stands apart botanically as being the only species in its genus. The forget-me-not-style flowerheads appear from the second year of growth in late spring, and vary from light to dark blue in colour (a white-flowering cultivar is also available.)

In the wild (which is indeed wild, with the Chatham Islands experiencing on average 225 days of rain each year, temperatures rarely warmer than 18° C, and strong winds), it grows where in the past, at least, the soils were generously enriched by roosting coastal birds. Keep this

requirement for high moisture and high fertility in mind when locating plants, and avoid frosty spots. The type of nutrition is important; one notable public garden sickened their forget-me-nots by overdosing with alkaline mushroom compost. Subsequently, more neutral compost turned out to be productive. The plants are most common on rocky bluffs or dunes enriched with organic material, so they clearly prefer good drainage; however, they will not tolerate drought. They propagate readily from freshly sown seed in moistened soil. The largest of the wrinkled glossy leaves die back over winter.

TOP Shore lobelia. ABOVE Chatham Island forget-me-not. LEFT New Zealand linen.

261

TOP TO BOTTOM *Pachystegia insignis*; peperomia; sand buttercup; *Raoulia hookeri*.

Pachystegia spp., Marlborough rock daisy

There are three formally recognised species of Marlborough rock daisy: *Pachystegia insignis*, *P. minor* and *P. rufa* (named for its distinctive reddish hairiness; although a threatened species, it is common in cultivation). Two more variants are possibly worthy of species status but currently are known only as *Pachystegia* 'A' and 'B'.

They all excel at living on impossibly steep rocky bluffs, especially on inland riverbanks, but out at the coast it is likely to be *Pachystegia minor* you see clinging to exposed faces. *Pachystegia insignis* is a favourite for gardens as it has the largest flowers of all the rock daisies. *Pachystegia minor* has less abundant flowers and they are slightly smaller, but it is no less attractive.

Pachystegia rufa has extremely limited distribution in the wild but has also become popular as a garden plant. All the rock daisies must have free drainage and preferably a sunny location. They are temperamental to strike cuttings from: growing from seed is recommended.

Peperomia urvilleana, peperomia

This is one of our succulents, and a stunning little plant by virtue of its fresh, glossy green leaves looking pert and enthusiastic even in the most unpromising of rocky locations. Upright flower spires are most decorative even though only pale green. It is quite a shrubby herb and seems to grow in shade as well as sun, which makes it well suited to its natural rock stack habitat. Being a succulent, it can handle life in a pot. Its juicy leaves, however, need to be kept away from frost, but it prefers warm climates anyway and in the South Island is found only at the northernmost tips. It grows easily from cuttings and rooted slips, as well as from seed.

Ranunculus acaulis, sand buttercup

No other buttercup has such plump, succulent leaves that glint in the sunlight. The plant occurs not just in New Zealand but also Australia, Chile and the Falkland Islands. In autumn the leaf colours seem to intensify, and it has a very long flowering season, during which time the mats are further spangled with tiny yellow flowers. Sand buttercup is well suited to life as a somewhat curious pot plant but it does prefer damp ground, so do not neglect the pots.

Raoulia hookeri

Although raoulias have widely spreading root systems naturally, they also make fine pot plants. Keep the substrate gritty or shingly as it is for them in the wild. They do not require fertiliser. In open ground they are sun-demanding and grow like ever-expanding polka dots. They blend happily with other creeping ground-covers, or keep them isolated like some remarkable giant patch of lichen.

Samolus repens, shore primrose

Samolus and *Selliera* are quite similar coastal herbs with small fleshy (succulent) leaves and white flowers. Those of *Samolus* are entire, whereas *Selliera* is known as half-star for good reason. Shore primrose is a versatile herb, shown here growing on hard clay, illustrating how it would be useful as a ground-cover on tricky sites. We tend to overlook small sprawling herbs as an option for ground-cover, but these succulent herbs are often the best solution. Shore primrose will also nestle into damp rocky sites and will be found around the edges of saltmarsh.

Sarcocornia quinqueflora, glasswort

This is the least likely plant to appear in a gardening book, as we usually see the succulent right in the splash zone, along rocky shores and quiet estuaries. Yet there is no reason why it shouldn't fill a nook or cranny in a salt-laden garden. The more stressed it is by full sun and salt air, the brighter the red tinges on its stems become.

Glasswort.

Selliera radicans, remuremu, half-star

Widespread around New Zealand (and other countries), you'll see this creeping mat herb in the sandy-silt and mud deposits of estuaries and coastal streams, forming lush green blankets of elongate but upright, paddle-shaped leaves. Its succulence allows it to survive in the splash zone of rocky shores as well. The density of the lopsided, crisply white flowers, sparkling like stars, can be stunning. It is widely available in nurseries and can be used for a robust ground-cover in sun or light shade. Although the flowers have a scent, you'd need to grow it in plant pots, surely, to be able to appreciate this! Ensure regular watering and don't overfeed it.

Selliera rotundifolia

Occasionally you may come across a damp sand flat so densely populated with *Selliera rotundifolia* it's as if a confetti-throwing bridal party has been through. The mat-forming herb, with its puffy little succulent leaves and distinctive lopsided flowers, grows in the damp dune hollows and sand flats of the Manawatu–Kapiti dunefields. For a long time it was considered merely to be a different form of the common *S. radicans* but better adapted to saline sand. It loves full sun and will make a great pot plant, although it must be kept damp. Every time an all-terrain vehicle passes across a sand flat, the future prospects for this little herb shrink a bit more. Perhaps gardeners can help it out.

TOP TO BOTTOM Shore primrose; remuremu; *Selliera rotundifolia*.

263

MONOCOTYLEDENOUS HERBS

Arthropodium cirratum, rengarenga

This amazing plant has a pantry in its roots stocked with starch and juices, allowing it to survive in the least accommodating of sites, on cliffs and clay bluffs along the rocky shores. Because it is frost-tender, it is not common south of East Cape and Taranaki, then it reappears around Cook Strait and northwest Nelson; whether occurring naturally or introduced there is not clear, but Maori have no doubt transplanted this root vegetable to new sites over the ages as it was a good food source

TOP AND ABOVE Rengarenga foliage and flowers.

for them, so now it is hard to know where its truly 'wild' locations once were. As gardeners know too well, it is 'snail-tender', requiring regular attention. The leaves often become infected with disease after frost damage, spoiling the plant's looks, so avoid frosty locations. Deadheading is well worth the effort to encourage a strong flush of foliage growth, but there is no need to remove the spent foliage, which acts as a mulch to both protect roots from drought and to restrain weed growth. In the wild, rengarenga will often grow in groups, so bulking it up in the garden echoes this communal growth. Often the greatest drama can be gained by growing it on steep banks or rock walls, or against a contrasting colour so that even when the plant is not flowering, the foliage can be 'working' for you. Nurseries frequently stock *Arthropodium* 'Matarangi' (which is large) and *A.* 'Te Puna' (which is small). These are selections from quite unique environments and may not truly represent your local character.

Astelia banksii, coastal astelia, shore kowharawhara

This Northland astelia grows hand in hand with pohutukawa on clay or rocky banks near the shore or on coastal cliffs. You'll find it perching on the lowermost boughs of pohutukawa, as well as on the ground among hound's-tongue fern, hook grasses and leather-leaf fern. It generally doesn't grow naturally south of Tauranga in the east or Kawhia in the west. It forms large

Coastal astelia.

clumps (up to 1 m wide). Like most astelias, this species has been selected for commercial purposes for varieties that dramatise the silvery sheen it can get on the leaves. The flowers and fruits (astelias have separate male and female plants) are not particularly colourful, but the plant fulfils a function in that difficult dry-but-shady zone under coastal trees where few plants thrive. Make sure it has good drainage.

If you want a way of remembering which astelia species is coastal, think of Joseph Banks, James Cook's senior botanist on his first voyage, seeing New Zealand from the shore and finding *Astelia banksii* growing on the banks along that shoreline. *Astelia solandri* was named after one of Cook's junior botanists, Daniel Solander, but it is not hard to imagine Banks having first dibs on naming the first plants found and Solander having to wait his turn, finding *A. solandri* perching on branches as they penetrated deeper into the coastal forest.

Astelia chathamica

This large astelia from the wild, windswept rocky coastline of the Chatham Islands has adapted well to gardens. Although astelias have good rain-trapping and water-storage capability to tide them over short dry periods, they will not thrive in constantly dry conditions (such as sand or pots).

Dianella nigra, turutu, New Zealand blueberry

This is a perfect ground plant for semi-shady bush edges and hard clay gardens, but the delicacy of the berries indicates shelter from wind should also be a consideration.

Astelia chathamica.

Turutu is a companion for other clay-bank species such as mingimingi, kumarahou, kanuka, totara, hound's-tongue fern and leather-leaf fern, and is easily raised from seed.

Libertia peregrinans, sand iris, mikoikoi

Of the *Libertia* species in New Zealand, this is the one that will grow right out in the open duneland. You may also find *L. ixioides* growing on clay banks, such as around estuaries or harbours, in a similar fashion to turutu. In full sun its leaves also take on a yellow tinge. Around Cook Strait the species found on clay coastal hillsides will be *L. edgariae*.

Sand iris responds to fertiliser by growing rampantly, spreading by horizontal stolons, but in the wild it is usually more subdued, sharing its dune hollows with wiwi and oioi, pimelea and spinifex. It does prefer the damper sands and soils, but the coppery hue of its leaves is usually a direct response to full sunlight, so keep this in mind to get the full benefit of its striking coloration. Its habitat of sand flats and hollows means it is often in the company of drifts of shells, and this combination, taken to its extreme in gardens where a shell mulch might be used around the plants, does complement the white flowering beautifully.

Phormium cookianum subsp. *hookeri*, wharariki, mountain flax

There are two forms of wharariki in the wild: a mountain form found through the South Island and in the Tararua Range that is quite stout in its

TOP TO BOTTOM Turutu; sand iris; wharariki.

265

growth; and a more limp form that, although it is still called mountain flax, is actually the dominant coastal flax along rocky shores and cliffs. Around Cook Strait the two forms appear to mingle and hybridise.

Perhaps it is easiest to describe wharariki by contrasting it with harakeke. It is by far the smaller plant (growing to only 1–1.5 m), with lax leaves; the seed pods dangle down from the flowerstalk stems (compared with the erect pods of harakeke). Flowers are a pretty yellow-orange mix dominated by red stamens, in contrast to the red flowers of harakeke.

Wharariki grows naturally in rocky sites or on damp mudstone bluffs. Its primary source of moisture is from crevices and fissures in the rock, where the collected rainwater will be enriched by weathering of the rock minerals. Many coastal cliffs and offshore islands appear smothered by wharariki. It is not killed by fire and, since it resprouts readily, can spread vegetatively and recolonise

A cultivar of wharariki.

faster than seed-dependent plants. Dense populations of wharariki may therefore reflect a history of burning.

Most modern flax cultivars are derived from wharariki and great efforts have been made to introduce coloration into the foliage. For a more naturalistic look, the dwarf selected forms known as 'Green Dwarf' and 'Emerald Gem' are more closely allied to the species.

Although wharariki can cope with salty winds, do not expect it to thrive in droughty, low-nutrient situations (such as sandy places) without irrigation and feeding. Having said that, wharariki is more tolerant of dry than harakeke—another reason it is a better suburban garden choice than harakeke.

Phormium tenax, harakeke, swamp flax

Harakeke has been in New Zealand and on Norfolk Island for 21 million years—and nowhere else. It truly is an iconic New Zealand plant and has supported Maori civilisation for centuries.

It thrives in well-drained but damp lowland soils or areas that are periodically flooded, such as the edges of swamps or streams, where it can reach heights of 2–3 m. Calling it swamp flax tends to misrepresent its true preferences. Although it is tolerant of both waterlogging and drought, it will not thrive within permanently wet swamp, preferring it when swamps are beginning to dry out and the top 200 mm or so of soil is aerated. It favours sites where there is flowing (oxygenated) nutritious

water replenishing the soils rather than stagnant water or waterlogged acidic peat soils.

Harakeke, therefore, dominates a zone where soil is periodically flooded, so you'll see it growing naturally around groundwater ponds that have fluctuating water levels and alongside streams. It fills valleys where wetlands raised by earthquakes are drying out or where the natural slow process of wetlands infilling with peat has raised the ground surface above the water table, such as many dune hollows.

You often see harakeke along beaches where seepages meet the shoreline, or where dunes have banked up to create a damp swale behind the foredune or shingle bank. Although harakeke can be grown in less swampy situations along the coast, it will not endure prolonged drought and will probably not reach

Harakeke seed pods.

Harakeke foliage fan.

its full stature. For example, you may see it scattered over dunes inland (and downwind) of dune hollows. Its lightweight seed has been blown onto the drier dunes, but these plants are rarely as healthy or strong as harakeke in damp soils.

Because harakeke was essential for survival of early Maori settlers, who used it as a (superior) substitute for pandanus leaves for weaving and fibre, not surprisingly a large number of old cultivars are recognised. In general, harakeke has erect growth and flowerstalks several metres tall bearing upright red flowers, although some forms have more lax foliage and seed pods vary in size. The variants are strongly correlated with both geographic areas and cultural migration routes, so it is not clear whether they are human-induced or reflect a natural variation in form. These days commercial cultivars are so rife that it is difficult to buy the wild forms of *Phormium tenax*.

Harakeke is relatively easy and cheap to plant out in bulk, and rabbits leave it alone. However, pukeko cause problems and, where they are present, it is recommended to bury the leaf fan by around one-quarter of its length.

Harakeke is important for native wildlife, supplying honey-eating birds with summer nectar and hosting a number of endemic invertebrates, including the flax snail of Northland. Two native moths lay their eggs in harakeke, and their caterpillars create 'windows' (the 'looper' caterpillar) or notches along leaf edges ('notcher' caterpillar).

Mealy bugs and scale insects can be common at the base of leaves (recognised by tell-tale white powdery or woolly patches, respectively) and can, in turn, encourage disease. In the wild, periodic flooding would keep these pests at low levels, but they can become prevalent in cultivated flaxes. In smaller gardens infestations can be minimised by cutting away old leaves and opening up the plant to sunlight. (Flax will become weak and straggly in shade anyway—the more exposure to full sunlight, the better.) Always cut leaves close to the base, at an angle to the fan of leaves (outer edge of cut lowermost) so that water cannot collect in cut stumps. The old flowerstalks make excellent kindling.

You can expect a few yellow leaves each season, but if an entire plant becomes yellow or orange, it probably has an infection introduced by a native hopper insect and all traces of the plant should be removed and burnt to prevent spreading the disease. This is the disease that helped bring the flax-rope industry to its knees.

Harakeke may not flower for five years, but once it does start flowering, a fan-replacement process begins, which results in a ring of fans surrounding a hollow centre. While this may not be desirable in a garden, it is perfectly normal. It is easy to see how flax can become a nursery-crop for the further establishment of native vegetation. Visiting birds kindly drop their seeds into the dead centre of the flax bushes and before long a new forest is underway. Note that this is a different process to interplanting a nursery-crop such as manuka with broadleaved species. When juvenile plants start life within the centre of a flax ring, they are less prone to damage by whiplashing flax leaves than they would be if trying to grow in between flax plants.

Phormium tenax from the Chatham Islands is a splendid variant on the species and so distinctive that it may well be given species status in due course; the same is true of the Three Kings Islands form. These stout, stately harakeke have very plump, erect seed pods and broader leaves.

Harakeke flowers.

Xeronema callistemon,
Poor Knights lily

The volcanic rocky crags of the Poor Knights Islands host this unusual plant. Thick, succulent leaf blades trap rain deep into the base of the plant (often built up with the slowly decaying fibrous mat of old leaves) to help it survive desiccation, while its roots penetrate rock crevices for nutrients and stability. This plant is therefore ideally suited to rock gardens or pots and, curiously, it seems that the more constricted its roots, the better it flowers. Give it full sun, an occasional dose of seaweed fertiliser, a tight fit and otherwise neglect it (until, of course, it flowers, when you won't be able to ignore the impressive red floral spikes).

TOP AND ABOVE Poor Knights lily.

CLIMBERS AND SCRAMBLERS

Calystegia soldanella,
shore bindweed

Shore bindweed makes its living out of the poorest of sands, shell beds and shingles by sending fleshy roots deep in search of moisture and nutrition. So while it may look on the surface as though it has trailing stems, really they reflect a subterranean network of taproots, and the gardener needs to bear this in mind and give the plant deep friable soils (or better still, the simple sands and shingles that are its natural habitat).

Bindweeds are promiscuous by nature and hybrids occur between species, in particular between shore bindweed and another common native coastal species, *Calystegia tuguriorum*. The result is a plant with slightly leathery leaves shaped more like the traditional convolvulus, and flowers that are very pale pink, bleaching to white (although not completely white as in *C. tuguriorum*).

Calystegia tuguriorum

This little species is barely noticed at the beach, where it likes to creep through other plants such as *Muehlenbeckia* or smaller shrubs, especially those of grey scrub, blending into their foliage and only revealing its presence when it flowers. Even then, these are modest little white flowers. It may not be a plant that gets deliberately planted, but it is a relatively benign addition and it would be a shame to weed it out on the basis of how its more aggressive

TOP TO BOTTOM Shore bindweed; *Calystegia tuguriorum*; *Clematis afoliata*.

Clematis forsteri.

cousin may behave. Wending its way through a hedge, it will be decorative rather than destructive.

Clematis afoliata

This is the joker of the pack and well worth introducing into a coastal garden, if only as a conversation starter. Mostly leafless, the clematis really stands out when its flowers turn to seed. Its preferred habitat is the dry eastern coastlines, where it decorates the grey scrub, preferring open, exposed sites to taller bush.

Clematis forsteri

Of all the clematis species in New Zealand, this is the one most commonly found along the coast, scrambling at ground level through small shrubs or winding through the branches of kanuka. As long as its roots are well shaded and protected from drying out, the tough foliage seems well equipped to survive most storms.

Fuchsia procumbens, creeping fuchsia

This delightful plant, the smallest flowering fuchsia in the world, is endemic to Northland coasts, scrambling among grasses and shrubs on both sandy and shingly beaches. Although it is surprisingly tolerant of disturbance, recent beach housing has removed it from habitat where it was already only sparsely distributed anyway. Pretty wee yellow fairy-cap flower tubes with magenta sepals are decorated with spectacular but miniature red filaments.

As if they aren't showy enough, they are followed up by relatively huge crimson berries. The long and wiry stems wind through other plants, spangling them with their tiny leaves to the point of smothering them. It is most versatile in gardens, growing in both full sun and dappled shade, and in both dry and moist conditions; it is readily pruned back (indeed, you'll probably need to). Every so often the trailing stems set roots, so new plants are easily created.

Creeping fuchsia.

Metrosideros fulgens

This climbing rata is special for providing winter flowering, attracting tui, bellbirds and humans alike. It is a rata for more sheltered bays and does need good support (preferably a tree) as it will become a heavy load with time.

Metrosideros perforata, white climbing rata

Everywhere there is or has been coastal forest you can almost guarantee that white climbing rata is also there, or remaining in bushy clumps even after the forests have been felled. It is probably the small

TOP *Metrosideros fulgens.*
ABOVE White climbing rata.

269

size of the fleshy leaf that allows this rata to live in salty conditions, but then all the ratas are very well adapted to wind. The way it climbs is to root at nodes along the climbing stems, so the support it requires is preferably organic, such as pongas. If left unsupported, it will bunch up with interlacing branchlets.

Muehlenbeckia australis, pohuehue
Muehlenbeckia complexa, small-leaved pohuehue

All the *Muehlenbeckia* scramblers may be found along the coast, but pohuehue, the one with the larger, thinner leaves, is pretty much confined to the shelter of forest, or sheltered bays and estuaries, whereas the low-growing small-leaved pohuehue can withstand the rigours of the open coast. Host to copper butterflies, this genus plays a crucial role not just for wildlife but for providing the shelter needed for smaller, less hardy herbs and ferns to become established behind or beneath their armoury. But be thoughtful with this climber in your garden as your neighbours may not thank you when it rambles off next door to smother their orchard.

Muehlenbeckia axillaris and *Muehlenbeckia ephedroides*, leafless pohuehue

Low-lying scramblers like these species are great tools for stabilising mobile gravels and coarse sands. Leafless pohuehue is mostly confined to the driest eastern coastlines, whereas *Muehlenbeckia axillaris* is

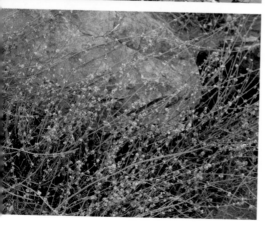

TOP TO BOTTOM Pohuehue; small-leaved pohuehue; leafless pohuehue.

270

more widespread, but they both dwell in the well-drained, infertile beach ridges and terraces where staying close to the ground is a wise precaution. At least their flowers will be pollinated and their fruits spread by sheltering lizards.

Parsonsia capsularis, *Parsonsia heterophylla*, New Zealand jasmine

There is hardly a coastal environment that does not contain native jasmine—from the old stable dunes to the gullies of a rocky shore—but which species it is depends largely on the dryness of the environment. *Parsonsia capsularis*, the fine-leaved species, can tolerate the arid east coast with its well-drained screes and shingle fans, whereas the broader-leaved *P. heterophylla* prefers the more benign, wetter western locations.

The species *Parsonsia capsularis* has been subdivided further into three varieties. One of these, *P. capsularis* var. *grandiflora*, does break the pattern and has broad leaves, which is rather confusing, but this variety is uncommon compared

Muehlenbeckia axillaris.

to the widespread *P. capsularis* var. *capsularis.*

And yes, these jasmine flowers really are scented.

Rubus squarrosus, leafless bush lawyer

Most coastal forests will contain bush lawyer, but the leafless bush lawyer offers the greatest interest to gardeners and botanists. It proliferates in the drier localities

Leafless bush lawyer.

and is not purely coastal, but where it does occur in coastal vegetation it can create quite a stir. It is not entirely leafless, but equally it can disguise itself as a barbed-wire fence without any trouble.

Tecomanthe speciosa

Frost-sensitive, light-demanding, winter-flowering and salt-tolerant—this rare vine from the Three Kings Islands now has a new habitat: gardens. It can take years for the flowers to appear, and although they hide themselves deep within the vine, giving their pollinating birds and geckos some shelter no doubt, their long seed pods make decorative dried ornaments for the sideboard. This vine is so vigorous in its search for sunlight that it can climb several storeys high and easily smother garages and pergolas. It must be well supported using widely spaced struts to allow for stem expansion, as it

TOP *Parsonsia capsularis.*
ABOVE New Zealand jasmine.

TOP AND ABOVE *Tecomanthe speciosa* foliage and flowers.

hangs on by twining the stem rather than using tendrils.

Tetragonia implexicoma (Tetragonia trigyna), climbing spinach

This species grows mostly in dunes, from the strand line on the beach and into grassland, but it is also found on coastal cliffs. It seems even more tolerant of saline conditions than New Zealand spinach. It will happily scramble up into the branches of coastal trees and shrubs, its leaves becoming larger and greener in

TOP AND CENTRE Climbing spinach foliage and berries. BOTTOM New Zealand spinach.

the shade. The berries are red and lack the horns of the fruits of New Zealand spinach.

Tetragonia tetragonoides, New Zealand spinach, kokihi

Despite its common name, we can't claim this coastal herb as our own as it is shared with other Pacific countries, but it is certainly a significant component of our natural coastal character. It appears in all sorts of situations: on beaches among the driftwood, in dunes, on cliff faces, on rocky beaches, and even within the margins of coastal forest. It isn't the 'true' spinach, but it certainly is edible and is commercially grown for culinary purposes. Although it is frost-tender, frost retards rather than kills the plant. Slight shading and rich soil will increase the leaf length and ensure a fresh green colour. Out in the open, leaves toughen up and become tinged with red.

New Zealand spinach grows in a sprawling mass and can trail for up to a metre. Be aware, though, that it only sporadically roots at nodes along these trailing arms and has no other form of attachment, so is not suitable to drape or climb in really windy sites as, without constant support, it will flail around. It does, however, mound and scramble and drape in sheltered locations to create a green blanket or veil.

The hard little horns on the fruit are a way of distinguishing the species from *Tetragonia implexicoma* (which lacks the horns and also has reddish stems).

FERNS

Adiantum hispidulum

Most of us would be surprised to find a maidenhair fern near the harsh coastal environment, but the *Adiantum* genus has some characters that are up to the task. Their fronds are stiff and well protected from salt, and although they are rarely out in the most exposed locations, you can find them growing under the shelter of shrubs and trees on hills surrounding estuaries and harbours, and in sheltered bays along rocky coastlines. *Adiantum hispidulum* is a large, highly decorative fern with black wiry stems and highly dissected fronds. It would tolerate the gardens on the south sides of houses in most of our coastal environments.

Arthropteris tenella

In dry coastal forest you may come across this unassuming but very pretty climbing fern, scrambling over tree roots and rocks. If you have an intimate space in the garden, perhaps

Adiantum hispidulum.

TOP TO BOTTOM *Arthropteris tenella; Aspenium obtusatum*, beautifully matched with a hebe on the Catlins coastline; shining spleenwort.

beside a shaded garden seat, this fern would attract the right sort of attention as it is usually overlooked in the wild. Although it needs sheltering from desiccating salt winds, it grows in dry places naturally.

Asplenium spp., spleenwort

Spleenworts are ubiquitous throughout New Zealand and most can be found at or near the coast. Even the older dunes can support these hardy ferns, although only the most succulent and leathery can endure the extreme exposure of both sun and salt spray. You might, for example, see isolated *Asplenium obtusatum*, the podgy hero of the rocky shore, tucked into crevices within the splash zone where nothing else survives. Look very closely and you realise that one of its survival tactics, apart from succulence, is scaliness. Aspleniums most commonly occurring at the coast are *A. obtusatum*, *A. polyodon* and *A. lucidum* (on southern beaches).

Shining spleenwort (*Asplenium oblongifolium*) will be familiar to people living in old dunes especially. It is pictured here with hound's-tongue, which shares its preferences for dappled light and a ground-cover of leaf litter. They make a good match, both with a shiny coating that helps to give a lift to otherwise shady places.

Blechnum (=Doodia) parrisiae, rasp fern

This northern New Zealand fern thrives on clay banks in both dappled light and full sunlight, and creates a cheerful ground-cover as it spreads to create pockets of colour in the coastal forest or shrubland. The more sunlight it is exposed to, the redder the fronds.

Microsorum pustulatum, hound's-tongue fern and *Microsorum scandens*, fragrant fern

In forests, these two climbing ferns can attain dizzy heights, but near the coast they are most likely found scrambling over rocks or logs within

TOP Rasp fern. ABOVE Rasp fern combined with *Libertia*.

the shelter of a coastal forest canopy or lower shrubland, and even out into more exposed sites if there is adequate rainfall or humidity. They are not often found growing in the same habitats, hound's-tounge fern, with the finer, skinnier fronds, seeming to thrive on drier sites and in more drought-prone climates than *Microsorum pustulatum*. Both are easy to introduce into gardens and provide excellent ground-cover. Their thick leathery fronds are a hint that they are very hardy in the coastal environment and will be found in duneland vegetation as well as along the rocky coastline.

Paesia scaberula, scented ring fern

Most of the ferns that cope with exposed situations are creeping ground-cover ferns, and this species is no exception. It can become rampant, so it pays to be circumspect about how you use it in a confined garden, but it is also very useful for covering large areas of moist, friable soil (preferably not sand) and will even compete with grasses. While it is one of the few ferns that enjoys full sun, it does require a soil that retains moisture. It dies back a bit in winter, which gives you the chance to remove the dead fronds in readiness for a flourish of greenery in early spring.

Pteridium esculentum, bracken

Bracken is a tough rhizomatous fern, widespread through many parts of the world. It grows tall (up to 3–4 m), although fronds tend to die back in winter and create a gorgeous autumnal palette of colour as they do. It has traditionally been cursed by gardeners but it is also an ally in the right situations.

Over half the biomass of bracken is underground, where a tangled mass of root networks and spreading rhizomes strengthens soils and boosts organic content of the soil. These extensive root systems are rarely destroyed by fire, thus bracken is often the first plant to reappear after a burnoff and the best protection possible against soil erosion. It also proved a productive food source for early Maori, who

TOP AND ABOVE Leather-leaf fern.

recognised that the starchy root could be cooked and processed into an edible flour—they weren't to know that it was moderately carcinogenic, however. The inclusion of bracken in Maori horticultural practices caused great loss of forest and shrubland throughout New Zealand.

In duneland the spread of bracken can be a blessing for stabilisation of sand hills. It can be problematic as a nursery-crop for interplanting, and a releasing programme must be maintained through summer (it dies back in winter), but it will eventually be shaded out by taller broadleaf plants. In the meantime it provides cool, moist shelter at ground level, a

rare commodity in most duneland. There would be no sense in trying to interplant with species *shorter* than bracken as it would only smother them.

Pyrrosia eleagnifolia, leather-leaf fern

This decorative little fern will climb trees, crawl over logs, sneak in among rocks and generally make itself useful in a garden, preferring dappled light to open sunlight, yet coping with sun if required. As it climbs, it is rooting into its support, which will need to be organic or very porous rock that can capture pockets of dirt.

SEDGES, GRASSES, RUSHES, REEDS AND RESTIADS

'Sedges have edges', as the saying goes. Indeed, sedges have three edges to their leaf blades (and often sharp cutty edges they are too). Grasses are flat-bladed, whereas the leafless rushes are hollow-stemmed (leafy forms are very similar to grasses). Reeds have strong, strap-like leaves. Restiads (*Sporodanthus*, *Apodasmia* and *Empodisma*) are rush-like, with photosynthetic stems doing the work of their almost invisible leaves.

Anemanthele lessoniana, gossamer grass

Even though this 400 mm-tall grass has become a popular garden plant and can even become invasive, ironically it has always been sparsely distributed in the wild. It is a plant

of edges, and the perfect habitat for it is created in sheltered bays where bush comes right down to the beach. The delicate misty flowerheads that envelope the tussock in spring often have a purplish tinge. It is very versatile in its habitat requirements, coping with dry soils in both sun and dappled shade, but not permanently damp soils. It is one of the few large grasses that can cope with living under a deck. Leaves have a rusty tinge in full sun.

Apodasmia (=Leptocarpus) similis, oioi, jointed wire rush

Great swathes of the orange-tinted restiad oioi are a common sight along the edges of estuaries, salt

TOP Gossamer grass. BOTTOM LEFT Oioi female. BOTTOM RIGHT Oioi male.

TOP AND ABOVE Toetoe.

marshes and damp sand flats. The massed effect of the jointed stems is a shimmering mistiness that is nevertheless imbued with colour. Oioi is readily propagated from root pieces and from seed. In the wild it generally grows where the water table is within 300 mm of the surface (and it can tolerate short-term inundation), but this relates to the seed germination requirements; in cultivation it can cope with a wider range of conditions as long as it gets full sun and regular watering.

Oioi has separate male and female plants, the main visual difference being the increased ruddy tinge to the female plants when seen at a distance.

Austroderia (=Cortaderia) spp., toetoe

Austroderia is a common genus in the southern hemisphere and we have four species native to New Zealand (and another few invasive intruders from South America we call pampas grass but that still use the *Cortaderia* genus name). As you move through New Zealand, you find different *Austroderia* species dominating. In the northern half of the North Island is it *A. splendens*, and this seems to be a predominantly coastal toetoe. Its name reflects its stature: this is the largest toetoe. *Austroderia toetoe* is most common through the lower North Island. In the South Island it is *A. richardii* that is more common, its flowerheads forming skinny, graceful pennants. These last two species inhabit the edges of swamps and estuaries where soils can be periodically damp. You can also find them in hollows within duneland. *Austroderia toetoe*, in particular, teams up with harakeke (swamp flax) and has the showiest flowerheads of all the species. The smallest species, *A. fulvida*, is a North Island species more commonly found along stream banks and in subalpine areas.

There is a common misconception that toetoe are swamp plants but they are really edge plants, preferring damp sites rather than permanently wet ones. Like most grasses, they are colonisers of disturbed sites (hence their prevalence alongside streams, mountain screes and floodable areas). This should indicate to the gardener that they will readily grow on difficult sites in large gardens and in poor soils. I suggest *large* gardens because after several years, without constant removal of dead leaves and flowerheads, they can soon look scruffy up close and are best positioned where they are mostly viewed from a distance. If you can position toetoe so that they are backlit by the sun, they will show off their flowerheads to best advantage.

To tell the toetoe species apart, look at the base of the leaf blade where it wraps around the stalk. They all have white waxy coatings on these leaf sheaths, but there is a brown collar at the base of *A. richardii* leaves, and the colour of the sheath itself is ivory on *A. toetoe* whereas all the others have green sheaths. *Austroderia splendens* is the only one that has hairy leaf sheaths.

There are several ways to tell the native toetoe apart from the two invasive pampas grasses: toetoe flowers in early summer and the flower plumes droop gracefully. In pampas, which flowers in autumn, the plumes are rigid, erect and, in the 'purple pampas', often tinged pink. The leaves of toetoe have many obvious ribs and old leaves drop away. Pampas leaves have only one conspicuous midrib and the old leaves accumulate like curled wood shavings (creating a fire hazard and attractive habitat for rats). The pampas leaf can be easily snapped (one of the reasons that pampas was propagated here for cattle fodder), and they do not have the white waxy leaf sheath of the native species. By the time flowering is over on both native and introduced species, they can look similar from a distance, so you need to get used to examining the foliage characteristics to tell them apart.

Austrostipa stipoides, buggar grass, estuary needle grass

Primarily a tall tussock of harbours and estuaries in northern North Island, Taranaki and Whakatane, this grass also occurs in the Nelson region. Its preferred habitat is mudflat (unlike the similarly tall sand tussock, *Poa billardierei*) but curiously it has also taken hold on volcanic rock shores around the Hauraki Gulf.

Carex pumila, sand sedge

This is one of the key sand-binding plants of the Pacific. Small, sparse and therefore often overlooked, this harsh, stiff sedge is a coloniser of moist sand. It will be found among the highest storm-thrown driftwood, on sand flats, fringing rivers and lagoons, and generally on the edge between moist and dry sand. It rarely grows densely, but the wiry rhizomes spread under the surface and intermittently send up tufts of harsh foliage. The leaves have a tendency to curl like party ribbons, and it does sport rather festive flowerheads down near ground level. During summer, micro-hollows become repositories for the abundant seed—you can pick up handfuls at a time. The promiscuity of the plant is cursed by at least one nursery manager, who swears never to grow it again after it flowered very promptly and spread its seeds through the entire nursery while her back was turned!

Carex testacea, trip-me-up

We have been through a phase in gardening where trip-me-up has almost reached saturation point. This naturally orange-tinted sedge has become even more strongly coloured in the hands of horticulturalists. In the wild it is found scattered through duneland, often colonising blowouts in the second or third line of dunes back from the beach. It has to compete with introduced species so is not as prevalent as it used to be. Full sun and low fertility are prerequisites for the plant. In the wild, although it often grows in family clusters (raising its babies in the precious shelter of its own leaf blades), it is rarely found in bulk—rather, it is scattered among other duneland grasses and sedges.

Chionochloa spp.

Chionochloa flavicans, C. beddiei and *C. bromoides* are geographically isolated but each fulfils an unlikely role on rocky bluffs, often with the sparsest of soils to bed into, breaking the general rule that grasses cannot readily establish in rocky sites because of their fibrous root mats. These ones appear to have an unparalleled ability to colonise rock crevices but then effectively build a nest of their own leaf litter to secure their perch. This tenacity makes them highly suitable candidates for rock walls and difficult banks, and this shows off their long

TOP TO BOTTOM Buggar grass; sand sedge; trip-me-up; *Chionochloa flavicans.*

foliage and drooping flowerheads to perfection. Of the three, *C. beddiei*, from Cook Strait, is the most upright. *Chionochloa flavicans* is commonly grown on the flat as well. To keep these grasses looking good, it is worth deadheading, but avoid removal of the leaf litter as it is only too easy to pull out live foliage with it accidentally. The leaf litter helps keep enough moisture around the roots, but keep an eye on whether it is rotting the plant bases. In the plants' natural steep habitats the mat of old foliage would be better drained than it will be in a flat garden situation. As a consequence

TOP *Chionochloa beddiei*.
ABOVE *Chionochloa bromoides*.

Giant umbrella sedge.

of this, the *C. flavican*s shown on the previous page lasted seven years before needing replacement.

Cyperus ustulatus, giant umbrella sedge, coastal cutty grass

Although this sedge does not reach the bottom end of the country, it is ubiquitous in damp coastal sites elsewhere—around estuaries, in dune swales, at stream mouths or edging rock pools. Not a lot of small gardens will have the kinds of locations this sedge thrives in, but pond edges, seepages and wet hollows on larger properties may offer ideal habitat. There are several native and exotic *Cyperus* species in the country, but giant umbrella sedge is the one most often found at the coast.

Ficinia (=Isolepis) nodosa, knobby clubrush, wiwi

Throughout not just New Zealand but the southern hemisphere, this stout, hardy coastal sedge will grow primarily in dunes, but also around estuaries and on stony beaches, as long as it is in a free-draining site in full sun. It forms large clumps because it is slightly rhizomatous,

TOP Knobby clubrush. ABOVE Pingao.

putting out short runners to extend its patch. Full sun brings out the orange-bronze tint to its stiff stems, but in shadier situations or in lusher garden soils it may be greener and more lax in its growth form. It looks fabulous when massed, but also holds its own as single clumps amidst low shrubs and herbs. It propagates readily from seeds or divisions. If your site is particularly frosty, this is a very helpful choice for the garden.

Ficinia (=Desmoschoenus) spiralis, pingao, golden sand sedge

The Maori use of the sedge pingao for weaving is legendary. Of the five key fibres used in weaving, this is the only one that dries to a strong golden colour, requiring no further dyeing. The toughness of the leaf fibre in life continues in death.

Once common throughout New Zealand's dunelands, pingao has survived in quantities today only through a huge conservation effort directed at planting and protecting the sedge from browse and competition from marram grass.

Although pingao is a good sand collector, it isn't as good at binding the sand as spinifex or marram grass, as it grows much more slowly and does not respond so speedily to erosion around its rhizomes. However, the dunes that form around it are generally smooth, so wind doesn't eddy around as it does among marram dunes.

Pingao's attributes relate to the harsh environment it colonises, and as a garden plant in more protected environments it may lose some of its golden glow and vigour but will nevertheless be a dominant showpiece, especially when it flowers. Be very careful when weeding (and grass seems to love germinating deep within the stems of pingao) as the stems are brittle and easily dislodged. A bent wire is the most useful weeding tool to use. If you want to harvest the leaves, cut rather than yank them off to avoid damage to the growing tips of the stems. Make sure the plant has full sun and no additional fertiliser.

Gahnia lacera

You can find gahnias displayed on banks and fresh slip faces all around New Zealand, but near the coast from East Cape northwards it is likely to be *Gahnia lacera*, growing on headlands within the shelter of coastal forest such as kanuka- or totara-dominated bush. This grass species is much more bamboo-like in its growth than other gahnias. Although gahnias are notoriously hard to cultivate from seed, do persevere (or at least let them self-seed naturally) as these large, clump-forming grasses are an integral part of northern coastal forest and a delight in the garden. Their foliage is so long that they need to be planted on banks or at the top of retaining walls, and they prefer dappled light. This is a very useful plant for dry shade.

Juncus kraussii var. australiensis, sea rush

There is little to commend this plain plant on aesthetic grounds but it is one of our most important coastal rushes, forming the first line of tall growth around the fringes of estuaries. It can cope with periodic inundation by high tides.

Lachnagrostis spp., wind grasses

Often overlooked in the wild as just another annual grass blending in with all the exotic species, this native genus (previously known as *Deyeuxia*) likes damper conditions than most. The edges of mud flats, estuaries and dune swales are home to *Lachnagrostis littoralis* (growing up to 400 mm tall) and *L. glabra* (a laxly sprawling,

TOP TO BOTTOM *Gahnia lacera*; sea rush; *Lachnagrostis billardieri*.

279

Jointed twig rush.

Oplismenus hirtellus

A sprawling grass of shaded coastal forest floors in dry parts of the North Island and around Nelson, the species can grow in large mats but rarely very densely. This is a pretty grass that, while small and sparse, cannot help but catch the eye. It is highly recommended in dappled light where leaf litter builds up and little else can grow.

Poa billardierei (*Austrofestuca littoralis*), sand tussock, hinarepe

This large, attractive duneland tussock grass is straw-coloured, erect and up to 700 mm tall. It used to be much more common on sandy shores as well as shingle beaches, but grazing has reduced it to threatened status—that's on the New Zealand mainland; on the Chatham Islands it has disappeared completely.

Don't confuse it with marram grass, which has long cat's-tail-like seedheads above the leaves. The seedheads on sand tussock are no taller than the leaves and look rather like barley seedheads. It may also become confused with buggar

Oplismenus hirtellus.

grass, which is another tall, stiffly upright tussock found through North Island and Nelson estuaries (but not common in sand).

Poa cita, silver tussock

This shiny tan-coloured tussock grass of clay banks and rocky sites prefers the hard life. As long as it gets full sun and very good drainage, that's all it needs. Although it has a preference for naturally fertile sites in the wild (i.e. rocky or clay sites, not sandy ones), do not overnurture it in the garden with rich soil and mulch as this will readily rot the base of the tussock if it retains moisture. If grown in the shade, silver tussock elongates and loses its upright stance.

bright green grass up to 300 mm or so tall). A more gregarious species, perehia (*L. billardieri*) is also found in Australia and can become quite widespread. These tufted grasses come into their own when their long, flexuous flowerheads are evident (when they were more prolific around the country, they featured regularly in flower arrangements). Wind grasses generally require a soil with nutrient- and moisture-retaining ability, not simply dry sand, although perehia is common in west coast duneland on older dunes.

Machaerina (=*Baumea*) *articulata*, jointed twig rush

The common name seems poorly suited to this robust, very tall, stiff-spiked aquatic rush that grows in the west of the North Island. The jointed part of the name refers to the cross plates in the hollow stem that are conspicuous even from the outside. While it grows in coastal ponds, it would be best to avoid planting the rush in windy locations as the tall stems are prone to damage and collapse.

LEFT Sand tussock. ABOVE Silver tussock.

Spinifex sericeus, spinifex, kowhangatara

A sand-binding grass of foredunes, spinifex was once widespread but has been largely replaced now by introduced marram grass—not just because marram grows more vigorously, but because spinifex is much more palatable to rabbits and is susceptible to a fungal infection in its flowerheads. A great effort is underway to reintroduce it to our beaches, as the dunes it forms are better shaped to withstand storms than the steeper marram-induced dunes.

The spinifex stolons stretch for metres, helping to slow drifting sand, and will assist in speedy recovery from blowouts and washouts along beach frontages.

The elegant pewter-green leaves become star-studded in summer when the tumbleweed seedheads of the female plants appear. The seedheads tumble along in the wind until caught by driftwood. Buried by sand, and sheltered from sun and wind by driftwood, fertile seeds will germinate, and as long as they are far enough above spring high tide, will start another colony of spinifex. The male plants have much more orthodox flowerheads.

Germinate the plump fertile seeds you have separated out of the whirligig seedhead the same way as nature does, keeping sand slightly damp and cool until they sprout, at which stage they can grow in full sunlight. Grow the seedlings on in a mix that is mostly coarse sand with just a minor amount of potting mix and slow-release fertiliser.

On the beach, bury the rooting base deeply (a stretched hand's depth) to protect it from erosion and dehydration. This isn't necessary in a stable garden situation. Although spinifex spreads steadily in the wild, in the garden it will not be so laterally vigorous but will still need a good depth of sandy soil for its long taproots.

Typha orientalis, raupo, bulrush

Our tallest reed, raupo can establish in water as deep as 1.2 m. It demands high fertility and thrives in the enriched ponds characteristic of today's pastoral environment. It has always played a role in the natural transition from shallow pond to swamp (and thus to drier shrubland),

TOP LEFT Female spinifex. TOP RIGHT Male spinifex. ABOVE LEFT AND RIGHT Raupo.

not only by trapping wind-blown and water-borne silts but by contributing huge volumes of leaf litter each winter as it dies back after flowering. The flowerheads are the familiar velvety bulrushes that dissolve into wind-borne fluff by late autumn.

These days raupo is not among the wetland plants recommended for planting in shallow ponds or lakelets, as it is difficult to prevent it taking over the entire waterway. Ponds deeper than 2 m are self-limiting for growth. On large properties, however, it is a welcome component of wetland areas and provides one of the most striking seasonal colour contrasts our otherwise constant native vegetation can offer.

Coast care

Coastal retreats

We have been aware of the rise in sea level since the 1930s. Rachel Carson alerted the American public in 1951 in her now classic *The Sea Around Us*, a popularist and global perspective on human relationships with the ocean.

Whereas no one really understood the reasons back then, seventy years of investigation has enabled us to identify causes for sea-level rise and the commensurate increase in storminess that accompanies a changing world climate.

The uptake of this knowledge by coastal developers and councils seems to have lagged behind the physical reality of coastal erosion that threatens roading, housing and property boundaries. Not only have we been losing land, but we have been losing public land, as the traditional Queen's Chain is gnawed away by the resource-hungry ocean. And by virtue of losing public land, more often than not this means we are losing the natural narrow fringe of coastal habitat squeezed between the water and developed properties. In places this strip has gone completely or is showing the signs of salt-water encroachment. Some duneland forest, for example, is being scorched off by salt damage, reverting to a vegetation type more akin to close shore habitats.

Coastal environment zones will march inland with the tide, perhaps even broaden if storminess increases in frequency and intensity as predicted. But, mostly, the salty zone encroaches on our developed land. Into our gardens. Over farms. Under siege, we want to blockade the invasion.

TOP There is no escaping the imprint of the developer on our coasts. As a result, many gardens become part of a healing process instead of simply a bonding between landowner and landscape.

Managed coastlines, designed to protect human property, come in various forms: solid structures such as rock revetments and walls and groynes. In sandy places, the effort to replant foredunes with native sandbinding plants has reaped rewards as shorelines accrete rather than retreat, in the short term at least. This is a far better approach than built structures, which usually create so much wind and wave turbulence that they actually increase scouring. Even tall trees such as Norfolk pines, a traditional favourite of coastal councils, can create an impediment to wind flow; in so doing they help scour out a sandy beach. Stormwater outflows also cause a problem by creating damp patches of beach that prevent the normal flow of dry sand up and down the beach. Where flow stops, scouring starts.

It is horrible to think of our gardens becoming museum piece legacies of lost natural communities yet, realistically, they already are, with some of our rarest species such as Tecomanthe vine, Chatham Island forget-me-not or Cook's scurvy grass doing better in gardens than in the wild. This may be the writing on the wall for a great many more coastal species.

So, rip out those agapanthus and gazanias and nuture our own heritage of plants for posterity instead! Few native ecosystems are as vulnerable as the salt-induced community. There is simply nowhere else for it to go.

The human footprint

As I write, a battle is being fought over the development of a 250ha coastal property north of Auckland that, although currently in pine trees, is adjacent to a stretch of beach hosting fairy terns. There are now only three nesting colonies of fairy terns in New Zealand – only 14 pairs in all – after decades of abuse by roaming cats, dogs, mustelids, vehicles and disturbance by beach-goers. Now this fragile sanctum is being threatened by human settlement. It is impossible for humans not to have detrimental affect on nesting birds. It also impossible for us not to meddle. We meddle with natural dynamics along the shore. We meddle with coastal vegetation if it is not stabilising dunes that threaten our livelihoods. I think of a South African example of a community wanting sand drift rectified by the stabilisation planting of foredunes. So successful was the dune creation that the locals lost their expansive swimming beach – complaints lead eventually to the council agreeing to destabilise the dunes once again, but in the interim development of the hinterland had occurred and now those house owners are complaining about the encroachment of drifting sands.

We meddle with estuaries if we would prefer to have causeways, rubbish dumps, flat industrial land. Our development feeds so much sediment into estuaries that mangroves invade and change shelly beaches to muddy expanses – so we get the bulldozers in once again (although we are rarely successful in reclaiming those lost shelly habitats).

We may well be part of the ecosystem, but the role we play is of predator, invader, polluter, suppressor. Sometimes out of ignorance, occasionally by accident and often motivated by greed.

Part of the difficulty in taking responsibility for the state of our coasts is that so many losses are insidious and have been happening over a long time frame. If you had lived in a quiet beach village at a rivermouth for sixty years you would have been aware that where birds once nested in the spring-tide debris, now none do. Since the arrival of motorbikes and quad bikes, and the exponential growth in the dog population over the last two decades, few birds even roost let alone nest. You are likely to mourn the days of full buckets of whitebait after a morning's fishing although you probably don't mind so much that there are no longer poisonous katipo spiders lurking beneath the logs you perch on while you wait. Where once you were surprised at the number of larks that sprung skywards as you roamed over the marram-clad dunes, now you notice the footprints in the sand of cats and weasels. But your children or grandchildren aren't aware of these losses and changes.

Unlike some landscapes, such as wetlands, which can disappear without trace into history, there will always be a coast. But what will it look like? Where, precisely where will it be?

ABOVE How many dotterel nests have they disturbed today? The riders wouldn't even know, so good is the camouflage of the bird and the scrape of its nest.

Acknowledgements

Special thanks go to Rudd (Castlecliff), Butterworth (Waiheke), Kundycki (Seatoun), Wilson (Cape Palliser), Sand Castle Motels (Pekapeka), The Library (Pakawau), Wild (Takaka), Nga Manu Nature Reserve (Waikanae), Forest Lakes Camp (Otaki), Millington-Braeyley (Marahau), Lucas (Lower Hutt), Pie Melon Farm (Waiheke), Hetet (Waiwhetu), Gibb (Kaipara), Barron-Ling (Whangarei) and Fern Glen (Auckland) for access to their properties. Access to Waitakere Council's living roof was arranged by Renee Davies, who instigated this innovative project, and her advice is appreciated.

I confess that not all the owners of the gardens featured in this book knew their gardens were being photographed, as the speedy technique of 'drive-by shootings' from the road to record great street frontages proved an efficient way to illustrate good ideas. I do apologise for this apparent rudeness, but hope that the owners involved take heart, indeed feel flattered, that their efforts were eye-catching and deemed worthy of sharing with more viewers than just their neighbours.

Many featured gardens are in public spaces, such as botanic gardens (Otari Native Plant Museum, Auckland Regional Botanic Garden), city waterfronts, corporate gardens and reserves. Where possible, professional designers and gardeners have been credited and contributions from other photographers gratefully acknowledged.

All photographs were taken by the author except: Rob Lucas, pp. 41 (top right), 53 (bottom left), 225 (centre left), 239 (bottom right), 242 (bottom right), 243 (top left), 248 (top right), 261 (top); Janet Gabites, p. 120 (centre); Louise Mantell, p. 130 (left); Peter Kundycki, p. 134 (top right); Jane Connor, p. 191 (bottom); Di Lucas, p. 202; Janice Lord, p. 205; Jeremy Rolfe, pp. 250 (bottom right), 275 (top), John Smith-Dodsworth, p. 255 (bottom left); Hamish Moorhead, cover.

Featured designers and gardens: Wraight & Associates (Waitangi Park, Wellington waterfront, Feist garden, Otaki Polytechnic); Isthmus Group (Hobsonville Point Park, Wellington waterfront, New Plymouth waterfront); Rick Rudd (Castlecliff, Garden of National Significance); Trudy Crerar (Ponsonby garden); Boffa Miskell (Point Dorset gardens); Margaret Philips (Britomart); Janey Christopherson (Conservation House); Cicada (steel manuka sculptures); Moorhead and Newdick Landscape Architects (Eastbourne garden).

Index

297